Jazz Migrations

AMERICAN MUSICSPHERES

Series Editor: Mark Slobin

Fiddler on the Move
Exploring the Klezmer World
Mark Slobin

The Lord's Song in a Strange Land
Music and Identity in Contemporary Jewish Worship
Jeffrey A. Summit

Lydia Mendoza's Life in Music
Yolanda Broyles-González

Four Parts, No Waiting
A Social History of American Barbershop Harmony
Gage Averill

Louisiana Hayride
Radio and Roots Music Along the Red River
Tracey E. W. Laird

Balkan Fascination
Creating an Alternative Music Culture in America
Mirjana Laušević

Polkabilly
How the Goose Island Ramblers Redefined American Folk Music
James P. Leary

Cajun Breakdown
The Emergence of an American-Made Music
Ryan André Brasseaux

Claiming Diaspora
Music, Transnationalism, and Cultural Politics in Asian/Chinese America
Su Zheng

Bright Star of the West Joe Heaney, Irish Song-Man
Sean Williams and Lillis Ó Laire

Romani Routes
Cultural Politics and Balkan Music in Diaspora
Carol Silverman

Voices from the Canefields Folksongs from Japanese Immigrant Workers in Hawai'i
Franklin Odo

Greeted with Smiles Bukharian Jewish Music and Musicians in New York
Evan Rapport

Resounding Afro Asia Interracial Music and the Politics of Collaboration
Tamara Roberts

Singing God's Words
The Performance of Biblical Chant in Contemporary Judaism
Jeffrey Summit

Cajun Breakdown
The Emergence of an American-Made Music
Ryan Andre Brasseaux

Jump Up!
Caribbean Carnival Music in New York
Ray Allen

Capital Bluegrass
Hillbilly Music Meets Washington, DC
Kip Lornell

Sound Relations
Native Ways of Doing Music History in Alaska
Jessica Bissett Perea

Instrument of the State
A Century of Music in Louisiana's Angola Prison
Benjamin J. Harbert

Jazz Migrations
Movement as Place Among New York Musicians
Ofer Gazit

Jazz Migrations

Movement as Place Among New York Musicians

OFER GAZIT

OXFORD
UNIVERSITY PRESS

Oxford University Press is a department of the University of Oxford. It furthers
the University's objective of excellence in research, scholarship, and education
by publishing worldwide. Oxford is a registered trade mark of Oxford University
Press in the UK and certain other countries.

Published in the United States of America by Oxford University Press
198 Madison Avenue, New York, NY 10016, United States of America.

© Oxford University Press 2024

All rights reserved. No part of this publication may be reproduced, stored in
a retrieval system, or transmitted, in any form or by any means, without the
prior permission in writing of Oxford University Press, or as expressly permitted
by law, by license, or under terms agreed with the appropriate reproduction
rights organization. Inquiries concerning reproduction outside the scope of the
above should be sent to the Rights Department, Oxford University Press, at the
address above.

You must not circulate this work in any other form
and you must impose this same condition on any acquirer.

Library of Congress Control Number: 2024003117
ISBN 978–0–19–768278–4 (pbk.)
ISBN 978–0–19–768277–7 (hbk.)

DOI: 10.1093/oso/9780197682777.001.0001

Paperback printed by Marquis Book Printing, Canada
Hardback printed by Bridgeport National Bindery, Inc., United States of America

For my father, Amram Gazit

Contents

Acknowledgments ix
Figures and Musical Examples xi
About the Companion Website xiii

Introduction: A Moving Scene 1

1. The Loop 32

2. Jam Session 56

3. The Scene 74

4. History 92

5. Home 114

6. The Village 132

Conclusion: Places that Move 156

Notes 163
References 169
Selected Discography 179
Interviews and Conversations 181
For Further Listening 183
Index 185

Acknowledgments

First and foremost, I'd like to thank the musicians whose stories I share in this book, and who taught me everything I know about New York's migrant music scene: Claudia Acuña, Kei Akagi, Matt Albeck, Melissa Aldana, Carter Bales, David Bertrand, Freddy Castiblanco, Matan Chapnizky, Sun Chung, Anat Cohen, Karina Colis, Ori Dakari, Vasko Dukovski, Leonor Falcón, Nitzan Gavrieli, Leo Genovese, Mariano Gil, Uri Gurvich, Ayumi Ishito, Michel Maurer, George Mel, Francisco Mela, Pablo Menares, Juan Lázaro Méndolas, Camila Meza, Alma and Rale Micic, Francisco Molina, Hironori Momoi, Vanderlei Pereira, Edward Perez, Franco Pinna, Prasanna Ramaswamy, Sofia Rei, Jochen Rückert, Rafał Sarnecki, Peter Slavov, Seth Trachy, Ariacne Trujillo Duran, Manuel Valera, Spike Wilner, Alex Wyatt, Kenji Yoshitake, John Zorn, and many others. Thank you.

I would also like to thank several people who were absolutely vital to the making of this book: to Mark Slobin and Lauralee Yeary for their encouragement and dedication throughout the publication process; to Sapir Midzinsky for his invaluable work in preparing and editing the transcriptions; to Ben Liebersohn for his help in preparing the maps; to Debby Stern for her close and careful reading in the later stages of the manuscript; Amanda Scherbenske for her helpful advice; Andrew Snyder for last-minute suggestions; the Valle Cupa writing group for their comments and wise discussion; the many members of the "Jazz Studies Collaborative" Facebook group for those missing bits of information.

I would also like to thank my PhD mentors at the University of California at Berkeley and Columbia University whose advice and support throughout the years continue to be a source of confidence and encouragement: Ben Brinner, Scott Saul, George E. Lewis, and Jocelyne Guilbault.

I am grateful to my colleagues at Tel Aviv University, Michal Grover Friedlander, Zohar Eitan, Nili Belkind, Hadas Peery, Neta Maimon, and many others, for reminding me to take deep breaths and keep moving.

To my friends who are family in Israel, the United States, and Italy, thank you for your love and support. Finally, to Valentina, Isabella, and Blu, you are the best I could have asked for.

Figures and Musical Examples

I.1	Map of jazz places discussed in the book.	3
I.2	Detailed map of jazz places in Greenwich Village.	3
I.3	List of jazz places discussed in the book.	4
3.1	Manuel Valera's New Cuban Express at Terraza 7, summer 2020.	82
4.1	Variation on the B part of "Bye Bye Blackbird," Keith Jarrett Trio, *At the Deer Head Inn* (ECM 1992).	105
4.2	Quote from Keith Jarrett, "Bye Bye Blackbird," Kenji Yoshitake Trio.	107
4.3	Sparse "Miles Davis" phrasing, Kenji Yoshitake Trio.	108
4.4	Dense "John Coltrane" phrasing, Kenji Yoshitake Trio.	109
4.5	Transition between blues and bebop phrasing, Kenji Yoshitake Trio.	111
4.6	Dissolving bebop phrasing, Kenji Yoshitake Trio.	112
5.1	Franco Pinna's modified drum set.	127
6.1	Jewish melodic markers in "Katzfiel," Uri Gurvich Quartet.	142
6.2	Jewish melodic markers in "Katzfiel," Uri Gurvich Quartet.	143
6.3	Lewis Nash drum call, "Sweet Georgia Brown," Anat Cohen Quartet (Anzic 2010).	150
6.4	Lewis Nash and Benny Green simultaneous syncopation, Anat Cohen Quartet.	151
6.5	Benny Green closely following and altering the harmony outlined by Cohen, Anat Cohen Quartet.	151
6.6	The quartet marks divisions of three against the $\frac{4}{4}$ meter, Anat Cohen Quartet.	152
6.7	Final cadence of Cohen's solo, simultaneous marking of chromatic line, Anat Cohen Quartet.	153

About the Companion Website

www.oup.com/us/jazzmigrations

Oxford has created a website to accompany *Jazz Migrations*, and readers are encouraged to take full advantage of it. The website includes a sound file to accompany Chapter 4 and external audio links to accompany Chapter 6. These recorded examples are signaled in the text with Oxford's symbol ▶.

Introduction

A Moving Scene

I walk hand in hand with Vanderlei Pereira, a visually impaired Jewish Afro-Brazilian drummer in his sixties. We head toward the 1 subway train on Broadway and 65th Street, just across from Lincoln Center. "So you are able to go downstairs like this with the drums?" I ask as we walk down. "Sure!" he responds. "I had to learn; I trained a lot. Counting the steps, the stops, etc. And now I know it by heart. It has to do with touch, timing, and memory. You have to study a lot to get to know the city." Finding the turnstile with his right hand, he quickly swipes his MetroCard and crosses to the uptown platform, where we part ways. As he boards the train, I can't help being astonished by how he navigates this hectic city, his home for the last three decades. Getting a feel for its streets, with his sticks and ears—using touch, timing, and memory.

Vanderlei Pereira's story weaves together several strains that will be crucial themes of this book. Pereira's visions of New York City—the dream of turning New York into a living reality—is shared by many of the musicians I collaborated with on this project. Indeed, visions of the city as a musical and educational utopia are among the most important motivations for the wave of immigrant jazz musicians who arrived in New York in recent decades.[1] Jazz critic Nate Chinen (2014) referred to this movement of musicians as the "polyglot stir of modern jazz," while jazz historian Dan Morgenstern (2001) acknowledged that "the number of players who've come to the US in the past few decades is legion."

This desire, the "jazz dream of New York City," has been circulated endlessly around the world through films, newspapers, magazines, and radio shows (Jackson 2012; Greenland 2016). Most recently, it has been livestreamed on social-media platforms during a global pandemic. It certainly was a dream of mine. As a teenager growing up in Israel in the 1990s, playing bass and obsessing over the intricacies of jazz, I constantly heard stories about Israeli musicians in New York—how they got there, where they went to school, and what famous musicians they had collaborated with. An implicit message was always present: "To play this music, to really know jazz, you have to be in New York. Listen and transcribe all the records you want; you've heard nothing until you've heard it where it happens." Like a brainless scarecrow or cowardly lion, to become a complete musician one had to go to jazz's Emerald City.

I finally arrived in New York for the first time in an unseasonably hot October in 2007, a twenty-three-year-old music student recently discharged from the Israeli Army jazz band. I came to New York to hear music, to see the city, but perhaps most of all because every other musician I had known growing up in Israel had already moved to New York. I was the only one among my peers who did not attend a jazz school in the United States. I stayed with one of my former bandmates, who was then studying at the New School for Jazz. From the couch of his small Brooklyn apartment, I carefully examined the back pages of the *Village Voice*, plotting my musical routes for the week. The Jazz Gallery, a humble performance space packed with folding chairs, featured the bands of guitarist Aquiles Báez and pianist Luis Perdomo, both originally from Venezuela. That same week, the Jazz Standard, an upscale club and restaurant on the corner of 27th Street and Park Avenue, was hosting the bands of two Cuban pianists, Omar Sosa and Manuel Valera. A short subway ride away, Israeli bassist Omer Avital's Band of the East, featuring some of my former bandmates from Tel Aviv, was playing at Joe's Pub on Third Avenue and St. Mark's Place. At Sweet Rhythm, the reincarnation of the Sweet Basil, Duduka Da Fonseka's sextet, was playing jazz samba. At the Blue Note, just a couple of blocks down West 4th Street, John Scofield performed with his electric guitar trio, while at the Village Vanguard, veteran masters Jimmy and Albert "Tootie" Heath had a weekly residency, maintaining the club's role as a bearer of tradition (Figures I.1 and I.2). The rumors were true. The sheer diversity of music and talent—along with the familiarity and intimacy—seemed magical, unreal, enchanting.

By the time I returned to New York for the initial fieldwork for a research project in June 2012, many of these venues had closed or moved to new locations, and some of the musicians I knew had left, citing visa issues or financial difficulties (Figure I.3). However, many had stayed, and many more had arrived: The "influx of jazz musicians . . . from every corner of

INTRODUCTION 3

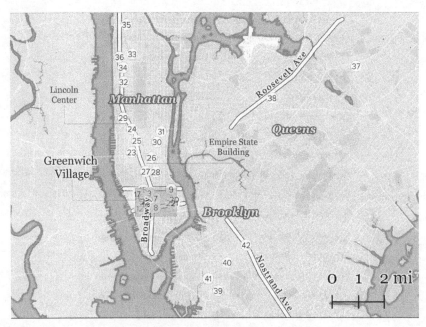

Figure I.1 Map of jazz places discussed in the book.

Figure I.2 Detailed map of jazz places in Greenwich Village.

Figure I.3 List of jazz places discussed in the book.

the globe" (Beuttler 2020) continued unabated. The changing of compositional languages and ever-expanding musical proficiencies I encountered on my first visit continued with greater verve. This seeming paradox of closing venues, struggling performers, and an ever-expanding wave of newly arrived musicians points to another crucial theme of this book. The desires and imaginations of New York jazz musicians often contrast sharply with the economic conditions of the jazz scene. These conditions are shaped in important ways by New York's role as an educational space. I am referring here both to the formal jazz education system, where many contemporary musicians are trained and later find employment, and to the ethos of jazz performers as perpetual "students of tradition," an ethos that carries economic and social implications as well as a sense of continuous struggle. These worlds—the dream, the school, and the gig—shape the musical biographies of musicians like Pereira, for whom straight-ahead jazz, Brazilian music, funk, and rock are intimate and familiar sonic vocabularies. These sounds interact in complex ways with his identity as an Afro-Brazilian, an immigrant, a converted Jew, and a visually impaired man. It is in this sonic space, on the border between identity and institutions, between musical skills and constructed ways of listening, that this book is located.

Jazz Migrations offers a new approach to the study of immigrant music by focusing on the musical practices of a multinational movement of artists, representing more than fifty different countries of origin, all living and performing jazz in the city at the time of the study.[2] Beginning with the material conditions that propelled the migration of jazz musicians to New York since the 1990s, it examines a wide range of practices (avant-garde, Balkan, bebop, Brazilian, Cuban, jazz-rock fusion, klezmer, trad-jazz) and actors (Anat Cohen, Leo Genovese, Melisa Aldana, Francisco Mela, Ayumi Ishito, Prasanna Ramaswamy, Camila Meza, and many others) as they explore new modes of musical belonging to the New York jazz scene. The book links them with key listeners on the scene whose impact on the lives of migrant musicians have seldom been told (club owners Freddy Castiblanco, Spike Wilner, and Lorraine Gordon; veteran musicians John Zorn, Daniel Carter, and Paquito D'Rivera). The book also takes an in-depth look at the impact of formal and informal jazz institutions: jazz schools like the New School and Berklee college of Music, cultural institutions like Jazz at Lincoln Center, major clubs such the Village Vanguard, migrant-led jam sessions, and multinational ensembles, offering a new perspective on the impact of migration and globalization on American jazz and the key roles belonging and exclusion play in its contemporary formation.

One crucial but often neglected question about the influence of immigration on American expressive culture revolves around its cumulative transcultural impact. Rather than focusing on the contribution of a single racial or ethnic group, I consider the co-constitution of immigrant cultures as an essential aspect for understanding American music today. Following Gloria Anzaldúa, we should listen for the ways "two or more cultures edge each other, where people of different races occupy the same territory, where under, lower, middle and upper classes touch, where the space between two individuals shrinks with intimacy" (Anzaldúa 1987). In this book I argue that jazz, constructed as an American music, provides us with a "borderland" music through which to examine the influence of immigrants on expressive culture in the United States.

Theorizing what I call a "musical border," *Jazz Migrations* explores the entanglements of migration, genre, and ethnic identity, showing how a music scene can provide motivation for immigration, a sense of belonging, and a sonic and affective home for a diverse group of migrant musicians. It also shows how the same scene can be packaged and resold as a global educational product, leading to unsustainable economic conditions and a growing exclusion of economic and racial minorities from its increasingly elite spaces. Finally, as it re-listens to the New York jazz scene, one of the most scrutinized musical spaces in the world, *Jazz Migrations* seeks to unpack the contemporary economic, institutional, and aesthetic implications of racial and ethnic frames of listening.

By "frames of listening," I mean the expectations that listeners develop before and during a particular performance. The way these expectations guide the listener's attention in the course of the performance, and the way they consequently shape listeners' aesthetic judgment, are key aspects of this study. Among the central listening frames addressed in this book are the continued historicizing of jazz in New York, the canonization of musical genius modeled on Western art music, and an emphasis on the relationship between genre and race. *Jazz Migrations* examines how these frames of listening become musical borders, sonic boundaries that migrant jazz musicians negotiate, reinforce, and cross. As expressive culture in American society continues to be firmly grounded in racial, ethnic, and national distinctions, musical expressions that defy such divisions become suspect, audibly clashing with widely held beliefs about ethnic differences and authenticity. By examining how musicians and listeners respond to the shifting subjectivities expressed in migrant jazz performance, *Jazz Migrations* considers a type of complex musical imagery that has been overlooked in studies of musical genre, music and race, and music and migration.

* * *

Sitting in a coffee shop in 2016, I asked Pereira what made him come to New York City. He told me that he first dreamed of coming to America in the 1960s, while listening to bands like Blood, Sweat and Tears; Chicago Transit Authority; and Kool and the Gang—bands that were combining jazz with pop and rock. The opportunity to move to New York finally came in 1987, when he was working as a drummer in the Rio de Janeiro jazz scene. Pereira met several New York–based Brazilian musicians and discussed his prospects in the New York jazz scene. Hanging out with the group was Susan Davis, a New York native, percussionist, and vocalist. The two hit it off. As their relationship grew closer, they planned to move together to New York. At the time, Pereira was dealing with the consequences of retinitis pigmentosa, a genetic eye disease that eventually turned him completely blind. He finally arrived in New York in the fall of 1988, and quickly made a name for himself as a sought-after drummer on the scene, recording and touring frequently in jazz and Brazilian music contexts. He told me:

> I got here November 26th, on a warm Saturday of Thanksgiving. The scene was amazing back then. There was so much work. As I told you, I got work on my second day here. I didn't even have a drum set.... There was work everywhere and I was the new guy in town, so I was like the "fruit of the month." There were a lot of clubs. There was Sweet Basil that was open, Blue Note, and I saw a lot of music. I saw Art Blakey, Billy Higgins, Roy Haynes, all my favorite drummers, a lot of jazz music back then. Things started to go down after the Gulf War in 1991, but I was able to gig a lot as a sideman and with my group The Blindfold Test all the way through the 1990s and 2000s. It was my dream getting here, and it became my life.

Pereira's story is a reminder of the limitations of identity categories in capturing the life stories of contemporary migrant musicians—a measure of the pace at which one can dream, fall in love, become blind, become an immigrant, become an American citizen, become Jewish, become a musician.

Listening to intermigrant sounds

Despite many calls for interculturality in music research, ethnic boundaries remain a surprisingly resilient framework in studies of music and migration (Brinner 2009). The past decade has seen a significant rise in writings on music and migration, with a focus on the music of the Mexican diaspora in the southern United States and along the US–Mexico border in the period leading up to the anti-immigrant policies of the Trump Administration (Byrd 2015; Chávez 2017).

Alex Chávez in particular considers the importance of institutional and cultural borders alongside national ones in his study of transnational music-making among Mexican migrants—what he calls the "smaller borders" that affect migrants' lives (2017, 2). Samuel Byrd's book *The Sounds of Latinidad* (2015) emphasizes how class and national origin continue to divide Latin music communities in Charlotte, North Carolina, paying close attention to how musicians in a southern US city respond locally to processes of globalization, while maintaining musical and social divisions between Mexican, Caribbean, and South American migrant music communities. These institutional and cultural borders are also felt far beyond physical borders. For example, as Su Zheng argues, strained US–China relations had a significant "bordering" effect on the lives of members of the diverse Chinese diaspora in New York, while the Trump Administration's so-called Muslim ban imposed in January 2017 had implications much broader than the restrictions on travel for immigrants from Muslim-majority countries (Zheng 2012; Tesler 2018).[3]

Evan Rapport (2014) shows that national borders and ethnic boundaries are palpable in the daily social and musical interactions of immigrants from the former USSR, many of whom settled in South Brooklyn and Queens in the late 1980s, propelled by the decline of the Soviet bloc. Rapport emphasizes the fact that Bukharian Jews continue to use specific instruments, repertoire, and improvisatory practices in an effort to resist assimilation and reinforce cultural boundaries between themselves and others. Carol Silverman similarly shows how musicians from the Macedonian Roma community in the Bronx claim that "music and dance help define them and set them apart from non-Roma," accepting certain essentializing attitudes such as innate musical talent while rejecting others (2013, 106). The important theoretical and methodological emphasis on transnationalism in these recent studies has led to a bounded view of New York–based immigrant communities. Transnationalism in these accounts is thus framed around the interactions of the specific immigrant community with the dominant population. Despite adding important sociopolitical context to the relationship between the United States and immigrants' countries of origin, musical interactions among immigrant communities within the city remain understudied, and scholarly accounts of everyday sociomusical exchanges among diverse groups of immigrants in New York remain relatively rare.[4]

Several recent volumes on music and migration have attempted to frame research around cities (New York, Groningen, Liverpool) and genres (particularly hip-hop and experimental art music) in order to cut across social and national boundaries (Toynbee and Dueck 2011; Sardinha and Campos 2016; Cohen 2022). Important antecedents to this book, these collaborative works conceive of cities not simply as locations of transnational interactions, but as theoretically rich frameworks for such exchanges, emphasizing genre (sub)categories and neighborhoods as facilitators of identity formation and belonging. These studies reflect a "post-migrant" perspective that attends to the ways in which music highlights temporal and spatial dimensions of migration (Çağlar 2016). The reality of immigrants' musical worlds is not limited to the religious, folk, or popular musics of their homeland, nor to their re-creation in new locales; rather, it involves a constant negotiation between instruments, people, musics, and memories carried over from the country of origin with those encountered in the host country. As Ulrich Beck and Nina Glick Schiller argue, "methodological nationalism" and "methodological ethnicity" fail to capture the increasing fragmentation and interrelations of ethnic groups in terms of language, place of origin, legal status, and social stratification, resulting in the exclusion of non-ethnic forms of social engagement and connection (Beck 2007; Glick Schiller 2008, 4).

Extant theoretical frameworks of immigrant musics in American urban centers are not readily applicable to a study of immigrants in the New York jazz scene (Shelemay 2012). This is because of several overlapping methodological assumptions regarding the ways in which the population under study is defined: first, most studies of immigrants focus on immigrants from a single country of origin; second, studies of immigrants often refer to a "community" constructed based on a shared "culture"; third, studies of immigrant musics often rely on musical markers to signify cultural difference, meaning that the group's cultural background and the music studied reflect each other; fourth, studies of immigrant music often assume shared racial and religious identity and underemphasize the influence of gender on transnational mobility and the immigrant experience; and fifth, in contrast to an immigrant community, the notion of "scene" is tied to a particular current locale (whether real or virtual) rather than previous place of origin, although these sometimes overlap (Bennett and Peterson 2004; Straw 1991).

In light of these crucial gaps, this book focuses on the lives of migrant jazz musicians in New York to show how migrant and minority cultures are reconstituted, not only in relation to a dominant culture, but crucially in relation to each other. It offers a critical view of New York as a musical meeting place, a romanticized, fetishized, and imagined "audiotopia" that has drawn thousands of migrant musicians since the 1990s (Kun 2005). It also aims at understanding how the active marketing of New York as a musical utopia by jazz institutions has created unsustainable economic conditions in the scene, transforming working musicians into perpetual students. Finally, it attempts to uncover the ways in which jazz, as borderland music, offers migrants and minorities of diverse backgrounds a mode of interethnic interaction, one that often goes unheard within US ethnoracial listening frames.

The musical border

As a musical genre, "jazz" is an elusive, maligned category, famously rejected by musicians themselves (Early and Monson 2019). Yet I insist on jazz as the framework for this examination of boundary-crossing migrant music. This is because "jazz" and (more broadly) "genre" are defined here not simply by what is included in the category, but also by how this category is used to exclude, deny, or implicitly accept certain musicians, compositions, and sounds. In other words, the framework encompasses the entirety of discourses pertaining to the musical category. It includes how sounds, musicians, and repertoire are discussed in relation to a musical genre, how listeners use these categories in their aesthetic judgment and interpretations, and how such categories impact the contexts for circulation and reproduction of music (Brackett 2016).

In his work on genres in popular music, Fabian Holt argues that genres are "a tool for essentializing connections between ethnicity, place, and music" (2007, 172). By focusing on musics that he hears as "in-between" genres, Holt draws attention to the fact that such musics are often overlooked in music research. Just as grouping music into genres is a collective endeavor, the exclusion of certain performances, instruments, and individuals from a genre grouping is also a collective action, negotiated by critics, scholars, producers, record companies, promoters, listeners, and musicians themselves (Drott 2013). However, the degree to which each of these actors influences inclusion and exclusion is highly unequal. We might say that certain actors are "purists" with regard to the musics they consider permissible, but the influence of a casual fan is not the same as that of a record promoter. Individual musicians often have the least control over the inclusion of their own music in a particular genre grouping. Because migrant musicians' impact on jazz is part of an actively contested discourse on inclusion and exclusion, and because much of this discussion revolves around the Americanness of jazz, about who and what is considered jazz, it remains the most appropriate musical category to frame this book.

I refer to the process by which individuals and performances are judged as part of one or more musical groupings and evaluated in relation to those groupings as a *musical border*. Musical borders are thus mechanisms of social inclusion and exclusion that are objectified, rationalized, and expressed through musical means and terminology. Although often attached to aesthetic goals or judgment, they are equally tools for the categorization and labeling of people and sounds as Other. Such borders can refer to specific musical parameters such as tempo, melody, harmony, timbre, and instrumentation, but they can also incorporate broader categories such as genres, repertoires, and musical traditions. Most commonly, they are ways in which perceptions of a musician, a sound, or an instrument's ethnic identity frame modes of listening. Musical borders can be communicated directly in the course of a performance, but they are often communicated verbally retrospectively in discussions about performances.

Importantly, while musical borders can create a sense of social inclusion, they can simultaneously limit (or "pigeonhole") the scope and meaning of cultural production to representations of perceived ethnic, racial, and gender identities. In other words, the perceived "Chinese-ness" of a particular saxophone solo, or the "Blackness" of a certain guitar riff, depends as much on its constitutive sounds as it does on the identity of the musician and instrument that produced it. Like the growing disparity between individuals crossing national borders, the experience of crossing musical borders is highly contingent on socially *visible* aspects such as race, ethnicity, gender, class, and religion, aspects that are often tied to musical parameters, or what Holt refers to as "codes" (2007, 22).

Musical representations of racial minorities in the United States often minimize the degree of interracial interactions, attaching particular sounds to specific racial identities. Roberts refers to this process as "sonoracialization," the organization of sound into taxonomies based on racialized conceptions of bodies and the incorporation of sound into a racial hierarchy (2016, 4). The process of sonoracialization thus creates a racial border between sounds created by Black, Asian, and White bodies. The ways in which listeners construct and discern racial identities based on sounds and the ways in which they assign different cultural, social, and political value to them has been referred to as the "sonic color line," which "produces, codes, and polices racial difference through the ear, enabling us to hear race as well as see it" (Stoever 2016, 11). The sonic color line is lodged not in the producer of sound, but in socially and sonically constructed ways of listening that racially code "sonic phenomena such as vocal timbre, accents, and musical tones" (Stoever 2016, 11). These codes are evaluated in relation to visible aspects of the producer (Eidsheim 2019). Importantly, both sonoracialization and the sonic color line are concepts that indicate the ways in which producers of primarily vocal sound are racialized and ethnicized by listeners, and the ways these racializations create sonic hierarchies. In jazz, the attachment of racial identity to instrumental sound (particularly the division between "hot" and "sweet" jazz) resulted in the creation of sonic and racial boundaries that are as old as the genre itself (Monson 1995).

Alongside race, gender and sexuality also serve as important listening frameworks in jazz. Tucker (2008) uses the metaphor of "straight lines" to argue that in jazz, heteronormative male listening functions as a "straightening device" that impacts the movement and direction in which female and queer bodies proceed. Such issues become ever more pressing when gender boundaries intersect with ethnic, racial, and national boundaries. Working with female jazz saxophone players, Yoko Suzuki (2013) suggests that for foreign female jazz musicians, womanhood, race, and foreignness represent boundaries with which they have to contend in male-dominated jazz circles. She cites Swedish saxophonist Amanda Sedgwick's remark that she knows she "can never become an insider by virtue of her birth and where she was brought up" (2013, 210). In contrast, Canadian trumpet player Ingrid Jensen emphasizes how visual aspects influence how she is heard: "[Trumpeter] Bobby Shew said after he heard me playing while he was backstage at a band festival, 'Damn, girl, I thought you were an old black guy playin' like that up there. What a surprise to see a young white chick'" (Enstice and Stockhouse 2004, 156). My own interviews with Asian and Latina musicians suggest that gendered, national, and racial discourses affect the way women are "heard" by listeners, their musical choices, employment opportunities, and ultimately their career paths. By choosing to conform to or reject such listening frameworks, female and queer musicians confront significant musical borders.[5]

The ways in which jazz musicians modify their sound in reaction to how they are heard and classified are crucial to understanding musical interactions across sociomusical borders. Because jazz listening intersects "with race, gender, class, modernity, nation" as social fields of power, Tucker's conceptualization of the pull of "straight lines" is helpful in considering how nationality, specifically US Americanness, functions as a straightening or bordering mechanism in jazz (2008, 3). As Tucker notes, jazz is often constructed as a straight line, moving from one inevitable style to another, from one genius to the next. Jazz listening is also constructed as a (straight) line of demarcation, a border separating "us" from "not us."

I am careful not to underestimate the multiple ways in which race, gender, and sexuality affect the lives of immigrants in the United States, and I do not wish to give the impression that interactions across jazz boundaries "fix" society's inequalities. I do, however, contend that to consider only immigrants from a single country of origin and ethnoracial grouping will render the important crossing of racial and other social boundaries invisible rather than highlight them. My aim here is thus to show the various strategies that jazz musicians use to cross both the physical borders of the United States and the social and musical boundaries of the New York jazz scene, without ignoring the inequalities of American society and the jazz world itself in relation to race, gender, religion, and nationality. An important aim of *Jazz Migrations* is thus to untangle the ways in which national and social borders in the United States are maintained through musical borders within which immigrants and minorities can operate, and to uncover how migrant and other minority musicians negotiate these borders.

Musical borders are often reflected in discussions of genre. As a result, they permeate the significant body of literature that focuses on the genre boundaries of the jazz canon. Scott DeVeaux examines the construction of the modernist narrative of jazz as a succession of mostly male, mostly African American individuals who pushed the music toward "artistic freedom," purportedly ending in the 1960s, when jazz "lost its way" (DeVeaux 1991, 2005; Lipsitz 2004). Others have asserted the political contours of the jazz tradition, identifying the "protective" function of boundaries but also their exclusions (Chapman 2018; Early and Monson 2019). It is important to note the difference between two types of canons: the jazz master narrative—constructed in jazz literature and film (one film in particular)—and the multiple, diverse canons shared by musicians in storytelling, autobiographies, and teaching and in the course of musical composition and performance. Whereas the latter are built on personal tribute and admiration, the former serve as the foundation for institutional and cultural politics (Gray 2005).

Boundaries in jazz are thus discursive constructs, tools of exclusion and inclusion. The jazz master narrative—as DeVeaux argues—is produced by elimination through a construction of difference. "Jazz is jazz because it emphasizes musical characteristics that are deemphasized in other forms or because it lacks those elements seen as central to other forms. It is defined through exclusion" (DeVeaux 1991, 528). In a later text titled "Core and Boundaries," DeVeaux makes this point explicitly: "It's not a matter of what to leave in, but what to leave out. It's a matter of drawing boundaries" (2005, 16). Jazz historian Eric Porter's contribution to the aptly named *Jazz/Not Jazz*, a volume dedicated to examining the boundaries of jazz, is similarly focused on these mechanisms of exclusion:

> The boundaries of jazz are maintained by calling attention to sub-genres or specific musical projects that some might view as jazz but that can also be seen as lacking some essential property (swing, improvisation, the fusion of African and European devices, spontaneity, sounds from black popular music, accessibility) or containing elements, such as commercial appeal, or sounds that some believe reside more comfortably in other musical genres. For example, jazz fusion is perceived to be "not jazz" because it uses elements from rock and funk such as electric instruments and a different rhythmic basis; the avant-garde fails the jazz test for some because it abandons swing and other fundamentals; and the neoclassicists are seen as deficient because they fail to understand that change is fundamental to the art form. (Porter 2012, 17)

Scholars have continued to deconstruct the master narrative of jazz by asserting the importance of community over individuals (Monson 1996; Jackson 2012; Greenland 2016); of women and non-binary musicians (Tucker 2001; McGee 2011b; Clifford-Napoleone 2018); of fusion and smooth jazz (Fellezs 2011; Washburne 2004; Gluck 2016); and of free jazz, experimental music collectives, and other crucial aspects that have been left out of the master narratives of jazz (Lewis 2008; Gebhardt and Whyton 2015; Heller 2017).[6] Rather than offering alternative canons, by paying close attention to the ways in which observers/listeners project national identity onto sounds, *Jazz Migrations* considers the impact of the jazz canon as a musical border, a listening framework applied in conjunction with visual cues to assign cultural, social, and political value to music.

An equally important strand in the literature has examined the global influence of jazz, exploring jazz as a symbol of liberal democracy as well as a sign of American global dominance (Starr 1994; Van Eschen 2004; Quirino

2008; Davenport 2010; Monson 2007; Kelley 2012; Atkins 2001; Jackson 2003; Marlow 2018; Garcia 2017; Kubik 2017; Nicholson 2014; Braggs 2016; Johnson 2019). Recently, a work on jazz from a global perspective, edited by Bohlman and Plastino, attempted to map and reconcile the many narratives of liberation and occupation associated with jazz as a global phenomenon (2016). Indeed, the meaning of jazz in the global context crucially depends on the perception of American involvement in these locales and the circumstances that brought jazz there. Taken together, these studies cover significant aspects of the relationship between jazz and the social boundaries and global influence of the United States.

These studies are crucial in framing questions that have been at the heart of US cultural politics for the last century, namely, the impact of immigration on American music. Due to the powerful role of listening in assigning national and ethnoracial meanings, and because the meanings of jazz outside the United States are highly contingent on hearing jazz as American music, a discussion of the ways migrant musicians are heard within the United States has much to tell us about the conflation of sound, place, and ethnoracial identity.[7] Here too, the musical border serves as a crucial theoretical framework aimed at teasing out the ways in which musicians and listeners attach nationality or ethnicity to certain sounds within and in relation to specific geopolitical contexts.

Migrating jazz bodies

This book rests on the premise that to understand the potential role of jazz in precipitating a musical migration, one must consider the role that location and social interaction hold in the study of jazz improvisation itself. When I arrived in New York in 2013 to begin a four-year-long study, my primary ethnographic tools were the upright bass, my body, and my musical proficiency or "chops." While interviews, archival research, and analysis of videos and recordings were important, the fundamental harmonic and rhythmic role of the bass positioned me physically and musically inside and in the background of countless musical contexts, social interactions, and formal and informal conversations. In order to become part of the scene, I had to practice daily, memorize intricate compositions, and work on weaknesses in my playing. I had to pursue performance opportunities, book gigs, and learn to navigate the subway system with a bass and an amplifier. I had to interact socially and musically with musicians on the bandstand and in the recording studio, pay other musicians, and get paid for my own work. Finally, I had to get home quickly and write down in detail the inner workings of the day's experiences. As an ethnographic tool, the bass and the musical proficiency it required had considerable advantages: as long as I was able to blend in musically, the bass provided access to experiences that would not have been possible otherwise. I was, for that moment and place, a migrant musician trying to integrate into a musical scene.

Scholars of jazz improvisation have argued that knowledge of improvisation is embodied, situated in a particular environment, and distributed among the participants in the musical act (Borgo 2005; Born 2005; Iyer 2016; Becker and Faulkner 2009). This gesture toward the specificity of improvised knowledge has important ramifications for our understanding of different jazz scenes around the world, about musicians' desire to know jazz, and about the possibility of doing so from afar or from the "outside." If knowledge of jazz improvisation is primarily *embodied* rather than textual or descriptive, the circulation of such knowledge depends not only on texts, scores, and recordings, but crucially on migrating bodies. If improvised knowledge is *situated*—and depends on the circumstances created in a particular location—then knowledge of jazz differs from one locale to the next. Finally, if knowledge of jazz improvisation is *distributed* among participants, then the people who make up the scene, the various musicians and audiences that populate it collectively, share and shape what jazz is for that time and place. When we consider what New York jazz is today, canonical historical texts and individual accolades can only tell a partial story. To know jazz is to be a *body* of jazz, to know New York jazz is to *situate* this body in New York, and to know jazz in New York today is to know the collective interactions of jazz musicians on the scene, rather than those of a select few.

Jazz musicians understand this in intuitive and subtle ways. As Ralph Ellison noted in the early 1960s, musicians travel to the New York scene in order to understand the conditions under which specific jazz performances were made prior to becoming texts, recordings, or transcriptions (2011, 208). Tadataka Unno, a Japanese pianist who arrived in New York in 2008, had steady work in Japan—recording opportunities and gigs almost every night. But performing, recording, and listening to records was not enough. "I needed to know the culture. . . . I wanted to meet my heroes, to play with them, to talk, to hang out," he said. "If I stayed in Japan that [would have] never happened" (Leland 2020). Could this desire for situated knowledge be enough to propel a mass musical migration? Certainly not by itself. But when an entire history of music is dedicated to enshrining one scene and one city, the gravitational pull might just be strong enough.

Philip Bohlman has argued that American music histories are based on the binary tension between "elite" and "vernacular" musics, or between the "cosmopolitan" and the "provincial" (2002, 130). The "elite" and "cosmopolitan" musics are based on traditions grounded in written notation, while "vernacular" or "provincial" traditions are often unscripted and therefore remain outside the purview of historical research. It can be argued that jazz, in all its diversity, has been moved (or pushed) along the social spectrum from a vernacular, embodied, situated music to an elite, textualized, cosmopolitan music, with contemporary jazz musicians being routinely counted among the winners of MacArthur "genius grants" and Pulitzer Prizes, serving as tenured faculty in Ivy League schools, and holding artist residencies at prestigious museums (Early and Monson 2019). As a result, US jazz in the last thirty years has been transformed from a music industry driven by audiences, labels, and festivals to a high art administered by private foundations and government institutions (Beuttler 2019). The decline of a jazz music industry was certainly aided by the rise of streaming platforms and by a general decline in recording sales across the music industry, but the decline in jazz audiences was well on its way long before Spotify and YouTube became household names (Nicholson 2014). It began with the decline of local scenes, where performers and audiences shared a specific embodied understanding of jazz (Williams 2014). As the United States moves its most prized jazz assets into the Ivory Tower, many of the musicians, audiences, and places where jazz was an everyday practice have been left behind.

The academization of jazz, as Thomas Owens notes, has created an international language, a lingua franca "serving as the principal musical language of thousands of jazz musicians. It also affects the way earlier jazz styles are played, and is the parent language of many action jazz ('free jazz') and fusion players" (1996, 4). The "lingua franca" Owens refers to is the growing transformation of jazz from a body-based practice to a text-based practice. In using Owens's term I do not wish to imply that jazz, like classical music, is primarily played from scores—something that has been going on since the 1920s. What I mean is that the ways in which jazz improvisation is studied today are based crucially on the global circulation of bebop texts (books, play-along records, YouTube videos) rather than on embodied knowledge as its primary source. These two processes—a decline of local scenes and a growth in the circulation of jazz texts—have created an urgent need for situated, distributed knowledge. As the United States continues to be the primary exporter of jazz texts, the absence of situated and distributed jazz knowledge has propelled, to paraphrase Vijay Iyer, a movement of musical bodies "without musical spaces."

Maintaining the conceptual boundaries described above, jazz scholarship has tended to focus on jazz as either vernacular and situated or as cosmopolitan and textual—as an expression of African American identity or of a global musical world—but the coexistence and confluence of these two conceptions of jazz within the United States have rarely been addressed (Ramsey 1996). Recognizing the situatedness and distribution of jazz knowledge thus brings us closer to understanding the impact of immigrants on the New York jazz scene. It also forces us to come to terms with the ways embodied, vernacular expressions of an African American sensibility are actively transformed by private institutions, academics, and governmental programs into a lingua franca—a cosmopolitan, elite music.

For Amiri Baraka, jazz was the "most cosmopolitan of any Negro music, able to utilize almost any foreign influence within its broader spectrum" (Jones 1999, 92). Baraka was referring here to the ways African American musicians such as Yusef Lateef, Randy Weston, and Eric Dolphy incorporated Latin American, South Asian, and West African musical influences. It is not clear if at the time Baraka recognized that jazz was also rapidly becoming cosmopolitan through its transformation into text: an increasingly disembodied, displaced, individualized music. I call this process a *second cosmopolitanism*, closely related to what R. Murray Schafer called the "schizophonia" of acousmatic sound—the splitting of an original sound from its electroacoustic reproduction. This split figures less prominently in recent writings on the use of jazz as a facilitator of transnational encounters and in ethnographic studies of American expatriates in jazz scenes across the globe (Ake 2010; Feld 2012; Braggs 2016). However, it is crucial to recent theories of sound and race and to the question of who is playing and who is listening (Ramsey 2001).

These two "modes" of jazz—jazz as a situated, embodied expression and jazz as a lingua franca—do not operate in separate musical spheres, nor are they split clearly by racial, national, or economic boundaries. Musicians of different backgrounds and understandings of jazz interact regularly, listening and adapting to each other's playing, learning from each other, and criticizing and reflecting upon the music of their fellow musicians. In other words, understanding jazz as a displaced individualized practice is becoming part of jazz's own "distributed knowledge." As jazz education increasingly departs from older models of apprenticeship in favor of structured and standardized instruction in academic institutions, vernacular and cosmopolitan conceptions of jazz clash regularly but also sustain one another in important ways (Wilf 2014).

A dream

"Now, that's a funny story!" Juan Méndolas, a Bolivian Quechua man in his seventies, recalls his past with a smile. He bangs emphatically on the table as he recounts his big break in the New York jazz scene. "I was just standing outside Sweet Basil. It was three or four o'clock in the morning, and Charlie Haden came out looking for some coffee. And he said, 'Hi, man, do you know where there's an open coffee shop?' And I said, 'Sorry, I don't know. I just came from Argentina.' 'Oh, you're from Argentina? Do you know Dino Saluzzi?' he asked. And I said, 'Yeah, I know Dino. I recorded with him a few years ago in Buenos Aires. We played folk music and so on.' And Haden said, 'Do you want to have a coffee with me?' And we went for coffee, and chatted a bit, and he asked what instrument I play, and I said 'I play flute, different kinds of flutes.' And he said, 'Can you come and play with me tomorrow?' I was a bit shocked, but how could I have said no? I said OK! I went back into Sweet Basil, crossed the room, and told my wife, 'I just had coffee with CHARLIE HADEN! And he asked me to play with him tomorrow!' The next day I went again to Sweet Basil and I brought my instruments, the quena and other flutes, and I went up to play. And Haden said, 'Play, I'll follow you.'"

"Wait, wait," I stopped Méndolas incredulously, momentarily interrupting his flow. "He invited you to play the gig?" "Yes! I played with him at the following gig! To a packed house! So I go on stage, and he says, 'Play whatever you want!' So I played my music, quena music, something very simple, like this [he begins singing the line of the quena], and Haden immediately followed me [he continues to seamlessly mimic Haden's bass line]. After the show, Haden talked to Carla Bley, his arranger, and they said they will write something for me, incorporate me into the Liberation Music Orchestra. We recorded Dream Keeper, and I toured with him for two and a half years. For me, it didn't matter if he paid me or not. I was flying. Me, with Branford Marsalis, Joe Lovano, Dewey Redman, Paul Motian on drums. . . . And I said to myself, 'Where am I? How did I get here?'"

Like the migration stories of many of the 1980s generation, Juan Méndolas's musical career seems incredible if not impossible. He grew up in the small community of Characoyo, a hamlet of five families near the city of Potosí, Bolivia. By the age of fourteen he had left his home on foot to find work in Argentina. While he was working on a construction site in the city of Mendoza, his fellow workers heard him singing and suggested that he take music lessons at the local conservatory. He began studying and quickly applied his newly acquired training in music theory, solfège, and flute to a wide range of woodwinds played in indigenous communities in the Andes, including the *rollano*, *ocarina*, and *quena*. Some years later he established the Andean folk group Markama, making his first album with them in 1975 and touring South America and Europe. The group traveled to the United States for the first time in 1980 with an invitation from Argentinian poet Bernardo Palombo, the founder of Taller Latino Americano, one of the longest-running immigrant cultural centers in New York (see Chapter 5). The band continued to tour South America, Europe, and the United States for seven more years, recording nine albums in the process. When they returned to the United States in 1987, Méndolas decided to stay.

Méndolas's story is but one example of the many everyday fairytales shared by older musicians in the New York scene. He arrived in New York at a watershed moment. Migrant musicians of his generation were a small but important part of the jazz scene, giving the music a broader sonic palette and an interpretative context without disrupting its boundaries. Many of them played instruments recognized as "external" to jazz, most importantly percussion.[8] Despite fiery op-eds in newspapers by Wynton Marsalis, Stanley Crouch, and others, what was considered jazz remained largely undisputed, and whatever influences were combined with it—rock, Latin, or Brazilian music, for instance—were clearly marked as Other (Washburne 2020). It is no coincidence that some of the most important fusion projects of the 1970s were led or co-led by migrant musicians, including Weather Report's Joe Zawinul, Alex Acuña, Miroslav Vitous, and Othello Molineaux, and the Mahavishnu Orchestra's John McLaughlin, Jean Luc Ponty, and Billy Cobham.

Like Méndolas, the majority of migrant musicians in New York in the 1970s and 1980s integrated into the scene as sidemen, building careers based on these associations.[9] For example, members of Miles Davis's groups in the 1970s and 1980s included English bassist Dave Holland and Panamanian saxophonist Carlos Garnett. Chick Corea's Return to Forever included Brazilians Airto Moreira and Flora Purim. Pat Metheny's group included Brazilians Naná Vasconcelos, Armando Marçal, and Nando Lauria, as well as Pedro Anzar from Argentina. Working as sidemen, playing instruments from their home countries, and performing vocabularies associated with the music of their countries, these musicians were often considered "auxiliary" to American jazz ensembles (Fellezs 2011). At a time when jazz-rock fusion was being criticized as detrimental to the swing and bebop tradition, the attachment of migrant musicians to fusion was becoming a professional liability in a scene switching to "neoclassical" jazz (Chapman 2018).

Importantly, it was bebop musicians such as Dizzy Gillespie, Art Blakey, and Oscar Peterson (himself a Canadian immigrant) who curbed these attitudes by hiring migrant musicians for their bands. It is rarely mentioned that prior to hiring the young Wynton Marsalis, Art Blakey worked for four years with the young Russian trumpet player Valery Ponomarev and Japanese bassist Isao Suzuki. Similarly, the bassist who took over Ray Brown's place in the Oscar Peterson Trio was Danish double bassist Niels-Henning Ørsted Pedersen, who worked with Peterson until the bassist's death in 2005. Perhaps most important in aiding the internationalization of the New York scene was Dizzy Gillespie's United Nations Orchestra, made up of African American, Panamanian, Brazilian, Dominican, Mexican, Cuban, and Puerto Rican musicians. While focusing primarily on Gillespie's Latin jazz numbers, the band provided young musicians such as Paquito D'Rivera, Danilo Pérez, Claudio Arditti, and Antonio Sánchez with important positions on the American bandstand. Pérez and Sánchez in particular would become role models for young migrant musicians, both through their command of straight-ahead jazz and through their participation in multiple musical "scenes." This sense of multiple affiliations would characterize the following decades in jazz (Beuttler 2019).

In the late 1980s several jazz scenes coexisted In New York City: a Brazilian jazz scene centered around Cafe Wha? and SOB's, a Latin jazz scene at the Village Gate and Nuyorican Poets Cafe, a New Orleans–style scene around midtown's Birdland and uptown's West End Café, a downtown avant-garde scene at the Kitchen and the Knitting Factory, a guitar-centric fusion scene at the 55 Bar, and finally a Greenwich Village straight-ahead scene centered around several clubs including the Blue Note, the Village Vanguard, Bradley's, and Sweet Basil. The musicians who performed routinely at these venues felt a sense of social and musical belonging to these scenes.[10] The association of scenes with genres was also manifested in clubs' booking practices. In the early 1990s there was an abundance of clubs specializing in specific genres. These clubs often had a weekly booking system, in which bands were booked either once a week for recurring engagements or for six-day residency cycles. These booking systems allowed musicians to sustain themselves in more predictable and dependable ways (Greenland 2016, 98).

The astronomical rise in rent in the post-9/11 years (leading up to the 2008 stock market crash), declining audiences, and the steadily growing number of musicians resulted in clubs seeking a faster turnover of acts to increase their appeal to a wider audience (Greenland 2016, 90). By the beginning of the 2000s, the boundaries between the separate scenes began to blur. Clubs such as the Iridium, Zinc Bar, SOB's, and Barbès began to book diverse, genre-crossing lineups featuring straight-ahead jazz alongside free jazz, Brazilian choro, and Latin jazz. The booking practices in these jazz venues indicate a growing openness in the scene, with Israeli, Cuban, Venezuelan, and Brazilian musicians having a prominent role in reconfiguring the meaning of jazz. At the same time, the "Big Five" clubs, such as the Blue Note and the Village Vanguard, presented a more conservative stance, with well-established musicians but an increasingly open attitude toward genre.

Changes in clubs' booking practices and genre affiliation highlighted a second transformation that took place between 1990s and the 2010s—a growing desire among musicians to reflect the complexity of their musical biographies, the range of scenes that they were part of, and the distances they traveled within and beyond the city.[11] In my conversations with Israeli-born composer and clarinetist Anat Cohen, who began playing in New York in the mid-1990s, she highlighted the cross-pollination between scenes during the early 2000s:

At some point I was part of the Colombian scene, the Argentinian music [scene], the Venezuelan music [scene], and the choro [scene], all from Latin America. I realized that between the gigs with [New Orleans jazz tubist] David Ostwald and gigs with Aquiles Báez, who's a guitarist from Venezuela, the thing I always loved in New York was that there were days when I would do two or three gigs a day—going to meet with guys in Columbus Square at 1 p.m. to open the banjo case and busk New Orleans jazz in the street, and go from there to play a small gig with the Diva Orchestra in some concert from six to seven, and then go play with a choro ensemble. And New York is one of the only places where you can do that.

Cohen's fond memories of daily travel across various musical worlds reflect changing attitudes toward musical knowledge, genre, and place of origin in the New York scene. For jazz musicians, the possibility of learning and practicing different musical traditions without leaving the five boroughs of the city has become part of New York's aura. The city encapsulates the best of the world's music. This "micro-cosmopolitanism" of the city is a direct result of the growing number of migrant musicians who became instructors of their own musical traditions (Radice 2015).

In the 2011 documentary *New York Jazzed Out*, Beninese guitarist Lionel Loueke expresses his perception of New York as a global music school: "We come to New York to have experience in the music. There's a vibe here you don't find anywhere else. We are here to learn. We can go around the world to present what we learned and what we do, but here is where we get the energy" (Mastin, Winckel, and Jeremiah 2011). These representations of New York as a hub for acquiring musical knowledge quickly bring to mind Josh Kun's notion of audiotopia, "a place where music points out the possible, to help us remap the world we live in now" (2005, 22). Perhaps because New York is so convincing as an audiotopia, "because of its uncanny ability to absorb and meld heterogeneous national, cultural, and historical styles and traditions across space and within place" (Kun 2005, 23), those already there are willing to make great personal sacrifices to will this audiotopia into reality. Dreaming of New York as a utopia, as a place of boundless musical learning, these musicians contribute their time and talent to the cause, often for little or no pay.[12] For Kun, the value of music is driven by what it can do. But it is precisely music's utopian potential that leads musicians to accept a life of perennial financial precarity.

Musicians describe the period of training, when one has to struggle to make ends meet, as the time for "paying dues." Paul Berliner describes this as "the trials and tribulations that accompany the learner's efforts to absorb and sort out musical knowledge" (Berliner 1994, 51). The concept of paying dues seems to be ever expanding in today's scene. The increase in the number of musicians led to growing competition for available gigs while also creating new musical possibilities and musical collaborations. While musicians continue to collaborate and develop their skills and knowledge, diminishing audiences mean that they are compensated less for this ever-expanding skill set. One's learning periods become longer and longer, a justification for longer hours, for rehearsals for little or no pay, and for one-off gigs. As long as musicians continue to struggle to make ends meet, these periods are framed as an endless apprenticeship.

A diverse musical skill set is thus not simply an artistic choice or a cosmopolitan affinity but also a survival strategy, a way to continue making music professionally. As Cohen put it in our conversation:

> Some people would say, "I only want to play jazz from the early 1960s, and that's *it*. When I don't do that, I go slice salami at the deli." Now, that's great: focus on one thing and do it really well. If you can reach the level where you are super-professional and you work all the time and they hire you because they need someone who can do that specific 1960s thing, and you are the best at it, that's great. But because New York devours its own inhabitants, it takes time to get to New York and be the best.

Cohen's use of the biblical phrase "a land that devours its inhabitants" (Numbers 13:32) alludes to the competitiveness of the scene and the resourcefulness needed to survive it. Cohen explained that her own way of addressing the economic challenges of the New York scene was to continue expanding her musical skills.

> I was always in several bands. At every given moment I played in two or three projects, with different people, because I always wanted to. From the Latin scene to the Brazilian scene to jazz, there's always something, and of course every now and then there's an "Israeli gig," perhaps at the consulate.... There's always something. In my music, with my quartet, it all comes out. There are all these influences, but it's all New York.... I am one of those people who has always liked to do many different things.

Cohen describes how her compositional process highlights different points in her biography, paying tribute to various musical people, scenes, and places. "The fact is that I could always do many different things in a kind of mishmash," she says. "There are all these influences. When you write music you don't say, 'I'll write music in the style of this and that.'" But Cohen's music is not non-idiomatic. Instead, it engages, critiques, and challenges musical categories directly. In her 2012 album *Claroscuro*, Cohen integrates original compositions and covers with a specific selection of guest musicians to represent her multiple musical worlds. But these worlds never appear in isolation, as separate entities.

In her cover of Artie Shaw's "Nightmare," Cohen pays tribute to her long participation in the trad jazz scene, and particularly to her engagement with Arbor Records jazz parties in Clearwater, Florida, where she performed with some of the elder statesmen of the swing generation, including Kenny Davern, Buddy DeFranco, and Bob Wilber. But rather than hosting musicians associated with the trad jazz scene, she chose for the recording her close friend and mentor, the Cuban composer, reed player, and conductor Paquito D'Rivera. Honoring her long association with the Wednesday residency of David Ostwald's Louis Armstrong Eternity Band at the Birdland club in midtown Manhattan, she invited trombonist and singer Wycliffe Gordon to take the lead, but rather than the light swing that an Armstrong tune would suggest, she added a laid-back hip-hop–tinged back beat. In her collaboration with Brazilian percussionist Gilmar Gomes—whom she met as part of her long engagement with Brazilian music and her weekly gigs at Cafe Wha?—she chose to cover Milton Nascimento's classic Brazilian rock song "Tudo O Que Você Podia Ser," as well as Pixinguinha's classic choro "Um a Zero." To make sure that the songs do not fall too neatly into musical categories, Gomes plays the percussion introduction on congas, a decidedly Cuban instrument, perhaps as a nod to D'Rivera (who shared the duet with Cohen). D'Rivera, as Cohen describes him, is "a person that does all music, and he finds himself in all music and represents himself just brilliantly in every kind of music" (Cohen 2013b).[13] Not surprisingly, the other members of her quartet—Jason Lindner, Daniel Freedman, and Joe Martin—represent connections Cohen made through Israeli musicians long associated with the Smalls scene, including bassist Omer Avital and guitarist Gilad Hekselman. It is interesting to note that Smalls, the club that gave Cohen her first break in New York in the mid-1990s, defines itself today as "strictly a bebop club" (Sidran 2017). Despite this, the kind of border-crossing music that Cohen and other migrant musicians make never falls neatly into such explicit labels and is often presented at the club.

Another musician whose work reflects the changing New York scene is Cuban drummer Francisco Mela. Mela was a member of the trios of Kenny Barron and McCoy Tyner during the 2000s (along with bassists Peter Slavov and Gerald Cannon, respectively), but he also performs in free improvisation contexts with saxophonist Daniel Carter and bassist William Parker, and as the leader of his own Cuban-influenced jazz ensemble Cuban Safari. On his album *Tree of Life* (2011), Mela recorded seven original compositions and three cover songs: a Jason Moran piece called "Retrograde," the standard "The Nearness of You" by Hoagy Carmichael, and the classic Chilean song "Gracias a la Vida" by Violeta Parra. On the last two, Mela sings in addition to playing drums. Presenting different aspects of Mela's musical biography and his association with different musicians, scenes, and places (including his Afro-Cuban roots), the album captures the changing positions of migrant jazz musicians in recent decades. It pays tribute to jazz-rock fusion in the fast-moving 4/4 rock groove of "Africa en Mis Venas," in Ben Monder's distorted guitar lines in the heavy 7/4 groove of "Toma del Poder," and in the angular saxophone lines of "Classico Mela." The piece "Yadan Mela," named after Mela's son, is a tribute to the new acoustic dimensions that jazz-fusion projects took on in the late 1980s. Through the flute playing of Haitian saxophonist Jowee Omicil and the singing of Esperanza Spalding, Mela pays homage to an earlier generation of migrant musicians, among them Juan Méndolas, Naná Vasconcelos, and Pedro Aznar, who brought wordless vocal timbres, traditional woodwinds, and percussion to the New York scene of the late 1980s. Finally, by choosing to perform standards, contemporary jazz, and a Chilean *nueva canción*, he places them all on equal footing as part of the contemporary jazz tradition. Featuring his long-time friends and collaborators—pianists Leo Genovese from Argentina and Elio Villafranca from Cuba, bassists Luques Curtis (a native of Connecticut who straddles the straight-ahead and Latin jazz scenes) and Peter Slavov from Bulgaria, saxophonist Uri Gurvich from Israel—*Tree of Life* is important not only in expanding the notion of what jazz is, but also in challenging understandings of subgenres like Afro-Cuban jazz, which carries its own essentializing ingredients and expectations, such as clave rhythms and *guajeo* patterns.

Such musical crossing is not always accepted by musicians who are firmly situated in a single scene. When Mela asked bassist Gerald Cannon, his long-time friend and collaborator in McCoy Tyner's trio, to comment on *Tree of Life*, Cannon replied, "These are interesting compositions, but it's not jazz—you should write a jazz album." "I understood right away that it wasn't something he really liked," Mela explained,

> so I asked him, "what is a jazz album for you?" And he said to me, "When we want to refresh our ears, do we go back to old records by people like Bud Powell or Art Tatum or John Coltrane? Yes, and what makes us do that? Because that's the real jazz. You have to write music that swings, music that puts you in a position where people can really hear you." And you know, we Latino people don't see that until somebody like Gerald Cannon tells us. We all think we're writing real jazz, but we don't concentrate on AABA tunes in 4/4 that swing. (Randall 2017)

Cannon's reaction was a clear demarcation of a musical border, of what is, and is not jazz. His reference to the jazz canon, to Bud Powell, Art Tatum, and John Coltrane, reflects its significance as a listening framework, one that was missing in Cannon's hearing of Mela. Most importantly, Cannon's advice to write music "that swings," music "where people can really hear you," attests to the power of listening frameworks to "mute" migrant musicians who cross musical borders, to make them inaudible to their audiences, and even to highly respected colleagues. Mela's reaction to Cannon's advice was to record a bebop-inspired album titled *Fe* (Faith) in 2016 (with Cannon and Argentinian pianist Leo Genovese), but to continue writing and playing free jazz with his new MPT Trio (with Cuban saxophonist Hery Paz and Venezuelan guitarist Juanma Trujillo).

Thus, the daily musical border crossings of Mela, a Black Cuban man and Jehovah's Witness, and Cohen, a White Israeli Jewish woman, reflect their compositional process and relationship to their audience. As we set out to discuss the ways in which migrant musicians cross borders in American music, we must also inquire who gets to delineate those borders. And when we consider the importance of the body, place, and social interaction to jazz knowledge, we must ask, who *knows* jazz? Who gets to defend jazz? Who is positioned on each side of the border, and what are the power differentials and stakes of being included or excluded from "jazz" as a category? How do inclusion and exclusion in American society with regard to race, gender, class, and religion influence passage through the social "checkpoints" or core values associated with jazz as a national American symbol? In the following chapters I hope to provide inroads into these challenging questions.

Chapter outline

Following a structure common to many migration narratives, this book traces the pathways of migrant musicians from the "margins" of the New York jazz scene to its "core," while simultaneously troubling this linear progression and the binary distinctions it suggests.

Throughout the book, I use the terms sound, movement, crossing, listening, space, and interaction as a gesture to the multi-directional nature of migrant musicians' lives and the complex relationship they develop with institutions that mark "straight ahead" trajectories in the New York jazz scene: educational institutions like the New School, cultural institutions like Jazz at Lincoln Center, and major jazz clubs like the Village Vanguard. To counterbalance these institutions, the book traces the informal, musician-led institutions that forge new relationships and pathways in the scene—house and jam sessions like the Vodou bar session, immigrant-owned jazz clubs and venues like Terraza 7 and Tomi Jazz, polynational bands and musical collectives like Legal Aliens. These institutions provide crucial spaces for defying and redefining the directional structures of the New York scene.

The title of each chapter and the ethnographic vignettes that open them are designed to capture a mid-point between theory and descriptive reality, between experience and reflection. The difference in tone between ethnography and analysis—although quite common in anthropological writings—may feel jarring to some readers. Its aim is to reflect the disorienting experience of migration that I experienced and sought to trace in this book, moving between countries, between languages, and across musical and academic worlds. Similarly, notions like *The Loop*, capturing the economic and educational, global and local nexus that shape the migration of the jazz musicians to the United States, or *jam session*, theorizing the social boundaries of the scene and the ways in which migrants cross them, are simultaneously theoretical and experiential concepts, remaining tethered to the concrete realities they describe. As such, their utility is lodged in the contexts they seek to explains. The concepts that guide the last three chapters of the book—History, Home, and The Village, are best understood as theoretical critiques, highlighting the complexity and frequent incongruency of these dominant concepts in the lived experiences of migrant musicians. In a sense, rather than expanding on existing theoretical concepts, the book seeks to destabilize their dominance as interpretative frames.

The first chapter, "The Loop," examines the relationship between the academization of jazz education and its contribution to the proliferation of migrants in the New York jazz scene. Building on recent literature on the growing centrality of jazz schools in jazz training, the chapter follows the globalization of jazz education since the 1990s through case studies in India, Israel, and the Bronx. It documents efforts by American jazz programs to recruit international students and traces the role of schools as conduits for migrant musicians into the United States through the facilitation of visas and award of scholarships. It then moves on to consider how the introduction of jazz education into elite social spaces has made it a crucial source of employment for migrant jazz musicians. It concludes with a discussion of the blurring of boundaries between educational institutions and performance venues, and of how such processes create an economic imbalance between studying, teaching, and performing jazz. The chapter argues that these processes have an important effect on the socioeconomic and racial makeup of the musician population in the New York jazz scene.

The second chapter, "Jam Session," describes the role of jam sessions in the incorporation of migrant musicians into the New York scene. It focuses on a Monday-night jam session at the Haitian-owned bar Vodou, located in the Bedford-Stuyvesant neighborhood of Brooklyn. It describes the historical role of jam sessions as places of border crossing between White Americans and Black Americans, and how musical proficiency was crucial in this process. Viewed from a contemporary perspective, the chapter describes how various social boundaries operate within the jam session, how they are policed, and how they are ultimately crossed. It concludes with a discussion of the extent and limits to which musical proficiency or "chops" allow musicians to cross social boundaries in the New York scene.

The third chapter, titled "The Scene," connects the notion of a "migrant jazz scene" to the lived time cycles of migrant jazz musicians. Framed around recurring monthly performances, weekly jam sessions, daily house sessions, and hours of individual practice, it focuses on the network of musicians associated with Terraza 7, a "jazz and immigrant folk" venue located in Jackson Heights, Queens. Through these cycles, it explores the bar owner's utopian vision of diversifying his clientele by programming artists who combine jazz with other musical traditions. Based on an analysis of performances and interviews with musicians, patrons, and the bar owner, Freddy Castiblanco, it examines the relationship between jazz as a cyclical improvisatory practice and the social cycles that constitute Terraza 7 as an immigrant jazz scene.

Chapter 4, "History," considers the ways in which migrant jazz musicians negotiate the jazz canon as a "musical border" in their performances. Building on recent debates about the marginalization and audibility of Asian American musicians in jazz scholarship, I analyze the relationships of several New York–based Japanese musicians to the African American jazz tradition. I then analyze a performance by the Kenji Yoshitake Trio at the Japanese-owned Tomi Jazz club to consider how these musicians evoke the African American history of jazz while negotiating demands for originality, sonic identity, and "freedom."

The fifth chapter, "Home," focuses on musical performances of "home" with the aim of destabilizing and challenging this elusive category. Drawing on interviews and analysis of musical performances at the Taller Latino Americano, Birdland, and other venues across the city, it considers the various ways in which Argentinian and Chilean musicians reconstruct home as an emotional and sonic category, reacting to fluctuating demands to express or suppress their sense of national identity and ethnic belonging in their music. It examines the musical use of cultural markers such as the zamba, the cueca, the *nueva canción*, and the legacy of Violeta Parra alongside rejections of such icons as simplistic and essentializing. Finally, it argues that in a time of mass migration and frequent territorial displacements, musicians create emotional attachments to new places through various sonic practices, thus capturing the fluctuating nature of home as a musical and emotional category.

The sixth chapter, "The Village," discusses the ways in which ethnic and racial frames shape how migrant Jewish musicians are heard, and the practices they use to subvert these listening frames. I focus on two performances by Israeli musicians Uri Gurvich and Anat Cohen, both of them at the famed Village Vanguard club in Greenwich Village, and both dedicated to renowned jazz musicians—John Zorn and Benny Goodman. By analyzing how markers of Jewishness (or the lack thereof) appear in their performances and how both the choice of an ensemble and the interactions within the ensemble subvert these markers, I ultimately show how migrant musicians actively work to decouple simple notions of race and ethnicity from sound.

The conclusion ties together the three main themes of the book: the meaning of jazz to migrant musicians, the place of migrants within the New York scene, and the ways these two inform musical practices, attitudes, and ways of listening in contemporary jazz. It begins by considering the optimism brought forth by the institutional recognition that migrant jazz musicians have received over the past decade and the disillusionment caused by the COVID-19 pandemic. It concludes by showing how the study of migrant jazz musicians in New York can offer new insights into migrant music performance and reception through the notions of musical borders and ethnic listening.

1
The Loop

For my fifteenth birthday my friend Matan gave me an audiocassette he had prepared for me. It included an alternate take of John Coltrane's "Blue Trane," in which he had overdubbed himself playing a recorder duet. One of the recorders was stuck in his mouth, the other up his nostril. We both thought it was hilarious. On the back of the cassette, he wrote a dedication in English: "See You in NYC." That night, on a dial-up Internet connection, I showed my dad the website for Berklee College of Music in Boston. He looked at it and asked, "How are you going to pay for it?" "I'll start saving money now, and there are scholarships," I answered hesitantly. "Forget it," he said. "That's more than your mother and I make in a year."

When I was twenty and about to finish my military service in the Israeli army jazz band, Matan and every other musician I knew was leaving for Boston or New York. I stayed in Israel and studied musicology at Tel Aviv University. I first went to visit my friends in the US in 2007. After that visit, there was no longer any doubt. I wanted to move there. My dad's question remained as relevant then as it had been when I was fifteen. In June 2013, six years, two degrees, and a six-day train ride later, I moved to New York City.

For migrant musicians, academic jazz institutions serve as the most important gateway into the United States. But the academization of jazz, it seems, also signals the exit of a significant share of the young, middle-class, and minority listenership. The National Endowment for the Arts has reported a decades-long decrease in the number of people attending jazz performances. Of those who do attend, a growing majority are older, White, and very highly educated (NEA 2019). In New York City, the rising cost of real estate and diminishing audiences have led to the closure of many landmark clubs, most recently the Jazz Standard, Cornelia Street Café, and 55 Bar.[1] On the other hand, the number of jazz musicians living and performing in the city continues to rise, partly due to growing numbers of migrant musicians.[2]

I refer to the impact of the academization of jazz on the social, racial, and economic makeup of the New York jazz scene as "the Loop." The Loop theorizes the process whereby precarious economic conditions in a crowded field (in this case, jazz performance) lead practitioners to pursue teaching to supplement their income.[3] In doing so, they train new musicians and inject them into an overcrowded jazz field. This second generation of musicians also pursues teaching to supplement their work, and so on. This general process is further exacerbated by academic institutions that mediate jazz training, socialization, and labor.

The Loop creates smaller social, economic, and racial loops that determine who can pursue a career in jazz despite the economic risks. As I argue in this chapter, one of the main causes of the rise of migrant musicians on the scene is the growing economic significance of academic jazz institutions, their global reach, and their impact on the city's club scene. I will begin this chapter by describing the global scope of this phenomenon and its impact on jazz migration to the United States. I will then examine its influence on the socioeconomic and racial makeup of academic jazz programs. I will conclude with a consideration of the ways in which the Loop impacts jazz clubs, the primary performance contexts of jazz musicians in the New York scene.

The academization of jazz

Academic jazz programs have been a rich topic of discussion among jazz scholars in the last two decades. Though virtually nonexistent in ethnographic studies of American jazz published in the mid-1990s, there has been a deluge of writing dedicated to jazz education since then.[4] This is not coincidental, as jazz became a subject of ethnographic research and part of the academic music curriculum around the same time. As Stuart Nicholson notes, the jazz-education industry grosses an estimated $300 million a year, with hundreds of millions invested in jazz education in colleges, universities, summer camps, and high schools in recent years. Data from 2014 suggest that more than 500,000 US high school and college students had been involved in jazz activities, and over 500 colleges were offering jazz-related courses for credit, with 120 programs offering a bachelor's degree in jazz studies (Nicholson 2014, 15).

Despite this precipitous growth, much of the writing on academic jazz programs deals with the tensions between the conformity of the college classroom and the idealized freedom and creativity embedded in jazz improvisation practice (Wilf 2014). The far-reaching social and economic implications of the rise of academic jazz programs and their disproportional impact on the lives of musicians remain largely unacknowledged. Ken Prouty notes that "the numbers of students who graduate with degrees in jazz have become a point of concern for some critics and musicians," particularly in relation to the number of venues, festivals, and ticket-buying audience members (2012, 46). Concerns notwithstanding, literature on academic jazz education tends to focus on teaching methods and on the kind of musicians that college programs produce, not on the social and economic implications of the schools themselves for the lives of musicians or their impact on the jazz industry more broadly. David Ake, for example, argues that "college-based programs have not only replaced the proverbial street as the primary training grounds for young jazz musicians, but they've also replaced urban nightclubs as the primary professional homes for hundreds of jazz performers and composers" (2010, 103). As I show in this chapter, college-based jazz education has not so much replaced as absorbed the "street" and the "road" into the university campus, incorporating struggling (but also successful) jazz clubs as collaborative educational institutions.

The issue at hand is one of overproduction. Unlike nightclubs, festivals, or other performance venues, each new class of jazz graduates injects a new stream of musicians seeking employment in a saturated field. For example, Berklee College of Music produces between 600 and 700 new graduates every year.[5] While college programs can offer a professional home to a small fraction of these musicians—and more often than not on a part-time or temporary basis—the supply will always exceed schools' demand for teachers.

In a conversation with Stuart Nicholson, guitarist John Abercrombie described this complex relationship:

> Well, there are so many players today, there are more players now than when I was coming up, but there're still no more gigs. It's terrifying. There're all these good musicians and there's no place to play, and a lot of my students wind up playing in these restaurants and they make $20 a night or something. I made $20 back in the 1960s. How can you live on that now? Back in the 1960s things were a lot cheaper—you could buy food—and if you made $100 a week, you were on top of the world. Now $100 a week will

keep you in cigarettes. I don't know how they're going to make it, so I always tell them, 'You really have to want to do this music because you love it. Sometimes I have a hard time working in this country, and if I have a hard time, you may be up against a wall.' So I try to be realistic with them, and I think they find that out pretty soon when they get out and start working, they see that there's not much there. (Nicholson 2014)

In fact, love has got very little to do with "making it." Nor are talent, dedication, and perseverance likely to resolve the basic issue of overproduction. As David Hesmondhalgh (2017) notes in relation to cultural industries at large, the choice to enter a saturated field has been explained as relating to a love of the profession or a sense of "calling," a tendency toward risk and uncertainty, and a desire to attain the non-monetary rewards cultural work brings, such as autonomy, sociality, and self-realization. These familiar tropes of the "starving musician" are indeed strong motivations for pursuing a career as a jazz musician, but there is a limit to how long a jazz musician can subsist on love, the thrill of risk, and self-realization, and it largely depends on their socioeconomic status and available safety nets. As Abercrombie notes, as the cost of living rises and compensation for musicians remains stagnant, the possibility of "staying in the game" becomes increasingly difficult.

Being trapped in an unsustainable economic situation can create complicated dynamics between jazz teachers and students. On the one hand, disabusing students of their dream of becoming musicians is likely to make them stop taking lessons with that teacher, costing an already-hard-up musician an important source of income. On the other hand, students often approach teachers seeking reassurance about their chances of "making it," or at least making a livable income in the jazz world. Keeping the student just optimistic enough is an unenviable task. One of my conversations with bassist Doug Weiss, a private teacher and ensemble instructor at the New School for Jazz in New York, revolved around gigs. At the time, I was playing a weekly restaurant gig in Williamsburg that was paying around $50 a night, and was picking up one additional gig every week or two. Witnessing some of my technical difficulties on the instrument, Weiss awkwardly tried to reassure me: "You are not trying to become a bass player, are you?" Weiss said. "You are just playing some gigs in Williamsburg." At the same time, knowing that I was about to complete my PhD and begin teaching at the New School myself, Weiss asked my advice about applying for an academic teaching position previously held by a well-known African American composer and improviser. The equalizing power positions between the highly respected jazz musician trying to find secure employment in academia and the inexperienced PhD student playing low-paid restaurant gigs in Williamsburg are one of the many symptoms of the shifting economic structure of the New York scene.

This situation is not unique to academia (e.g., Hesmondhalgh 2017), but the disproportionate investment in schools compared to other types of cultural institutions and venues in the jazz world, combined with shrinking audiences, has created a loop in which growing numbers of musicians have no clear avenues for income in music outside of teaching. The shift to music-streaming services over the last decade and the sharp drop in revenue from record sales points to a discouraging conclusion: musicians have few viable ways of earning a living in their field outside educational contexts (Hesmondhalgh 2017). By training new cohorts of jazz students at a time of declining performance opportunities, jazz schools necessarily contribute to the growing number of underemployed musicians.

The overproduction of jazz musicians in academia is not unique to the United States. As of 2001, there were 141 degree-granting jazz programs across Europe, with dozens more in the United Kingdom, Russia, South and East Asia, Africa, and South America (McGee 2011a). New York–based guitarist and composer Prasanna Ramaswamy, who founded the Swarnabhoomi Academy of Music in Chennai, India, in 2008, explained to me the recurring loop between his own studies at Berklee College of Music in Boston in the 1990s, the opening of his school in India, and students arriving in the United States to study today:

> Now there are a lot of Indian musicians who come here [to the United States], a lot of Indian students who've come to Berklee. Berklee is packed with people from India now. When I was there, there were two people, you know? And there are other Indian folks, people who went to Swarnabhoomi Academy. Many of them have scholarships in Berklee. . . . At the time that I came in the 1990s, I had to be in America to be able to do certain things, but now it's possible—You can live anywhere and you have access to all these things.

For Ramaswamy, the opening of the Swarnabhoomi Academy meant that Indian students did not have to travel to the United States to study jazz. As it turned out, however, the school has had the opposite effect: the overall number of Indian students at Berklee College of Music, including Swarnabhoomi Academy graduates, has increased dramatically.[6]

Once again, the business aspect of American jazz schools is a major motivation.[7] According to the Institute of International Education, a nonprofit organization administering the entry of many international students into the United States, international students alone contributed $40.1 billion to the US economy in the 2022/23 academic year (Banks 2023). For public institutions—such as Queens College (City University of New York); William Paterson University in Wayne, New Jersey; and the University of North Texas—international students represent an important source of income because they contribute higher out-of-state tuition fees, taking the place of diminishing state funding for public universities.

For private institutions like Berklee College of Music and the New School for Jazz, the picture is more complicated. International students do allow the school to qualify for federal grants based on ethnic diversity by lowering the ratio of White to Black students, but this is not their primary significance for private schools.

Their significance is largely that international students compensate for the loss of enrollment of low- and middle-class students, who cannot afford tuition of $40,000 a year (even with financial aid). The dominance of academic jazz programs has led to a steady increase in college-trained jazz musicians and a corresponding increase in tuition, which rose from $7,700 at Berklee in 1990 to $41,000 in 2020. In order to continue charging such high tuition, institutions must maintain small numbers of star students who keep up the school's prestige, an "active" waiting list, and a long list of rejected applicants (around 70% in 2016, according to the Integrated Postsecondary Education Data System [IPEDS]). In other words, the field of applicants cannot just be watered; it must be saturated to create sufficient demand. With employment in jazz becoming increasingly difficult to obtain, only the most affluent can afford the expensive academic training and diminishing returns of a jazz performer's life. Most others combine performance with private and institutional teaching, primarily of students from well-off families. With resources for advanced jazz education available only to higher-income families, the so-called jazz community has become increasingly White and affluent.

It is not unreasonable to assume that the jazz musicians who pursue college studies in the United States are those who are able and willing to pay the expensive tuition. But a college education is often thought of as a necessary condition (or sacrifice) for pursuing a music career in the United

States, a decision that is often not adequately informed by knowledge of the economic conditions of jazz musicians there. Moreover, the relatively early award of scholarships at the college-admissions stage advances the misconception that through a college education, improved musical competence will be financially rewarded in the future. Students who are admitted to higher-education programs in New York and Boston encounter considerable financial challenges.

The stereotype of rich international students supported by their parents does not reflect the socioeconomic background of the musicians I encountered in my fieldwork. George Mel, a drummer who came to Boston from Tbilisi, Georgia,[8] in the mid-1990s, recounted to me his experience of arriving in the United States:

> I was still basically illegal in Holland and got this big thing to look forward to [a scholarship from Berklee], all indications that I had to wrap it up. I went back to Georgia, sold certain family belongings to get money for my flight ticket and first-month living expenses at Berklee, and got the visa. The American embassy had just opened in Tbilisi, and by May of 1996 I was in Boston. I started working at the voice department, hooked up with the rock faculty to gig outside the city, played with a local blues band—that was my bread and butter, different kinds of jobs to support myself—and at night I would transcribe the recordings of the lessons with a dictionary because my English wasn't "there."

Through partnership programs with music schools outside the United States and "global extensions," American academic institutions such as Berklee College in Boston, the New School for Jazz, and New York University (NYU) lower the barriers for international students to enter the United States. In these extension programs, students often begin their degree in their home country and complete it in the United States. When I asked Matan Chapnizky, a Berklee graduate and the current head of the New School for Jazz extension in Tel Aviv, Israel, how he conceived of the prospects of graduates of the program, his reply reflected the circulation of jazz overproduction between the United States and Israel.

> When you and I were growing up, there were a handful of jazz musicians who were teaching; most of them had graduated from Berklee. They came back to Israel and opened the Rimon School of Jazz (an extension of Berklee

in Israel), which is where I went to school. After Rimon, I went to Berklee myself. And after six years in Boston and New York, I came back to Israel. Here, I was able to get the occasional tour and one or two festivals a year and play every now and then at the one club that features live music nightly. Everyone is competing for these gigs, so obviously you can't live on that. So at first I started teaching part-time at Rimon, then in several other jazz schools, and now I have started running the New School program here in Tel Aviv. We prepare our students for their studies in the US at the highest level, but beyond that I don't know where they're heading. That's a tough question.

The stories by Ramaswamy, Mel, and Chapnizky indicate that for aspiring musicians, jazz schools are important gateways into the United States. American jazz programs are well equipped to solicit applications from foreign musicians, audition them, facilitate their travel, and sponsor their visas. As the case below demonstrates, they have done so for decades.

Pulled-in: A school for visas

The experience of Japanese-born pianist Toshiko Akiyoshi is illustrative of the far-reaching pull of academic jazz programs, but it requires some context: until the 1950s, immigration from Japan was prohibited under a section of the Immigration Act of 1924 designed to prevent the entry of immigrants from Asia and to deny Asians citizenship. These regulations were gradually relaxed following World War II as part of the United States' diplomatic efforts in the region. In those years, jazz garnered growing popularity among the Japanese public, and a small scene of local musicians emerged in Tokyo (Atkins 2001). Through her acquaintance with American jazz musicians serving in the US Navy and stationed in Japan, Akiyoshi applied to study jazz in the United States, and in 1956 she became the first Japanese musician to enroll as a full-time student at Berklee College of Music. In her conversation with Anthony Brown after receiving the 2008 National Endowment for the Arts Jazz Masters Award, Akiyoshi recalled the importance of Berklee in facilitating her arrival in the United States:

[T]he school, basically, gave me a full scholarship [to] advertise the school. And in those days, you couldn't come to the States unless you had a student visa or a working visa, one or the other.... I still remember the student visa was called an F-form visa... and in '56, January, I came to this country. It was Pan-American number one. (Akiyoshi 2008)

Akiyoshi was breaking an important racial barrier by entering the United States and was breaking an additional gender barrier by enrolling in Berklee: she was the first Japanese person and probably the first woman to graduate from the school. She is also among an elite group of international students who have attended Berklee College and other music schools in the past sixty years, using them as launching pads for careers in the United States. Some of the most important foreign-born musicians of the sixties and seventies, such as South African trumpeter Hugh Masekela, Ethiopian vibraphonist Mulatu Astatke, and Austrian-born pianist Joe Zawinul, began their long tenure in the United States on visas sponsored by academic jazz programs.

In the last three decades, the overwhelming majority of migrant jazz musicians have arrived in the United States as students. Data published by academic institutions located in the New York metropolitan area suggests that international students make up around 30–40 percent of total enrollment in college-based jazz performance programs today (Marshall 2012). Schools have made progressively greater efforts to boost international enrollment. Beyond the "global extensions" mentioned above, academic institutions now offer prospective students abroad the possibility of auditioning remotely by sending video recordings of their performances and organizing live auditions in various locations around the world in an effort to expand their international student body and streamline the visa application process. In an interview, saxophonist Ayumi Ishito recalled the process of obtaining various visas in her first seven years in the United States:

> F-1 was easy to get. I was studying. I was taking lessons with a saxophone player that was kind of famous in Japan, and he wrote me a recommendation letter for Berklee. So I could just get in, very easy. I had to send them a lot of documents, like my financial background or my school transcripts, but that's it. I had to go the interview in the embassy. And I just told them, "I'm going to study music," and they said, "OK. No problem." F-1 was very easy.

After graduating, musicians on student visas often make use of an "Optional Practical Training" (OPT) period that allows them to extend their stay in the United States for an additional year. During that year, they carry an employment authorization card, which allows them to work within their field of study, that is, only in music-related jobs. As mentioned above, some find work as music teachers, but many work in the unofficial service economy, playing cash gigs at weddings or in restaurants to make ends meet.

Ishito arrived in New York after graduating from Berklee in 2009. She described to me the process of obtaining the OPT: "I think everyone needs to apply [for] an OPT. Anyone can get it. I just submit some paper to somewhere [in the] government, and they send the OPT card a few weeks later. I could use it as my ID, and it has an expiration date of one year." With the restrictions on work permitted by the OPT, Ishito had difficulty finding employment immediately after moving to the city:

> It's very difficult to get a music job here. It's easier in Tokyo if you're good. I started to work [in New York] at a Japanese grocery store. After that I worked at Somethin' Jazz [a now defunct jazz club in midtown] for a while. I didn't get a lot of gigs at first, [but then] I got some gigs from my friend who played saxophone, and sometimes he couldn't make it, and he would call me as a sub, and the bandleader liked me and he kept calling me for the gigs.

The OPT year is often used to prepare a professional portfolio to support a request for an O-1 artist visa.[9] This visa recognizes a musician as having "extraordinary abilities" that justify his or her stay for an additional period. Preparing a portfolio and obtaining an O-1 visa often entails a considerable financial burden in legal fees and extensive clerical work. One musician, who asked to remain anonymous, recounted:

> I had to apply [for] the O-1. A lot of my friends did the same thing. I used a lawyer to help me. I think I got her contact through one of my friends and I heard she was good at the O-1 visa for music, one of the famous ones, I think. I had to get a lot of recommendation letters from faculty from Berklee or other musicians or somebody I knew; I got like twenty letters. I talked to people and wrote emails to ask for the letters. I think most of them I just wrote by myself and they signed them. My lawyer sent me a lot of sample letters. I had to show them to her first, and she would say, "OK, it's good." I had to make a contract with some people or a band that I [would] work with, and also an agreement that shows that I was hired for

the next three years, and I was going to play in this and this place. I asked my teachers for that. It was just fake. No one knows where they are going to play for the next three years.[10]

Connections with faculty and peers during the school year are thus crucial to obtaining the knowledge and techniques required for maintaining legal status in the United States. These musical immigration "techniques" are embedded in the institutional and personal relationships international students develop during their school years. Students depend on relationships with teachers to receive supporting letters of recommendation, but the stakes here are not whether or not they are hired for a position, but whether they are deported. Similarly, they depend on teachers and peers to agree to participate in what one might consider a legally dubious act—a guarantee of future employment that cannot be guaranteed. While some migrant musicians are indeed hired to play in their teachers' bands, such contracts rarely if ever last three years.[11]

The quality and depth of student-teacher relationships do not always provide the conditions necessary for obtaining a guarantee of three years' paid employment (even if only on paper). In these cases, migrant musicians search for other individuals in the music world who are willing to sign a formal letter guaranteeing secure employment. One of the most remarkable tactics used (but rarely discussed) by migrant musicians is to pay for such sponsorship: In exchange for a yearly fee (of around $200), an American citizen with some tenuous ties to the industry produces a letter attesting that they are the direct employer of the musician petitioning for a visa.

Once the Department of Homeland Security has recommended approval of a visa, the musician must leave the United States and await final approval by the US embassy in their home country. The embassy then issues the new entry visa. In this final approval process, the visa portfolio is reevaluated, and at times new supporting documents are requested. Before receiving final approval, musicians are interviewed to ensure that they meet the visa requirements. They are likely to be asked questions along the lines of "Have you won a Grammy?" or "I like jazz. If you are such a good musician, how come I haven't heard of you?" The O-1 visa allows musicians to remain and work in the United States for up to three years. Obtaining and renewing an O-1 does not lead to permanent residence and a green card; if musicians do not show sufficient progress in their careers within the visa period, they are likely to lose their status. Even a stellar record of achievement does not guarantee the reissue of a visa. Macedonian clarinetist Vasko Dukovski, who had lived in New York since 2003 and had earned a master's degree from Julliard, told me that he was recently denied reentry after his visa renewal was rejected—forcing him and his partner (who is Chinese) to give up their teaching positions, concert contracts, many of their belongings, two cats, and their car.

The application process, the additional costs associated with hiring a lawyer, and the various visa application fees have a significant impact on the everyday lives of musicians. Woodwind player David Bertrand, who arrived in New York from Trinidad in 2010 to attend Queens College, gigged frequently and worked as a music teacher but was at one point forced to sell his secondary instrument—a bass clarinet—in order to pay a lawyer to have his visa renewed (Bertrand 2013).

Although the increased restrictions on immigration introduced by the Trump Administration created new obstacles for musicians, visa denials are nothing new, even for the most celebrated musicians. During the 1990s, Cuban trumpet player Arturo Sandoval was repeatedly denied a US visa despite having been invited several times to perform at the White House during the Clinton Administration. The denial was due to his previous membership in the Cuban Communist party, which he had joined only as part of his years-long efforts to obtain permission to leave Cuba and eventually request asylum in the United States (Navarro 1997).

Creating jazz capital

> How was teaching today? Normal. Lots of farting. You have to pay attention to the farting. You have to ask: Everything OK? It's better than if they shit their pants.... My piano student today—he is five—he told me, "I can't play this." I asked him, "Why can't you play it?" "I need to poop." I have another student, she is seven, she stops, smiles at me and farts, then starts laughing. Horrible. So you have to catch them before, when they start farting; otherwise it's a mess. Because if they shit their pants during piano class you have to ask the parent to go inside, and then they hate you and never come back. But yeah, a lot of farting today.

This scatological conversation between myself and a colleague who teaches piano to young children captures the way in which the jazz education loop permeates wider contexts of the jazz-education economy. The rising cultural prestige of jazz among upper-middle-class New Yorkers and the growing supply of jazz musicians in economic need have broadened the range of ages that can receive a first-class jazz education. As I show next, jazz education is now available to toddlers less than a year old. Unfortunately, this trend has narrowed the range of socioeconomic backgrounds that have access to the same educational opportunities.[12]

Over the past decade, Jazz at Lincoln Center, the largest jazz organization in the United States, has been offering "WeBop," a program aimed at children from eight months to seven years old. The program "invites families to stomp, strut, and swing to the joyous rhythms of jazz." According to WeBop's promotional material, the program facilitators "strongly believe in children's natural ability to improvise . . . and are committed to exploring their creativity through fun interactive classes."[13] Taking place at the heart of the Lincoln Center complex in midtown Manhattan, just a few steps from Dizzy's Club Coca-Cola, the program serves the Central Park area and the Upper East and West Sides, among the wealthiest parts of the city. While the program is designed as a "child-adult" experience (and explicitly not as a "drop-off" program), the reference to families remains vague. As one of the piano accompanists in the program—a migrant musician in his thirties—explained to me, because the program operates on weekdays and during work hours, "there are virtually no parents or adult family members around—only nannies and trust-fund babies." The relationship among jazz education institutions, migrant jazz musicians, and New York's upper classes is thus one of increasing dependency, shaped by the framing of jazz as a form of elite education and cultural capital, akin to ballet, classical piano, and violin lessons.

Teaching private music lessons to young children is one of the most common jobs jazz musicians take to supplement their income. This is particularly true for migrant musicians, as teaching music is one of the few jobs allowed by their work visas (they are permitted to work only in music, their field of expertise). Depending on the types of instruments they can confidently teach, their desire to remain available for gigs and tours during the school year, and their intuitive proclivity for interacting with children, musicians have several options: they may decide to manage their own roster of private students who pay them directly but are often less dependable; they can seek a formal position in a music school (which often pays less but guarantees a certain number of lessons and ensures student attendance); or they can open a school of their own, managing their own teaching schedule as well as that of other musicians. The distinction is important because managing an active list of private students; attending to scheduling, cancellations, and rescheduling; handling payments and debts; and (in some cases) traveling to students' homes all add up to a significant share of the overall time spent preparing lessons and teaching. Keeping private teaching cost-effective is thus a delicate balance.

The time spent managing an active roster of students has to be counterbalanced by maintaining availability for touring or gigs. As Israeli saxophone player Uri Gurvich explained to me, accepting a three-week tour outside the United States may result in losing a teaching position in a rigidly managed school, but with proper preparation (arranging for a substitute, giving sufficient prior notice) it can increase the legitimacy and prestige of the teacher as a performer in the students' eyes.[14] Despite teaching children and young adults in several schools and institutions, Chilean saxophonist Melissa Aldana recently explained: "Even though I love teaching, I don't fully consider myself a teacher. . . . [T]eaching is not my main focus. My heart is in performing" (Aldana 2018). In practical terms, the choice between negotiating relationships with students and parents oneself and relying on others means that musicians have to include the time expenditure that goes into the teaching schedule in pricing private lessons. For both adult and young students in New York, the price could be as high as $90–$100 per one-hour lesson.

Singer Alma Micic and guitarist Rale Micic, who immigrated to the United States from Belgrade, Serbia, met during their studies at Berklee in the mid-1990s. Like many of their classmates, they moved to New York in 2000, and they toured the United States, Europe, and Japan in the years following graduation. Realizing they could not sustain themselves on gigs alone, they taught music privately at first and later joined the faculty of the Music Conservatory of Westchester in White Plains, New York. In 2010, however, dissatisfied with the long commute and having discussed the matter among themselves and with fellow musicians/teachers, the couple decided to open their own school: the Riverdale Music Studio, located on West 235th Street and Hudson Parkway in the Bronx. They recruited some of their friends and colleagues, many of them migrant jazz musicians themselves, to join them in a space that emphasizes comprehensive musical training for students with the flexibility needed by performing musicians. Israeli pianist Nitzan Gavrieli, who has worked at the studio since it opened, frequently recounted to me how different it was to work for Alma and Rale than for other schools where he had taught: "It's never weird. I can always call them and explain what's happening and they will do what they can to help. I didn't get enough gigs this month—they'll try to find more students. If I have too many, they'll help with finding a sub. They understand because it's the same situation for them."

Located in the northern corner of the Bronx, Riverdale is among the most affluent neighborhoods in New York City. The proximity to the wealthy community of Riverdale and the relatively low rent in nearby Bronx neighborhoods where many musicians live proved key to the success of the studio.[15] This success is measured in part by the number of students who have gone on to attend the prestigious LaGuardia High School of Music & Art and Performing Arts (which has a strong music program) and Berklee College of Music. "I prepare a lot of students for LaGuardia and for Berklee," Alma Micic said, "and a lot of our students end up going to those schools, or to whatever they envision for themselves" (Lassauze 2019). The possibility of attending music school is closely related to access to private music education at a young age. While migrant musicians live in lower- and middle-class neighborhoods, they teach and open music schools in upper-middle-class neighborhoods where parents can afford to invest in private lessons. This musical infrastructure contributes to students' chances of acceptance to prestigious music schools. Thus, the very loop that forces jazz musicians to supplement their income by teaching leads to higher numbers of affluent, often-White students in music high schools and college-based music programs. Students from upper-class backgrounds with strong support systems are also less likely to be concerned about the feasibility of an economically sustainable career in jazz.

The case of the Riverdale Music Studio presents one of the crucial contradictions of the New York scene. On the one hand, it captures how an international group of migrant jazz musicians can create a system that allows them to support themselves and one another economically in an environment mindful of the irregularity of jazz musicians' income and performance schedules. On the other hand, the musical training they received in their home countries and in higher education programs in the United States is passed on primarily to affluent White students. While there are many fantastic musicians from lower- and middle-class backgrounds, specific knowledge about audition requirements, ear training, and theory levels may vary widely between musical education contexts. This creates an increasing gap in the specific training students receive before applying to prestigious jazz programs. As I show below, these disparities create a racial and economic loop within college-level jazz institutions.

The racial loop

When I worked at the New School in 2016, the impact of the racial and economic loop seemed evident, if only anecdotally. My classes consisted primarily of upper-middle-class White students, a substantial number of international students from middle-class backgrounds, and a very small number of US-born middle-class minority students, mostly African American. The New School's own reporting confirms these subjective perceptions: in 2012, the proportion of New School jazz students who identified as Black or African American was 9 percent, whereas 40 percent identified as White, and 34 percent were international students (Marshall 2012). Similar figures were reported by Berklee (40% White, 6% Black, and 30% international students) (IPEDS 2019) and by LaGuardia (46% White, 11% Black).[16] These data represent a significant departure from the overall demographics of New York City high school students, the lion's share of whom are minority students, particularly Asian (16%), Black (25%), and Hispanic (40%) (New York City Council, n.d.).

The intersections of race and economic status with immigration data paint a complicated picture. Alongside an increase in upper-middle-class White jazz students, there has been an increase in international jazz students. The enrollment of US-born Black students, on the other hand, continues to decline. The overall population of jazz programs in the schools examined seems to be remaining stable. The result is a widening economic and racial gap in jazz education, one in which academic jazz programs use international students as "fillers" of ethnic diversity.

While some of these international students are people of color, the racial makeup of international students is not documented in institutional reports. The high cost of a college education seems to suggest that migrant jazz musicians come from higher socioeconomic backgrounds in their own countries, and this might be true. However, as George Mel explained in our conversation, the prestige attached to studying abroad, particularly when some scholarship funding is offered, can be enough to persuade international students with minimal resources to make significant economic sacrifices (e.g., selling family belongings). The relative racial and economic homogeneity of globally renowned private jazz schools can also be the result of better access to information about alternative public school options. In a conversation with Tim Ford, a second-generation Jamaican American drummer from Brooklyn, he suggested that students who grew up in the New York area are less likely to take the financial risks involved in enrolling in a private school, opting instead to attend one of the public institutions in the area such as City College (CUNY), Queens College (CUNY), or William Paterson University in Wayne, New Jersey. My own experience teaching at CUNY in 2017 suggests that public institutions are also significantly more racially diverse than private schools, which can enhance their appeal to minority students.

Private college-based jazz programs are highly conscious of their widening racial gap. Discussing the racial imbalance at the New School for Jazz in an internal report on the diversity of its student body, a senior school administrator stated:

> Despite our diverse environment, we lose a lot of students of color every semester due to financial issues, poor academic performance and a growing perception that getting a college degree isn't important. Students of color need mentoring, academic support (due to lack of preparation), scholarships, programming around Black History Month, etc., perhaps a "club" where they can talk about issues they face. (Turenne and Villa Lobos 2009)

Once again, the financial burden and lack of infrastructure lead even those students who are able to attend a prestigious music school to drop out. An alternative explanation to the analysis proposed by the school administrator is that the main issue experienced by lower-income students is again a result of the loop: if their parents cannot afford to pay the high yearly tuition and living expenses at the New School or Berklee (around $40,000), they themselves must have a respectable middle-class income from another source. This would suggest that achieving financial stability in a music career is not dependent on earning a college degree. The average total earnings of a unionized jazz musician are around $23,300 a year (DiCola 2013). Even if they do not know exactly how much they can expect to earn themselves, lower- and middle-class students are well aware that they will be struggling to pay back student loans with money they are not likely to earn.

Clubs as schools, schools as clubs

One of the main reasons both migrant and native-born musicians choose to enroll in academic jazz programs (aside from instruction in harmony or orchestration classes) is the opportunity to meet and interact with well-known faculty members and a large group of peers. As previously noted, schools and teachers have a decisive impact on international students' immigration status and a disproportionate role in shaping students' economic conditions, but they also have a dramatic influence on where and with whom musicians play and "hang." In other words, schools shape the social networks and connections students make. These networks map onto the scene in ways that influence musicians for years to come, extending far beyond the time spent in the classroom. These collective networks, sometimes referred to by musicians as "hangs," are essential social formations for jazz musicians trying to make music for a living. With the shift in emphasis from jazz clubs to schools, academic jazz programs have become the basis for the formation of hangs, while clubs continue to reinforce existing school networks.

When Mitch Borden opened Smalls Jazz Club in 1994, it quickly came to be associated with a new generation of jazz musicians, many of them migrants. Representing an alternative to the more established Sweet Basil (closed 2003) and Bradley's (closed 1996), it featured residencies by Argentinian pianist Guillermo Klein, Chilean singer Claudia Acuña, Spanish drummer Jorge Rossy, Israeli bassists Omer Avital and Avishai Cohen, Miami-born saxophonist Myron Walden, Brooklyn-born pianist Jason Lindner, and many others. Although regulars such as Mark Turner, Kurt Rosenwinkel, Guillermo Klein, and Jorge Rossy had studied at Berklee, Avital and Acuña had no formal jazz education (though both had training in classical music).

Anat Cohen, an Israeli-born Berklee graduate and a regular in the Smalls scene since its beginning in the mid-1990s, told me about the atmosphere at the club in its first years:

> The first gig that I played there was in 1996, with Jason [Lindner's] big band. Daniel Freedman and Jason and Omer Avital, they were all playing there a lot. They were there all night every night. And they became a *jama'a* [a hang]. And a scene developed there. They're all people who came from a jazz tradition, and they just simply gradually started writing their own music because it's such a free, calm place. Mitch Borden [the owner] was doing the booking, and I remember I had just moved to New York. It was

like, "You want a gig?" "Oh, what about next Thursday?" "OK, sure." It was from one day to the next, from today to next week, and people just wrote music. It was very fertile ground for creating, and there was always somewhere to play. You'd go in for free, or pay ten dollars and stay for a night full of music.

Many musicians today fondly remember the inclusive atmosphere at Smalls in the mid-1990s (it was also celebrated by jazz critics at the time; see Watrous 1996; Ratliff 1997). But even then, the increasing number of musicians, the closing of nearby clubs, and the growing dominance of school-trained musicians were starting to have their effect. Jason Lindner (a graduate of LaGuardia High School) recalled the conditions and challenges that allowed him to lead a big band with some of the best young musicians in the city:

> A lot of people I had in the band were regulars at Smalls and a lot of them didn't last. It's a tough world... because you have to be willing to sit through a gig, which we rehearsed and then played three sets. And didn't get paid hardly anything. I think it was $20 and we were there from 6 p.m. to 3 a.m. Nobody would do that now, except if you were very young and eager to learn, which I guess we were. (Lasky 2015)

The idea that if you are young and eager to learn, or if you love the music, you can subsist on $2 an hour was embedded in a particular artistic-economic logic: education and experimentation became the justification for low pay. Alto saxophonist Myron Walden explained at the time: "[W]e're not necessarily making a lot of money, but we can try things out at Smalls. We can sit down and have a conversation with the owner—not only about the music, but about life" (Ratliff 1997).

For decades, getting performance experience in clubs was considered the "jazzman's true academy." In 1986, when saxophonist Arnie Lawrence founded the New School for Jazz, one of his first initiatives was to establish a weekly student-run jam session at the Village Gate club on Bleecker Street. Initially, the Village Gate session was a place for young musicians such as Larry Goldings, Peter Bernstein, Brad Mehldau, and Roy Hargrove to hear and be heard (and hopefully hired) by the old guard of the New York scene. Meanwhile, New York clubs began shifting their hiring practices to reflect the growing number of student performers in the city, keeping the musicians' wages low while raising the price of admission and alcohol. Clubs became endless summer internships, with only those with sufficient financial support able to take $20 gigs to build a reputation, without relying on them for their livelihood. Over time, the number of musicians from lower- and middle-class backgrounds—and hence the number of African American musicians—dropped (Jeffri 2003).[17]

Upper-middle-class White listeners were always important in maintaining the jazz scene's "business model," but by the early 2000s clubs were becoming increasingly dependent on upper-middle-class musicians to sustain them, both as performance venues and as educational platforms. Like many other club owners in the post-9/11 years, Borden was struggling to keep Smalls open due to a decline in customers and rising rent. In 2003, he was forced to shut down. Three years later, Smalls reopened with the help of longtime regulars, pianist "Spike" Wilner and poet Lee Kostrinsky. As Wilner describes it, the financial aspects were never a consideration:

> Smalls was open when I started playing professionally. It was a place we played in and hung out at a lot. I got to know the owner, Mitch Borden, quite well. We became very good friends. I never intended to be a club owner, and I kind of still don't really want to do it, but I did it because Smalls was closing. Mitch was looking for somebody to be his partner and invest in Smalls. I thought it was the only way I could keep my gig, so I decided to go for it. I owned an apartment in Harlem that I decided to mortgage. I dove in headfirst into the jazz club business and had to take some time to really learn what I was doing. I'm still learning. (King 2019)

Wilner, who grew up in an upper-class Jewish family, benefited from precisely the kind of infrastructure that is required to be a jazz musician in New York today: he received music lessons as a young kid and had a piano in his house. He joined a high school jazz band and enrolled in a private college jazz program. To secure weekly gigs, Wilner would donate his own private pianos to several clubs around the city. When his weekly gigs playing stride piano at Smalls came to a halt because of the club's financial difficulties, he became part-owner, mortgaging family-owned real estate to keep his gig. Although the history of the Smalls closure and Wilner's involvement in its resurrection is unique (and by now has risen to the level of jazz mythology), it reflects the changing demographics of the jazz scene. It shows that extraordinary measures may be taken—by those with the means to do so—to ensure continued performance opportunities.

As briefly mentioned in the introduction, under Wilner's direction Smalls's booking practices changed. Instead of an environment that welcomed experimentation and sonic innovation, much of it led by migrant musicians such as Guillermo Klein and Omer Avital, the new Smalls became a competitive proving ground for contemporary straight-ahead jazz musicians, many of them recent graduates of the nearby New School program. While the Smalls scene continues to draw a significant share of migrant musicians, Wilner explicitly emphasizes that "Smalls is a bebop club." This can create contradictory situations: for example, Wilner asserted that while "everything gets played [at Smalls] to some degree, we don't really tolerate Brazilian music down there, for example". (Wilner 2017). Nevertheless, Brazilian musicians such as Helio Alves and Duduka Da Fonseca perform at Smalls regularly, and their material frequently includes covers of Brazilian music and rhythmic and melodic elements derived from Brazilian music. What sounds too "Brazilian" or "rock" or "bluesy" to be played at Smalls thus depends on Wilner's perception of who and what is included in the category of bebop.

The case of the Stone, a venue formerly owned and operated by composer and saxophonist John Zorn, is similarly illustrative. Zorn opened the venue in 2005 on Avenue C in the East Village, just a couple of blocks above Houston Street. The venue was originally conceived as a not-for-profit performance space dedicated to avant-garde and experimental music. Zorn was in part motivated to open the Stone because of the impending closure of another Lower East Side club, Tonic. As Amanda Scherbenske (2018) notes, in its initial years Zorn had to financially "float" his venue to keep it viable. The goal was to relieve musicians of their concerns about audiences and subsequent performance invitations if ticket sales did not cover operating costs. To open the venue, Zorn initially invested $80,000 of his own money. In addition, the Stone depends on donations through fundraising concerts and benefit albums (in which musicians donate their performances), as well as spatial subsidy (rent below market rate).

This hybrid model worked until 2017, after which Zorn decided to relocate the Stone to a new space at the New School performing arts building on 13th Street. Absorbing the venue into its facilities, the New School demonstrated the financial power of private jazz schools, but also the complete transformation of venues into educational facilities, primarily catering to jazz students and faculty as both performers and audiences. This sense of ownership was recently made clear by Richard Kessler, executive dean for the performing arts at the New School. In an interview with the *New York Times*, Kessler explained: "This is not just, 'They're using our space.' It's something we own, something we're responsible for. We have skin in the game. We're seeing it as shared, as much ours as John's" (Woolfe 2017). As we unpack Kessler's quote, we must keep in mind that the Stone's reputation as a space for creative music was established, sustained, and paid for through the talents and relationships of musicians who donated their time and labor in an economy that was ruthless to experimental music. After thirteen years, this reputation was moved into an institution that charges its students $40,000 a year. The tuition of ten New School students could have kept the Stone in operation for an additional fifteen years.

It is important to carefully disentangle the relationship between the New School, which charges students around $40,000 a year, owns extensive real estate in Manhattan, and has an endowment of $400 million, and the Stone, an artistically influential forty-seat nonprofit venue with a yearly gross income of $25,000, mostly from benefit concerts and album sales.

The move reflects the growing centrality of experimental music in academia and its establishment as elite music.[18] Representing himself and other avant-garde artists of the Stone scene, Zorn said they are no longer "marginalized over on Avenue C and Second Street. We're in the heart of the Village, in a serious space. I think it's going to help the visibility of the music and the artists" (Woolfe 2017). This description is somewhat anachronistic, considering the growing visibility of avant-garde and experimental jazz in institutional contexts in the last two decades. As Scherbenske (2018) notes, framing Avenue C in the East Village as a marginal space is a potent reminder of the spatial politics of the jazz scene and the importance of schools in shaping these musical geographies.

In Kessler's quote, he is expressing a sense of risk and ownership of Zorn's performance space, or "skin in the game" as he puts it. When we consider what (or who) is the game that Kessler is talking about, and whose skin it was that they now have, the New School's choice to incorporate the Stone into its facilities rent-free becomes a corporate acquisition, the purchase of a reputation developed through years of musicians' fundraising and volunteer work only after the value of the Stone as a critically acclaimed venue was established. In other words, the main risk for the New School was not the loss of investment or the overhead to keep the Stone open, but that the Stone might lose its significance as the core of the avant-garde scene as a result of entering the institutionalized hospitality of the New School.

Conclusion

The erosion of boundaries between the club and the school—between earning money and paying tuition—means that low- and middle-class musicians cannot afford to attend jazz programs (or take out student loans) without a realistic prospect of a stable income. This leads to a growing racial and economic imbalance within these programs. It also suggests that academic programs must bolster international student enrollment in order to compensate for the loss of lower- and middle-class American students due to increased tuition and decreased employment. College-based jazz programs are thus investing resources in pursuing international students. These include global outreach and auditioning efforts, the proliferation of Berklee and New School extensions around the world, and the significant role of schools in facilitating student and artist visas. These international students arrive in the United States with the promise of a scholarship and the hope of becoming working musicians in the scene, but with incomplete knowledge about the economics of contemporary jazz and the immigration hurdles facing them once they arrive. For many, teaching becomes a crucial economic foundation. As I have argued in this chapter, this loop makes the New York jazz scene increasingly Whiter and more affluent, but also more international than ever before.

Spike Wilner's decision to buy Smalls Jazz Club in the early 2000s demonstrates the complicated ways in which academic jazz programs have changed the jazz scene's socioeconomic structure. Wilner's claim that he bought Smalls to "keep his gig" demonstrates the inverse relations created between a young musician and his place of work. Imagine, for example, a grocery-store employee buying the struggling grocery store where they work in order to keep their job. This scenario may seem like a paradox, but placed in a context in which students invest tens of thousands of dollars a year to attend academic programs, the idea of investing money or a piano in a venue to keep one's job starts to sound reasonable. Indeed, the boundaries between "the club" and "the school" seem more porous than ever when financial considerations are secondary. As academia becomes the "jazzman's true academy," jazz musicians turn into perennial students and teachers in an endless cycle of underpaid apprenticeships. Even with multiple sources of income from music, going so far as to buy a venue or donate a piano in order to keep one's job requires a considerable socioeconomic safety net, one which few middle-class musicians have.

With the growing racial and economic imbalance in jazz programs, and the growing prominence of schools themselves, the hangs and sociomusical groups associated with particular clubs and venues are becoming increasingly uniform. In a recent piece for *DownBeat* magazine reflecting on racism and Whiteness in the Brooklyn scene, Trinidadian composer David Bertrand explicates the loop experienced by Black musicians: "If the Black musician ... observes the lion's share of opportunities mostly remain within pre-existing cliques—often fostered by US graduate programs only affordable to those with generational wealth—he or she must decide whether to continue supporting a scene that doesn't reciprocate professionally or emotionally" (Bertrand 2020). The pre-existing cliques Bertrand is referring to are not limited to graduate programs. Travis Jackson described the formation of such cliques in the early 1990s (Jackson 2012, 84). The racial and economic implications of the academization of the New York scene have made the path of Black migrant musicians like Bertrand that much harder. On the one hand, Black migrants represent a minority within a minority—a fraction of the student population in jazz schools. On the other hand, like other migrants, they depend on connections made through schools to obtain visas and to secure gigs. These racial and economic boundaries will be further explored in the next chapter.

2
Jam Session

April 2014: I walk down Nostrand Avenue towards Vodou Bar, a Haitian American nightclub on the corner of Halsey and Nostrand. On Monday nights this small neighborhood joint hosts a jam session led by the Common Quartet: Seth Trachy on tenor saxophone, Alex Wyatt on drums, Pablo Menares on bass, and Nitzan Gavrieli on piano—two Americans, a Chilean, and an Israeli. Tables are lined up along the outside wall amidst the cars and the human traffic of Nostrand Avenue. Familiar sounds hit me as I walk in. My eyes slowly adjust to the dim lights. The place is still empty. A couple is sitting at the bar with their backs to the band, chatting with each other. Trachy nods hello. The others are playing, wrapped up in the music. Maya, the bartender, extends her hand to greet me: "How you doin'? What can I get you?" I sit at the bar to watch the band's opening set. Tucked in a small niche at the front of the room, the band discusses the next song: A Miles Davis tune? A ballad? A Bb blues? They play the song "as is," allowing it to lead them in different directions without having to decide much in advance. The first set comes to an end and the band takes a short break. Trachy, the saxophonist, announces that the second set will be opened for a jam session. More musicians trickle inside. I recognize some: Juliata, an Argentinian saxophonist, Mark, a bass player from Toronto. Others I see for the first time. "Ofer!" Pablo says as he walks over to the bar. "It's nice to see new faces!" he adds jokingly. "How are you, man? You want to play?"

For recently arrived musicians, jam sessions are an important gateway into the scene. To begin with, they are a place to try out new ideas, learn new tunes, or experiment with new harmonies. As George Lewis explains, jam sessions can have an "explicitly experimental atmosphere [where] musicians explore the contours, borders, and possibilities of the bebop language" (2008,

18). An equally important aspect of jam sessions is that they allow outsiders to use their musical skills to enter a new music scene. In their first days and months after arrival, migrant musicians attend jam sessions frequently, stick around for long hours, talk to other musicians, and embed themselves in the social scene. They practice "how to hang" in a social as well as a musical sense, performing at a high level despite the diverse challenges the jam-session context can present.

In migration studies, the notion of "incorporation" is used to describe the way migrants negotiate social boundaries in the new society. Migrants encounter highly divergent experiences in their incorporation in the United States, affected primarily by racial constructs, religion, and socioeconomic conditions (Alba and Nee 2009). In a city like New York, where one out of three adults is a first-generation immigrant and two out of three adults are either first- or second-generation immigrants, the "host" society is itself a composite of immigrants (Kasinitz, Mollenkopf and Waters 2002; Foner 2013). The incorporation of migrant musicians in New York is therefore influenced by the long history of immigration to the city and the dominance of ethnic minorities in the city's institutions and cultural life. Whether they attend a jam session in Manhattan, Brooklyn, Queens, or the Bronx, migrant musicians are likely to encounter other migrants or children of immigrants performing there.

Historically, jam sessions allowed some crossing of social boundaries. During the 1930s, in the back rooms of Harlem nightclubs, in hotel rooms, and in private apartments, Black and White musicians performed together without the repercussions of American social and legal segregation (Monson 1995). The possibility of crossing the racial line was generally unidirectional, available only to White musicians entering predominantly Black spaces. While Black musicians did not completely exclude White musicians from jam sessions, they made use of competition to establish the criteria for entering. Through musical competence, jam sessions became gateways into a close-knit community of African American musicians (Walker 2010). Through "cutting contests," competitive trading of musical ideas, African American musicians raised the level of musical competence required for acceptance. By making the music faster, longer, and more harmonically, rhythmically, and physically challenging, they made sure only the most capable musicians participated in their jam sessions.

In his essay "The Golden Age, Time Past," Ralph Ellison famously called jam sessions "the jazzman's true academy" (2011, 208). Ellison recalls that in jam sessions at Minton's Playhouse in Harlem, players new to the scene got a chance for recognition and an opportunity to test their improvisational skill and physical endurance in competition with established musicians. He mentions, for example, that "it was here [at Minton's] that [British pianist] George Shearing played on his first night in the United States," but says little else of migrant jazz musicians who performed at the club (Ellison 2011, 208). Discussing the musicians who were visiting the club at the time of his writing (1959), Ellison suggests that jam sessions at Minton's might actually have been more important for foreign musicians than for Americans:

> Dutchmen and Swedes, Italians and Frenchmen, German and Belgians, and even Japanese ... study the discs on which the [bebop] revolution is preserved. Such young men (many of them excellent musicians in the highest European tradition) find in the music made at Minton's a fuller freedom of self-realization. ... [T]hey come, fresh off the boats and planes, bringing their ... startlingly innocent European faces. ... [P]erhaps Minton's has more meaning to European jazz fans than to Americans. (Ellison 2011, 205–206)

In his romanticized account, Ellison shows appreciation for European musicians' commitment to jazz, but he considers them primarily as tourists, pilgrims, or fans rather than aspiring jazz musicians. Moreover, he does not mention Latin American musicians in his descriptions even though many of them performed in Harlem clubs and presumably participated in jam sessions as well (Gazit 2020).

For Ellison, the jam session is the "true academy" in yet another sense, contrasted with academic music institutions and tied to the role of jazz in African American history. In Ellison's day, jam sessions were a place where veteran musicians would school a younger generation in the folklore of the art form and its political and social significance. While the African American legacy of jazz is still central to migrant musicians' lives through stories, anecdotes, and the rigorous study of recordings, today, as Eitan Wilf shows, migrant musicians are more likely to learn about the broader political and social meanings of jazz through books and formal academic training than in jam sessions (Wilf 2014, 100).

These historical accounts align with more recent studies of exclusion and inclusion in jam sessions. Anthropologist João H. Costa Vargas writes that in the jam sessions at the World Stage in Los Angeles, a majority of the participants are African American, but that there are White, Latino, and Asian American musicians as well. Moreover, "players from China, Indonesia, Japan, Sweden, Denmark, England, Canada, Australia, Russia, Brazil, Poland, Israel, South Africa, Mexico, Cuba, Argentina, Italy, Spain, France, Germany, Colombia, Haiti, and from various U.S. states appeared at the venue during the time of [his] research" (2008, 323). Costa Vargas, a bass player who immigrated to the United States from Brazil, sees exclusion and openness as related primarily to racial (and gender) boundaries and an "ethic of openness" among some of the African American musicians attending the session. Although he claims that as a Black Brazilian rather than an African American he was only a "relative" insider in the group, he nonetheless considers himself an insider. His Brazilian identity did not bar him from being incorporated into the group. In fact, his ethnographic anecdotes from the jam session are written in the first-person plural.

> He [Billy Higgins] set up the tempo for "A Night in Tunisia" and cued the rest of us to come in. Just relax, he said. So we did, in spite of the furious pace. He nodded in appreciation and reassurance. We were doing fine, and began to settle in the changing grooves, alternating between an Afro-Cuban feel and a fast-paced hard bop. (Costa Vargas 2008, 320)

While some migrant musicians purposely frequent jam sessions with a large African American contingent, such as the Tuesday night Evolution sessions at the Zinc Bar in Greenwich Village, the rationale for attending is grounded in a desire to interact with a particular group of contemporary musicians and not with some putatively "true" African American context. At Vodou Bar, migrant musicians similarly seek interaction with a particularly diverse group of peers, and not necessarily the approval of the largely African American audience.

Migrant musicians' experience of jam sessions is highly contingent on their ability to perform competently. Benjamin Brinner defines musical competence as "[i]ndividualized mastery of the array of interrelated skills and knowledge that is *required* of a musician within a particular tradition or musical community and is *acquired* and developed in response to and in accordance with the demands and possibilities of general and specific cultural, social, and musical conditions" (1995, 28). Reframing Brinner's definition, I propose that individualized mastery of musical skills and knowledge can serve as credentials for acceptance in a sociomusical event such as a jam session. That is, the skills and knowledge developed by migrant musicians in widely divergent cultural and musical contexts can be adapted over time to meet the specific requirements of a musical community or sociomusical group. The shared repertoire and techniques of jazz as a musical lingua franca are crucial to this process.

What attracts migrant musicians to jam sessions is the potential for harnessing their musical competence to cross social boundaries between themselves and local jazz musicians. But this immediately raises further questions: How does musical competence affect the crossing and blurring of social boundaries between migrants and hosts? Can musical competence facilitate the crossing of any social boundary, or are some boundaries impenetrable? At what point do the social boundaries of the jam session begin to blur? How does an individual migrant's race and gender affect acceptance into the group? Finally, how does the ethnic diversity of the group influence immigrant incorporation?

Vodou Bar, Bed-Stuy, and frontiers of race and gender

> Freddie, a conguero in his sixties, is sitting close to the stage, clutching his drum between his legs. His hands tap the skin of the drum ever so slightly, making no sound. It's still early; the house band is playing its opening set. Fabio, an Italian architect, is sitting next to me. He looks intently at the band, then at Freddie, then back at the band. Leaning over, he asks, "When is the Black guy going to play?" All his expectations of American jazz are compressed into this single sentence. "When they open up the session," I answer briefly, fully aware that he does not possess the background knowledge to make sense of my answer. "Why don't they want him to play with them?"

Vodou Bar is located at the heart of Bedford-Stuyvesant, or "Bed-Stuy," a historically Black neighborhood undergoing rapid reinvestment and gentrification (Wilder 2013). Gentrification, generally suggesting changing demographics and rising real-estate prices in the area, naturally affects the regular clientele of the Vodou Bar, but it has its own characteristics here (Atkinson 2005; DeSena 2009; Freeman 2006). Most of the patrons of Vodou are African Americans, men and women in their twenties, thirties, and forties, sharply dressed, part of Bed-Stuy's growing Black middle class. In a conversation with me, Carlton Brown, an African American architect and urban designer who arrived in the neighborhood from Mississippi in the early 1980s, described the people of the neighborhood as "mostly civil servants, teachers, lawyers, and business owners, extended families living side by side."

The neighborhood is still home to the largest African American community in the city, but a growing number of Caribbean and African migrants have moved in. Called the "Islanders of Bed-Stuy" by Paula Marshall more than thirty years ago (Marshall 1985), today Caribbean and African migrants are an important demographic in Bed-Stuy and make up a significant part of the Black community.

Immigration affects music in Bed-Stuy in several ways. In the 1960s, clubs such as the Blue Coronet and the East featured local jazz luminaries Slide Hampton, Freddie Hubbard, Max Roach, Randy Weston, and Wes Montgomery.[1] Since the 1980s, the growing number of migrants from the Caribbean and Africa has diversified the music offerings in the neighborhood, with musicians hailing from these migrant communities performing at venues and in local events, most notably during Carnival (Allen 2019). Today, dancehall, reggae, rasin, soca, reggaeton, and Afro-pop reverberate from cars, storefronts, and family barbecues.

In Bed-Stuy, borders between local and foreign have become increasingly blurred. Historian Robin D. G. Kelley (2004) wrote about local businesses and venues coming together in the Central Brooklyn Jazz Consortium (CBJC) and about the involvement of churches and educational institutions in promoting jazz in the neighborhood. In the last decade, the growing diversity of local audiences and performing musicians has been increasingly reflected in the CBJC's programs. Napoleon Revels-Bey plays Caribbean arrangements of well-known jazz compositions; Eddy Bourjolly's group Mozayik blends jazz with Afro-Haitian rhythms and plays tributes to John Coltrane and Thelonious Monk. These performances are a part of an ongoing incorporation process in the neighborhood, a blurring of social boundaries between the African American and Caribbean communities. They reflect a century of interactions between various Caribbean communities and African American migrant communities, but they are also an assertion of specific dual cultural identities.

At the Haitian American–owned Vodou Bar, which derives its name from the Haitian religious practice, patterns of incorporation can be found both in the music and in the menu. "American" dishes like mac and cheese, turkey sliders, and grits are served alongside Creole coconut shrimp, vegetarian empanadas, and teriyaki chicken wings. The music, too, is a panorama of "Americanisms" and the diverse backgrounds of the DJs and bands performing: Reggae Thursdays, Soca Fridays, and R&B Sundays. Mondays are jazz night at Vodou Bar.

Despite its location in a predominantly African American neighborhood, the jam session at Vodou Bar attracts only a small number of Black musicians. Most of the regular participants are White, with smaller numbers of Latinx and Asian musicians. I asked David Bertrand—a Trinidadian flautist who attended the session regularly for a while but later stopped showing up—why he wasn't coming anymore. David explained that as a flautist he felt he wasn't welcome. I found that very curious, and very intriguing. "You mean you are discriminated against as a flautist?" "Yes," he said. "I mean, it just didn't feel particularly friendly."

Seth Trachy, a member of the house band with a strong influence on the social dynamic of the session, agrees that few Black musicians participate in the Vodou session, but that there is not much he can do about it beyond inviting people to take part. "Why would any of George's friends come to Vodou? They have their gigs on Mondays. They're making money. George wouldn't have come here either if it wasn't literally across the street from his house." George is George Burton, an African American pianist who attends the session regularly. He has been featured on numerous albums and tours regularly with established musicians, personifying for Trachy the kind of people he wishes would attend the session in greater numbers.

Unfortunately, not all musicians can be young and successful. Freddie, the conga player mentioned above, was in his sixties, one of the few Black musicians coming to the session regularly at the time of my research. Forty years senior to most of the musicians attending, Freddie would arrive early and sit close to the stage for most of the evening. He would engage in brief conversations, greet the musicians he recognized, and shake hands with members of the house band, but for the most part he would listen intently and play. Playing conga, a percussion instrument used in Afro-Cuban music, put Freddie in an auxiliary position, outside the rotation of regular "kit" drummers. It meant he did not need to alternate with anyone or ask permission to play. On several evenings, Freddie was asked by a member of the house band not to play every song. While it is true that no other musician in the session played *every* song, musical convention and aesthetic judgment were used here to mark and reinforce social boundaries. In the competitive tradition of the "cutting session," it was considered acceptable for a house band member to "cut off" an inept player in order "to make room for the real musicians." At Vodou, it was considered acceptable for a house band member to ask Freddie to stop playing. Musical competence is often vital social armor. It may seem fairly simple at first for a musician of color to cross the racial and social lines of the session, but it is difficult to do so without the protective coating of musical competence.

In the male-dominated space of a jam session, musical competence alone does not always provide sufficient protection. Women are a minority at the Vodou Bar jam session; on a given Monday night anywhere from one to eight women participate, many of them pianists, but also singers, saxophonists, drummers, and bass players. The majority of women are migrants, primarily from Japan and South Korea, with smaller numbers of American-born, Latin American, and European participants. Ayumi Ishito, a Japanese saxophonist and Berklee graduate, shared with me the particular concerns and challenges she experienced while attending the Vodou session.

ISHITO: I went to the jam session for a while to meet people or to listen to other people and play there. I would always go with my roommates because it's very late at night, and I am a woman, so I don't really feel safe by myself to go there. And the drunk-drunk people like to talk to me. [Imitating a drunk man's voice:] "You sound great. . . . You can practice with me. Come over to my place." Something like that. So I couldn't really trust if they want to be my friend, or talk to me just because I'm a woman.
GAZIT: So you go with other people? You stay safe with other people?
ISHITO: Yeah, I try to ignore them, but some of them really play good! Good musicians! Still, I try not to be too close. After being there for a couple weeks I could tell which is which. I also met some friends—Carter, those people. I've seen some other women there, you know. Melissa Aldana, she was there a lot of times, and Chelsea. It wasn't only me, so . . .
GAZIT: So you would go more if there were more women playing?
ISHITO: Yeah, or if it was earlier, people wouldn't get so drunk.

The social boundaries of the jam session can be tricky for women attending for the first time to negotiate. In her work on women's big bands in the 1940s, Sherrie Tucker states that she was surprised to learn that women were "welcomed at after-hours jam sessions." She was astonished to hear that "the burden of proving to men that women musicians can 'really play' [can be] presented . . . as an occasion for fun, rather than as a perpetual nuisance" (Tucker 1999, 71). But as Ishito mentioned in our conversations, a generally welcoming environment can sometimes turn into an arena for unwanted sexual advances, particularly with increased alcohol consumption in the late hours of the night. Women attending the session to increase their involvement in the scene and establish themselves as professional musicians are crossing into a male-dominated space. They have to discern the difference between wanted collegial and professional attention and unwanted sexual intentions in a professional guise, including invitations for joint practice sessions, gigs, and professional collaborations.

Unfortunately, the latter behavior is rampant in New York City jam sessions. Due to its stable core of attendees, among them a growing number of female musicians, Vodou Bar is a relatively safe environment. As Ishito explained, attending the session regularly helped her get to know the musicians there and develop friendships and musical collaborations. As I discuss next, musical competence is crucial for blurring not only gender boundaries, but ethnic, educational, and professional boundaries as well.

Hangs and sociomusical groups

I was sitting outside chatting with Gavrieli when Menares called me inside to play. Nelson, a drummer from Chile who'd been coming to Vodou often, sat at the drums. There were only one or two pianists that evening, and no one approached the keyboard. We waited a while to see if one of the pianists would sit in, but eventually we decided to just start playing. One of the tenor players called "Countdown," John Coltrane's fast and harmonically challenging tune. I gasped and took the challenge: "Yeah, let's do it. I need to look at it for a second, though." For some reason, I always accepted these "suicide" offers. I took out my phone and looked at the chord changes in the Real Book app one last time before we started. The saxophonist snapped his fingers: "Clack!" We were off. I held it down in the first choruses as best I could, as fast as I could. Just looping the changes, again and again. The saxophonist standing next to me seemed fine with what I was playing. We knew where we were, and I marked the beginning of each chorus clearly. After a few minutes, while the tenor guy was taking a solo, Gavrieli came and sat in at the piano. What a relief to have someone else to carry the harmony with me—humanitarian aid! I wasn't sure how long I'd be able to keep going at this pace without losing my place and confusing everyone. Eventually things started to fall into place. I was still frantically trying to keep the harmony together, but at least I wasn't alone. Trachy, who was listening in the back, stepped forward and picked up his saxophone. That was a good sign. Gavrieli was there to help, but Trachy wouldn't have risked a rhythm section he didn't think would hold, especially not on "Countdown." At the end of the song, he walked over and said, "Nice quarter note, man." That didn't happen often, and it felt surprisingly good.

To understand how musical competence can be used to blur social boundaries, I begin by asking what constitutes a social boundary in the context of the Vodou session. In general, musicians in the session have social and professional networks that they have developed through three main sources: "the home group," that is, musicians with whom they grew up or went to high school; the "college group," with whom they attended jazz school or college; and the "New York group" of musicians, with whom they have played or worked in New York. Musicians who have lived elsewhere might have developed additional group affiliations in these locales as well. Because of New York's unique status as a hub for jazz musicians, many musicians maintain active professional and social relationships with members of one or more of these sociomusical groups while living in the city (Greenland 2016; McGee 2011a).

For migrant jazz musicians, the home group consists of musicians from the same country or region of origin rather than the hometown. My own home group, for example, was developed mainly during my service in the Israel Defense Forces (IDF) jazz band and while I was living in Tel Aviv, Israel's cultural capital. Many of the musicians I played with back then relocated to New York or Boston for college, creating their college groups there. Of those, approximately thirty still reside and perform in New York City today, and we meet on various musical and social occasions. Through members of my home group I came to know, work with, and collaborate with other Israeli musicians I had not known while living in Israel, and they became members of my home group as well.

Through interaction with my home group I came to know non-Israeli members of their college groups. While I was not initially part of that milieu, some of my home group's college group members eventually became part of my New York group. Connections within the New York group are often contingent upon active and frequent interactions, while membership in the two other groups is less sensitive to location or relocation. Haim Peskoff, an

Israeli drummer who did not attend a college-level jazz program, explained to me that he feels the connections made between alumni of the same college are often stronger and last longer than the musical connections he was making through his New York group, despite his playing extensively with a fairly regular group of musicians.

The Vodou jam session is one occasion where such sociomusical groups meet, interact, and sometimes converge. Members of the Common Quartet invite their own (sometimes overlapping) groups of musician friends to participate in the session. Gavrieli and Wyatt are alumni of the New School jazz program and are likely to invite people from that milieu; Trachy and Menares met when Trachy was living in Chile, and they have many contacts in common; Menares and Gavrieli's home groups of Chilean and Israeli musicians are also frequent attendees of the session.

Language is the first and most evident social boundary in the session. At Vodou Bar, conversations in several different languages, particularly Spanish, Hebrew, Japanese, and heavily accented English, are common. While most conversations both on- and offstage are in English, musicians will switch to their native language when all participants in a conversation are native speakers. Switching back to English often suggests an acknowledgment that one of the participants does not speak the language and requires the conversing parties to verbally accommodate and welcome him or her into the conversation. While speaking one's native language is an important way of establishing connections within one's home group, sharing the experience of speaking English *as a second language* allows musicians in a session to bond outside their ethnic/linguistic community. Emphasizing one's own accent, jokingly mimicking a fellow musician's accent, or sharing linguistic misunderstandings provides a means for foreign-born musicians to engage across social boundaries.

Ethnic identity, particularly among compatriots, constitutes another important boundary in the session. Musicians in the same "home group" often arrive at the session together and often (but not exclusively) interact with one another. One way in which musicians cross these ethnic boundaries is by referring to them explicitly, by pointing out a fellow musician's affiliation with a specific social group. On several occasions, after I introduced myself, a fellow participant would inquire where I was from. When I said I was from Israel, they proceeded to name the Israeli musicians they had played with (members of their college or New York groups), mentioned Israeli musicians they appreciated, or told me about their last visit to Israel on vacation or on tour. Demonstrating knowledge of fellow musicians' ethnicity is a way of acknowledging and communicating across ethnic differences.

The third social boundary at Vodou Bar is the New York sociomusical group. Belonging to a particular group of musicians through professional interactions asserts an unspoken structural hierarchy. Answers to the twin questions of where and with whom one is playing indicate one's professional standing in the scene. Musicians will gauge another musician's abilities based on their judgment of the latter's peers and collaborators. Most importantly, a New York group is the sociomusical network migrant musicians try to construct by going to jam sessions. It is the very group into which they are trying to incorporate.

When I first arrived at the Vodou session, before anyone there had heard me play, I was accepted as a peer by members of my home group, many of them well established in the New York scene. Musicians who did not yet know me well misidentified my home group as my New York group, which placed me on a higher plane than my actual standing in the scene merited. In fact, at the time I did not yet have a New York group, since I had not yet developed any professional associations there. My associations with established Israeli musicians earned me introductions to other musicians and eventually helped me develop my own New York group, but they could not come in place of demonstrated musical competence.

Because of the importance of professional connections to social acceptance, musicians are likely to mention not only those musicians with whom they have played most frequently but also those most respected and esteemed by other musicians. Venues and gigs similarly indicate prestige and standing in the scene. When Trachy responded to my question regarding the number of Black musicians attending the session, his answer reflected precisely this hierarchal construction of the scene: "Why would any of George's friends come to Vodou? They have their gigs. . . . They're making money." He was actually referring to the absence of George Burton's New York group, which is predominantly African American, and not really answering my question about Black musicians in general.

A fourth and rarely acknowledged symbolic boundary relates to one's choice of instrument. To put it bluntly, musicians who sing or play instruments other than the six core instruments of jazz, namely, trumpet, saxophone, trombone, piano, bass, and drums, and to some extent guitar, are accepted into the session with some reservation. Freddie, the conga player discussed above, not only was outside all the social groups in the session, but was playing an instrument that was only provisionally acceptable to the house band. In contrast, Itai Kriss, a flute player from Israel who went to the New School, was always a welcome presence at the session because of his high musical competence and because he belongs to three sociomusical groups associated with the session. Instruments, in short, have a profound influence on one's ability to meet the musical requirements of the Vodou session, but Kriss's network connections and competence were sufficient to override the outsider status of his instrument.

By now it should be clear that, along with race and gender, each group affiliation has a question and social or symbolic boundary associated with it. "What instrument do you play?" "Where are you from?" "Where did you go to school?," and "Where and with whom have you played?" are all questions likely to be asked by a member of the house band, and the answers affect the participant's experience in the session. The boundaries delineated by these questions may all be crossed by demonstrating high-level musical competence and may be blurred by attending the session over time, eventually becoming a close collaborator with members of the Vodou session. During the time of my research, several migrant musicians became closely connected to members of the house band as participants, collaborators, and even substitutes in the house band. However, the boundaries do not completely disappear. The question remains: What happens when you are not affiliated with the same groups as any of the musicians in the session? What happens when you face all the social and symbolic boundaries of the session, including gender, race, and musical instrument?

The art and practice of being a newcomer

On his first night at Vodou, Pavle Jovanovic, a Croatian guitarist who studied in Austria, played every tune he knew, trying to demonstrate his wide knowledge of standards. He had heard of the session through Rale Micic, a Serbian guitarist who has been living in New York for many years. He said he wasn't too interested in playing the standard jazz repertoire, but felt he had to play standards well in order to meet other musicians. I also learned that he was a fan of John Zorn and Israeli bassist Avishai Cohen and that we had a mutual acquaintance, Eran Har Even, an Amsterdam-based guitarist with whom I had played in the IDF jazz band.

Most of the migrant newcomers I spoke with during my research had heard of the Vodou session through musicians they had met at other jam sessions and gigs. They often mentioned similar goals for attending: to become involved musically in the Vodou Bar scene and to meet other musicians through it. However, their ways of achieving these goals varied considerably. Several first-time attendees decided to explicitly showcase their virtuosity, calling particularly difficult tunes at cutthroat tempo in an effort to impress other musicians, both onstage and off. Other musicians who attended the session for the first time while I was conducting my research preferred a different approach. Some kept to themselves at first, listening to others perform and assessing their abilities. In most cases, this was not a sign of lesser musical ability or hesitancy, but rather a way of getting experience: evaluating the social and musical norms of the session before participating. In his first night at the session, drummer Shareef Taher chose to sit in the back and listen to the band "to see what the vibe was like." He did not introduce himself to Alex, the house band drummer, until the very last song. Instead, he preferred to listen to the various groups, engage in conversation with fellow musicians, and mostly keep to himself. Similarly, Jihee Heo, a Korean pianist, sat by herself for several tunes before deciding to play. When she finally joined in, it was with a solid bass player and drummer she found compelling. By listening and studying the session and its participants in advance, she orchestrated the situation to complement her playing.

The house band decides which of the participants will perform each song. This decision is based on the number of players of each instrument present, the order in which they arrive, and the preferences of the musicians themselves. There are also other, less obvious factors. Members of the same social group, for example, often arrive together and prefer playing together in the same ensemble. Sparse attendance of pianists may reward (or burden) a pianist with playing several songs in a row. In cases where the house band has a special interest in one or more of the musicians participating, the quartet will suspend the "first come first play" policy and take the stage to perform a tune—often with someone from its "New York group."

Once the participants are selected, the group will convene to choose a song to perform. The process requires a quick negotiation among the players; the presence of an audience waiting to hear the band adds an element of urgency to the decision, particularly for newcomers who have a stake in choosing an appropriate song to demonstrate their musical competence. As they negotiate which song to perform, newcomers must balance their own knowledge and experience with those of other participants.[2]

While anyone can propose a song, a newcomer will often be asked what he or she would like to play. This is a courtesy gesture but also a moment of evaluation. The choice of song is an important indicator of taste, influence, and in some cases overall competence. A newcomer suggesting a tune that is considered part of the amateur jazz musician's repertoire risks marking themselves as an amateur. Numerous tunes in this category, including "Blue Bossa," "Cantaloupe Island," and "Autumn Leaves," are rarely played at the Vodou jam session and are likely to be declined by other participants. Conversely, suggesting a challenging composition by a renowned African American musician, such as Cedar Walton's "Bolivia," indicates knowledge that is highly appreciated in the Vodou session context.

Acceptance of a song has to do with the musical role of each instrument in the jazz context. Most commonly, the decision is made jointly by the horn player (or players) responsible for the melody and the bassist and pianist responsible for the harmony. Drummers tend to have less of a say in choosing a song due to the nature of their instrument. For a newcomer, declining a song is a loaded issue. While not knowing an "obscure" tune is acceptable (and these are less likely to be suggested), limited knowledge of the repertoire may hinder the newcomer's effort to become accepted into the session. Eitan Wilf discusses the time and effort jazz students spend creating and playing musical games that help them commit to memory both the titles and musical content of tunes. As Wilf notes, these games have an important social purpose as well (2014, 189).

Despite the loaded implications of knowing the repertoire, some blind spots about the specifics of a song may be acceptable; in response to a song suggested by the guitarist or pianist, a horn player can say, "I haven't played this in a long time. Can you take the head? I'll follow you." At that moment the pianist may agree to play the melody or ask the horn player to suggest a different tune. This option is not available to a bass player, who must know (or figure out) the song's harmony completely and cannot defer this responsibility to a different member of the band. The repertoire of the jam session is thus limited to the tunes the bass player and pianist in a particular setting can both perform with confidence (Wilf 2014, 214).

Newcomers are sometimes confronted not only with particular songs they are not familiar with but also with ways of playing to which they are unaccustomed: horn players who just start playing without calling out the name of the tune, drummers who superimpose various polyrhythms on the beat, pianists who scold a guitarist for accompanying during their solo, singers who request that a song be transposed on a moment's notice. The various social and musical norms and accepted behaviors of the session take time and repeated participation to learn.

Vibing

An Argentinian singer and a guitarist chose to play "You'd Be So Nice to Come Home To." The singer knew the song well, but the guitarist who accompanied her was playing it for the first time, reading the chord changes off his phone. When the singer marked the speed of the song, she counted the tempo twice as fast as she intended to sing it. I realized what she meant and slowed down to half the speed. The guitarist was confused, unable to figure out the pace at which he was supposed to move from one chord to the next. He looked at me, as if to say, "What's going on?" I responded verbally, marking the move to a new section as "going to the B part." That was not a good solution. The transition between chords was still not clear to him. I then switched to stating the names of the chords, one by one, as I played them. Trying to communicate my position confused me as well, and on several chords I played a wrong chord tone or played out of tune. I was getting piercing looks from the drummer. Because of the instability of the song, none of the horn players present wanted to take a solo. The awkwardness continued for a while before the singer decided to sing the head in an arbitrary location in the form. I reset my position and returned to the top. The guitarist did the same. This time we played a whole chorus of the song with the proper harmonic rhythm. It was done. What a relief!

Playing with an unfamiliar musician affects one's ability to communicate and demonstrate one's musical ability. Even experienced newcomers will find it hard to communicate ideas freely and perform their best when playing with less proficient musicians. In case of a mistake or confusion, an experienced player who is teamed up with an unstable ensemble will assertively articulate their own position in the song's harmony.

A mistake can frustrate even the most experienced musician (Monson 1996, 133). Responses to such events depend on the musician's personality and mood. They range from mild to harsh, from a surprised or stern look to a highly offensive verbal attack. Musicians refer to this as "vibing," as in "giving a bad vibe." Vibing is actively scolding a musician during a performance by musical, gestural, or verbal means. It is a way of indicating to a musician that they are messing up or are otherwise out of line. It is also among the first idioms newcomers learn upon arriving on the scene.

The most common reason for vibing is loudness. Drummers are frequent offenders, but any instrument can be too loud in certain musical contexts and to certain ears. Initial vibing is usually expressed through stern, piercing looks. A vibing musician may express discontent musically through loud, rigid playing accompanied by a facial expression and hand gestures. Finally, yelling over the music can express even harsher disapproval.

Because newcomers want to impress other musicians, jam sessions are prone to long soloing and overplaying. While this is sometimes expressed in the literature positively as "stretching out," long solos often attract negative responses from other members of the band and are a common reason for vibing. Andrew, an English pianist, recounted the feeling of being "trapped in the song" while a saxophonist took a long, loud solo that lasted over ten minutes: "I should have just gotten up and left but I couldn't get myself to do it. It was horrible. I'll never play with that guy again." Saxophonist Dan Blake remembered a traumatic jam session in his younger days in which he played with some older, respected musicians. Eager to demonstrate his abilities, he stretched his solo too long. After a few minutes, the musicians had had enough and they stopped playing completely, leaving him alone on the stage.

Vibing can happen to the most experienced musicians and in the most welcoming of jam sessions. Although musical competence reduces the likelihood of vibing, even friends and frequent collaborators "vibe" each other from time to time when they engage in musical dispute. For newcomers to Vodou, being vibed during a performance by the musicians from whom one seeks approval is a difficult experience, a clear delineation of a social boundary.

Conclusion: Jam sessions as sites of incorporation

Throughout this chapter, I have argued that the jam session at Vodou Bar is a site of incorporation for migrant musicians, yet I have continually introduced borders and boundaries that restrict, delay, and hinder this incorporation. Boundaries, as James Clifford reminds us, are not only places of control, but also places of contact where identities are made and remade

(Clifford 1997). Through sustained contact and interaction among host and migrant musicians of different genders, races, classes, and national origins, the jam session can turn strangers into musical collaborators.

Musical competence and sustained contact do not fix society's exclusions and inequalities. Despite the inclusive stance of the house band and the majority of participants, race and gender construct different experiences for musicians attending the session. Linguistic and ethnic affiliations sometimes contribute to a sense of belonging, but they can also create a sense of isolation and alienation. The experience of a college education can bring people together, but it does not close the gaps between musicians of different means and economic backgrounds. Finally, professional affiliations in the New York scene can produce unspoken hierarchies, making some musicians feel welcome and others unwanted.

Despite its hidden exclusions and hierarchies, the Vodou session privileges incorporation precisely because it generates personal contact that would not otherwise be available. It requires no invitation, no prior acquaintance with any participant, and no affiliation with any particular group. It includes participants of different racial, gender, and ethnic groups and facilitates interactions across racial, gender, and ethnic lines. Most importantly, it privileges musical competence, a set of learned skills, over other markers of social belonging.

3
The Scene

September 10, 2017: My last week in New York. One more gig left, one last day of recording the new album, and clearing out my apartment. After an emotional goodbye dinner at our favorite Uruguayan restaurant, my partner Valentina and I walk down the block to Terraza 7, a jazz club in Jackson Heights and the heart of the local music scene. I push the heavy wooden door open and hold it. A bit too quiet. The lower floor of Terraza is relatively empty. It seems there's no jam session tonight. Just a few people sitting across the elongated table. I look around at the Día de los Muertos decorations hanging from the dark red walls, the beer barrels doubling as bar stools. I think back on the many shows I've seen down here, looking up from underneath the elevated stage, quickly moving away from the occasional trumpet or trombone player emptying spit from their horn, or up on the terraza itself: Argentinian vocalist Sofia Rei, Moroccan pianist Amino Belyamani, Edward Perez's Big Band, and many more, too many to recall now. A whole world in one bar, one neighborhood, one city.

In the previous chapters, I explored how dreams of musical knowledge become entwined with bureaucratic and economic systems that enable migrant musicians to arrive in New York, and how the very same knowledge allows musicians to build sociomusical networks and enter jazz scenes in the city. In this chapter, I explore how knowledge of musical events, and the musicians, genres, and venues associated with them, are crucial to formation of migrant jazz scenes.

For many of the musicians I worked with during my research, New York had a unique quality. It was an island full of islands, where most other places, peoples, and cultures existed simultaneously. This line of thinking, connecting New York to a kind of internal global mobility, is as old as the city's first immigrant neighborhoods. Visiting these neighborhoods was sometimes associated with racial and sexual fantasies of the Prohibition era and has been the subject of popular jazz songs, Broadway shows, and movies (Hiroshi Garrett 2004). But the desire to see other ways of living is not restricted to the exoticism of upper-class Whites who wish to see "how the other half lives." Migrants of various racial and religious groups, classes, and legal statuses were equally interested in crossing ethnic boundaries within New York City but with a different set of motivations; rather than tourists, they sought to become neighbors in a strange new place—to know and be known by their fellow New Yorkers.

The majority of studies on immigrant music in the United States reflect the rich musical practices the immigrants brought with them from their home countries, the transformation of these musics as a result of migration, and the role of music as a marker of ethnic identity (Glasser 1995; Slobin 1995; Shelemay 1998, 2012; Reyes 1999; Zheng 2012; Rapport 2014). As mentioned in the introduction to this book, scholars such as Nina Glick Schiller have criticized use of the ethnic community as the basic unit of analysis in migration studies. She urges scholars to move beyond "methodological ethnicity" because it fails to capture the increasing fragmentation of ethnic groups and excludes non-ethnic forms of social engagement (Glick Schiller 2008).

In an effort to rethink the relationship among music, ethnic identity, and place, Kay Shelemay (2012) constructs a geography of "ethnic" places—churches, immigrant-owned businesses, public meeting places, and immigrant media—in which music plays a constitutive role. To understand the particular ways in which migrant jazz places operate, it is important to keep Glick Schiller's critique in mind as well. First, restaurants, community centers, and churches are important aspects of the migrant jazz experience in New York. They not only provide a sense of home to members of the same ethnic community, but can also represent a variety of migrant experiences and affinities. Second, private homes often hold special meaning as ethnic meeting places for more than just their residents, particularly during religious holidays, celebrations, and bereavement. Similarly, much of the jazz music performed in New York every day is played in the homes and studios of musicians rather than in public venues. As Shelemay shows, ethnic meeting places give immigrants a sense of familiarity. While this is certainly true of places where migrant jazz musicians hang, the relationships between music and national, ethnic, and racial identity are often more complex. I propose that a more appropriate term for describing these complex relations is a migrant jazz "scene," which connects people through shared expressive practice. What, then, could a "migrant jazz scene" mean?

The term "jazz scenes" describes the various sociomusical worlds migrant musicians move between. Following the work of Will Straw, Barry Shank, and others, I understand a "scene" as a social network connected through a discourse of cultural expression. In this sense, it overlaps somewhat with the concept of musical genre, but goes beyond it. The scene encompasses the expressive and technical musical discourse that people use to interact with one another, the places in and about which they interact, and the people involved in the conversation. In many ways, a scene functions as a spatial and social "home" for an expressive practice (Straw 1991; Shank 2011). Similarly to Shelemay, theater scholar Sabine Haenni sees an "immigrant scene" as representing the public culture of an immigrant group: a set of visual and sonic representations used by an immigrant group to mark their own spaces in the urban landscape, as well as a stereotype used in theatrical and cinematic depictions of immigrant enclaves. It can include grocery stores, newspapers, restaurants, musical performances, and other signifiers of cultural identity (Haenni 2008, 16–17). These various definitions apply to the migrant jazz scene in New York, but the scene extends beyond them. Rather than marking community boundaries, the migrant jazz scene amplifies sonic crossing. Like the overlapping soundscapes of Chinatown, Little Italy, and Russian Jewish tenements on the Lower East Side in the early twentieth century, the contemporary migrant jazz scene resonates with and against other musical scenes. It encompasses overlapping migrant expressions—sonic, verbal, and visual.

Michael Heller's work on the Lower East Side loft jazz scene in the 1970s shows that African American musicians were able to make a place for their music by creating collective organizations and establishing privately owned multipurpose spaces in which to live, work, and curate their own concerts: "The lofts' identity as mixed-use living and working spaces already blurs the boundaries between home, office and public venue. . . . The lofts could use strategic markers of domesticity in order to foreground their liminal position between home and nightclub" (Heller 2017, 70).

The loft scene illustrates how a community of musicians can construct a scene by associating a music venue with a real and metaphorical home. It emphasizes musicians' ability to make a place for their music by repurposing existing spaces, physically creating new performance venues, and organizing concerts. More importantly, it shows the reciprocal process whereby music becomes identified with the kinds of spaces in which it is performed and vice versa.

Among the most crucial aspects in the formation of a music scene, beyond the physical spaces and people identified with it, is the regularity with which events in the scene take place. A scene gains its sense of familiarity from the predictability and reliability of encounters that take place within it. Henri Lefebvre (2004) referred to this predictability as a kind of pulse or social rhythm to which participants in the scene orient themselves. As Anat Cohen told me in one of our conversations, "People who go to the office every day don't say, 'It's Tuesday night. I can go [to the Village Vanguard]. I'll probably find one of my friends there.' We [jazz musicians] don't need to make plans with anyone. I can just know: tonight I'll go to the Vanguard and I'll find [my] people there." The rhythm of the scene thus revolves around the recurring cycles of interaction among musicians, audiences, and the venue or venues in which a scene takes place.

In this chapter, I discuss the relationship between the sense of belonging and the cycles of encounters that create a "migrant jazz scene." These encounters are centered around Terraza 7, a migrant jazz hub in Jackson Heights, Queens, that has an explicit utopian agenda: using jazz to enable migrant musicians and audiences from different backgrounds to interact. I look at the construction of the Terraza 7 scene through three time cycles: monthly residencies, weekly jam sessions, and daily practice. Through these cycles of encounters, musicians, audiences, and one club owner created a migrant jazz scene around a small bar. I analyze how this bar and its surrounding community function as both a home and a place to form new relationships and develop new musical material.

Terraza 7: Locating a migrant jazz scene

January 16, 2016: On the border between Elmhurst and Jackson Heights, just past the small plaza at the intersection of Gleane Street and Roosevelt Avenue, Freddy Castiblanco is renovating again. Castiblanco, the owner of Terraza 7, moved to New York from Colombia in 2000. He opened Terraza two years later in June 2002 and has been building it ever since. The two-level bar, with its iron "terraza" (balcony) hanging above patrons' heads, attracts mostly local middle-class men and women in their thirties and forties. On most nights, a live band plays on the upper level. Freddy promotes the bar as a "jazz and immigrant folk" venue, with the ambiguity of the terms jazz, immigrant, and folk serving to accommodate the variety of musics performed at Terraza. The sounds of Afro-Peruvian jazz, Karnatic rock, or Moroccan Gnawa are equally likely to fill the room along with lively chatter and clinking glasses.

Hailed as one of the most diverse communities in the world, Jackson Heights is home to some 100,000 people. Two-thirds of them are foreign-born, representing 160 different languages. Bounded by the Brooklyn–Queens Expressway on the west, the Grand Central Expressway on the north, Junction Boulevard on the east, and Roosevelt Avenue on the south, it was not originally intended to be the Tower of Babel it is today. Jews and African Americans were banned from living in the neighborhood until the late 1940s and 1960s, respectively. As a consequence, "The Queens Jazz Trail," a promotional tourist map of the homes of legendary jazz musicians who lived in the borough, takes a conspicuous detour around Jackson Heights, moving quickly to Louis Armstrong's home in the adjacent Corona neighborhood. In the 1950s, with the suburbanization of New York, declining real estate prices began attracting artists and entertainers to the neighborhood, among them a large LGBTQ community. After the enactment of the 1965 Immigration and Nationality Act, immigrants from dozens of Asian and Latin American nations arrived in the neighborhood. Large Ecuadorian, Colombian, Mexican, Bangladeshi, Chinese, Indian, Dominican, Peruvian, Pakistani, and Filipino communities formed, with no single group dominating. The 7 train, running above Roosevelt Avenue, is the lifeline of the neighborhood. Cutting through the skyline and dominating the soundscape, it is sometimes referred to as the "international express," taking local commuters to and from midtown Manhattan for their day's work and bringing tourists and patrons to the neighborhood's restaurants and bars.

In our conversation, Castiblanco described his intercultural vision for Terraza 7:

> When I started my place, I tried to do something that many people would share. I noticed that the people [who came] tend to be from the Colombian community, and at some point [they] tried to separate from other cultures. I noticed that people from Colombia started saying, "Oh, our place is getting every day more Mexican or Ecuadorian," and that wasn't the concept that I wanted here. So I started bringing live music from Mexico, from Veracruz, like *son Jarocho*, and the people from Colombia, Ecuador, from other

cultures, started to admire expressions from Mexico. I also brought music from Peru, like *cajón peruano*. Through different musical expressions, the people began to appreciate the diversity and real value of each culture.

Through Castiblanco's booking practices, Terraza 7 became a crucial point of encounter for various migrant music scenes, including the *son jarocho* and fandango traditions (Williamson 2018). It was Castiblanco's explicit desire to create encounters among members of the different communities living in the neighborhood and migrant musicians of various backgrounds. Jazz played a significant role in facilitating these encounters. For example, Texas-born bassist Edward Perez, who lives a few blocks away from Terraza, told me of the importance of Terraza in his encounter with *son jarocho* music.

> I did get to hear music from Veracruz at Terraza, and I heard it there for the first time. One of the cool things about this group [Radio Jarocho] is that they set up on the floor, not onstage but on the ground floor. And I remember one of these nights they played until really late, and it just kind of turned into a jam session, and one of the guys said, "You know, the strings of the *leona* [a four-string, guitar-like bass instrument] are tuned in fours. You could play it." And he just handed me this thing and I just played with them. A little bit, just one vamp, but it was a really cool experience.

The many ways in which boundaries between performers and audiences are blurred at Terraza are particularly striking in Perez's description. On the one hand, a significant number of audience members on any given night are likely to be musicians themselves. As Perez recalls, an audience member who is there to support a friend performing or just to hang out in a familiar environment may become a guest performer for a song or two. Tellingly, the language Perez uses to describe his experience is jazz language. The *son jarocho* performance becomes a "jam session" and his playing the *leona* is just a little "vamp."

By explicitly booking live music from various cultural contexts, Castiblanco created a space for interactions of musicians and audiences across migrant community boundaries. To Castiblanco, diversity did not mean promoting the traditional musics or cultural practices of his own home country, but rather creating a new musical sensibility and sense of home drawing on memories of the past and present experiences in New York. In choosing to curate live musical performances from different countries of origin, Castiblanco was able to reorient audiences' expectations regarding the identity of the place as an "immigrant folk" venue.

As early as 2004, Castiblanco began to curate ensembles that used jazz as an aesthetic and conceptual framework. Among these were Sofia Rei's group and the Afro-Peruvian jazz ensemble of Yuri Juárez and Jhair Sala. Importantly, the groups Castiblanco booked deconstructed nostalgic representations of "home," creating music deeply rooted in the diversity of New York's musical cultures, including free jazz, bebop, and the big-band tradition. Castiblanco recalled:

> I wanted something that would help us to dialogue among cultures, something that we can find in this community, meaning New York. I thought jazz would be really good and also bring "acoustic memories" to that new culture. Jazz is also very malleable; I mean, I admire the plasticity of jazz. You can express your memories, your cultural acoustic memories, through jazz very well.

Castiblanco's explicit attempts to make an immigrant music scene in which jazz played a key communicative role was not an imposition of a musical aesthetic, although it certainly gave Terraza a particular overall sound. Instead, the choice reflected ongoing musical practices used by migrant musicians when playing outside their own native musical traditions. Castiblanco's crucial role in the formation of a migrant jazz scene was in creating regularity—a dependable, recurring opportunity for musicians and audiences of different backgrounds to hear and get to know one another's music. As I show next, musicians attribute the sense of home and trust they felt at Terraza to this regularity.

A monthly residency

Among Castiblanco's most important curatorial decisions was the creation of regular monthly residencies in which musicians could develop new material, experiment with collaborations, and write for unconventional ensembles. In discussing his work at Terraza over the years with me, Cuban pianist Manuel Valera emphasized the importance of his regular gigs at Terraza in his creative process.

My first gig in the Terraza was with my own group Cuban Express, with Ernesto Simpson on drums, Ricky Rodriguez on bass, Yosvany Terry on saxophone and Mauricio Herrera on percussion. That was in 2010. It was probably one of the first gigs of this band. Freddy was super supportive of the band, we ended up playing there once a month, around that much, so we definitely got a lot of stage time. It was a nice chance to workshop the material, and figure out where the band is going. A lot of that happened in Terraza.

The stability afforded to the band by regular gigs at Terraza allowed Valera and his bandmates to solidify and refine the band's sound. The sense of trust built between Castiblanco and Valera stemmed from the former's conviction that witnessing a new band grow and develop original music over time would be enough of a draw for Terraza's audience. A decade after his first performances at Terraza, Valera recalled this enduring feeling of trust with regard to developing new material for his more recent big-band project:

In 2019 I received the Guggenheim fellowship, and part of this fellowship was to do a big band project. And I didn't want to do a big band where you just played [the material] once or twice and then you never play it again. Unfortunately, this happens to a lot of big bands because most people don't have the luxury that I have of having a place [like Terraza] to play that music all the time. My big band started . . . a residency in March 2019 and that's how I developed all that music. . . . [S]ince I knew I had that gig, it gave me a purpose to write the music. I wrote thirty arrangements that year. It was like a safety net. Anything was possible. Nothing was forbidden or off limits.

In describing Terraza as his place (I had to verify with Valera that he wasn't referring to his own private studio), Valera makes clear the contribution of Terraza to his own creative process, and the luxury of having such a space where projects have room to develop (Figure 3.1).

Guitarist and composer Prasanna Ramaswamy similarly emphasized to me the central role Terraza plays in facilitating his own encounters with migrant musicians in the neighborhood:

I met Freddy through Yuri Juárez, a great guitar player from Peru. I went to see him at a gig at Terraza, and Freddy was there and we started talking. And he asked, "Can you do a gig ten days from now?" At the time, I was playing

Figure 3.1 Manuel Valera's New Cuban Express at Terraza 7, summer 2020 (photo: Freddy Castiblanco, used with permission).

in big venues, classical concert halls like Symphony Space, or with Vijay Iyer at the Jazz Standard, but at Terraza something struck me as very informal, a homely kind of a venue. For the gig, I got [Cuban drummer] Francisco Mela on drums and Max Zbiral-Teller on hammered dulcimer, and it was wonderful. After that, Freddy said, "Why don't you do something different every month? The audience that is coming for your concerts is a very interesting mix of people, and this is exactly what we want to do here at Terraza."

Several aspects of Castiblanco's ability to build trust with the musicians performing at Terraza come across in Prasanna's telling. Prasanna explicitly mentions the informal, homey, conversational context in which his first gig at Terraza was booked. Moreover, the trust that Castiblanco bestowed on him in his monthly residencies allowed Prasanna to try out new projects every month, essentially delegating some curatorial responsibilities to the musician. It was this trust that cemented Prasanna's commitment to the Terraza scene.

A lot of people are surprised that I chose one venue and that I am taking so much time in doing this. Usually, if you have a steady gig, in jazz terms, it's a gig for you to write new songs, try out things, and do whatever you want. Yes, that's true, but for me it's not about that. It's about these people. If these guys are willing to travel so far to come and check out one hour-and-a-half gig and drive back in this weather, what can I do that makes it meaningful for them? So not only do we do music; we connect with people. Freddy is very passionate about that. We both are. It's not just a gig.

In his description, Prasanna suggests that in his monthly residencies at Terraza, the relationship among new musical material, new ensembles, and new audiences is different from that at other jazz venues. For him, both the compositional process and invitations to other musicians to collaborate in his concerts are meant to connect with a wider range of audiences. Prasanna was referring to fans coming to hear his concerts not only from nearby neighborhoods but as far afield as New Jersey and Philadelphia. By writing new music every month and inviting musicians who were members of diverse migrant communities to collaborate in his residencies, Prasanna was able to contribute to Castiblanco's vision and create new opportunities for encounters across musical communities.

Castiblanco's monthly efforts also included creating encounters and collaborations among musicians. In our conversation, bassist Edward Perez mentioned Castiblanco's role in facilitating his own musical encounters and creating new "acoustic memories."

> I've been playing at Terraza for almost ten years. Freddy has introduced me to different musicians there who played different styles. He encouraged certain Colombian musicians to call me for their gigs, and there were certain styles that I played for the first time through that. We used to play a lot of Afro-Peruvian music mixed with jazz. For example, Freddy put together a group for Javier Ruibal, a Spanish singer-songwriter with some flamenco influence. I played bass in that group, Manuel Valera was on piano, Ludwig Afonso played drums, Yosvany Terry was on saxophone. The guy didn't usually have saxophone on his gigs. That was Freddy's idea.

The monthly rhythmic cycles created by Castiblanco thus connected musicians like Valera, Prasanna, and Perez to the Terraza scene in several ways. It created a reliable space for developing new material for specific ensembles, from Valera's early work with Cuban Express to his more recent big-band projects. It allowed musicians like Prasanna to experiment with new ensemble configurations and new instrumentation, thus attracting new audiences. Finally, it created opportunities for musicians like Perez to encounter new musical contexts, connecting them to other musicians as they collectively formed the Terraza migrant jazz scene. But Castiblanco's determination to use jazz to cross the neighborhood's social boundaries extended beyond these monthly cycles. Weekly jam sessions were an important way to introduce local musicians to one another.

Weekly jam sessions

May 5, 2014: John Benitez is sitting above my head on the elevated metal platform. The sound of his bass reverberates through Terraza as if a train or earthquake were coming. A loud son clave is hammered on a cowbell; timbales and congas interlock their patterns. A trumpet player and keyboardist trade lines: higher and louder, higher and louder. The PA system is pushed to its limits. Sharp feedback pierces the ears. Benitez begins to sing, getting the audience to respond to his call "Qué como fue?" The people echo: "Qué como fue?" He repeats the phrase again, setting up a steady vamp. The people ask: "Qué como fue?" He begins to improvise—syllables, words, his voice rising over the chanting crowd. "Qué como fue?"

On Sunday nights, Terraza holds its weekly jam session. For many years, including during my first visits to Terraza, the jam session was led by Puerto Rican bassist John Benitez. In the sketch above from my field notebook, the band was playing "Qué Como Fue?," a piece by the celebrated Afro-Boricua ensemble Batacumbele, with whom Benitez began his professional career. Benitez was performing a *soneo*, an improvisational vocal practice in which the singer introduces rhyming lines of extemporaneous text that respond to the lyrics of the chorus. Following Benitez's lead, the musicians in the band and the audience sang the repeating choruses in response to the vocalist's solo improvisation.

The practice of *soneo* fits in well with Benitez's approach to running the session. By involving both audience and performing musicians in the accompaniment, Benitez was applying some of the values advanced by Castiblanco to musical arrangements. Venezuelan violinist and Jackson Heights resident Leonor Falcón remembered Benitez as being unlike any other session leader in the city. "He was always very inclusive," she told me, "getting everybody in, singing, playing, no matter their level, what instrument, whatever." Benitez's inclusivity stands somewhat in contrast to the more exclusive attitudes seen in other jam sessions and discussed in the previous chapter, in which gender, instrument, and the divide between musicians and audience serve as boundaries to be crossed through competitive musical competence.

The relationship between the format of the Terraza jam session and its inclusive stance is integral to the Terraza scene. Rafał Sarnecki, a Polish guitarist who has lived in Queens since 2005, described to me Benitez's influence on the atmosphere as well as on the structure of songs in the Terraza session.

> My favorite moments in Terraza were the vamps at the ends of the songs. Benitez would call a standard song, everybody would play a solo, and then we [would] play the head-out. Then at the end, someone plays the montuno [a repeating harmonic pattern]. There would be four percussionists playing. Everyone [was] shifting the rhythm in many interesting ways, and then John would sing a melody [for] the other members to sing. Then everyone would vamp on that for a while and we would have more solos!

As in the example of *son jarocho* described earlier, Benitez uses a montuno vamp, a repeating groove or bass line, as a tool for musical and social inclusivity. One might also describe Benitez's vocal instruction and the *coro* itself as type of vocal vamp that encourages the audience to participate through repetition.

While the jam session often retained some aspects of straight-ahead jazz such as the use of standard songs and solos, other aspects were adapted to the particular musicality of Terraza. "Not too long ago," Edward Perez told me, "we were playing a bunch of swing with Benito González, but he's from Venezuela and there was a singer from Venezuela who wanted to do Venezuelan merengue. [At the session] you might play 'It Could Happen to You' or you might play a bolero." In expanding the musical repertoire selection beyond the standards in the Great American Songbook, the Terraza session created conditions that encouraged musicians to familiarize themselves with new songs, but also to reconsider the boundaries of the "standard" repertoire and practice. The influence of such reconsideration went beyond the bounds of the session, opening up new creative possibilities for musicians in the scene.

Edward Perez recalled how the structural and instrumental influences of the jam session and social connections formed through it gave him additional creative impetus.

One time, Freddy called Gabriel Guerrero, Juan Felipe Mayorga, and myself to lead the jam because Benitez was out of town on tour. Since I knew I would be playing with two Colombians, I wanted to write a tune for the occasion. What I had in mind was a tune that was truly a jazz tune but could be played with a cumbia groove. I actually didn't finish it in time for that gig, but just the fact that I was doing a jam with the Colombians was my motivation for the tune.

Once again, in Perez's description the jam session creates anticipation and musical reaction—a large-scale rhythm to which musicians respond in creative ways. As I show next, social and musical encounters created through the Terraza scene extend beyond the rhythmic cycles of the venue and enter the homes of musicians through daily practice session and rehearsals.

Daily sessions and genre ambivalence

September 2014: I get off the 7 train at the 82nd Street stop, carefully stepping down from the elevated platform, trying to orient myself toward 34th Avenue. Karina Colis, a drummer and singer from Mexico who has been living in Jackson Heights since 2006, invited me to a session at her house. Walking upstairs, I could hear some furious scales practiced on soprano saxophone on the second floor. A bassist was bowing long notes on the third. In Karina's room, set up with a single bed to leave space for her drum kit and a keyboard, she is able to practice, compose, and host sessions. We talked about her upcoming trip to Chennai, India, where she teaches drums at Swarnabhoomi Academy of Music. When I asked her how she came to teach in India, she told me that Prasanna had invited her. She has been going there for the spring semester for the last two years.

The session at Colis's house was a completely ordinary affair, part of the everyday practice of many jazz musicians in the city. As I mentioned at the beginning of this chapter, private homes have been important contexts for performances since the beginning of the New York jazz scene, in the Harlem "rent parties" of the 1920s and the downtown "loft jazz" scene of the 1970s (Heller 2017; Early 1991). It is safe to speculate that the majority of jazz music performed daily in New York is played in the homes of jazz musicians—in small apartments, basements, studios, and rehearsal rooms in what are generally referred to as "house sessions." These sessions connect the monthly and weekly rhythmic cycles of the migrant jazz scene to the everyday lives of musicians, and give migrants a sense of home.

I argued earlier in this chapter that a sense of home is tied to the reliability of musical events in the scene. By musical events I am referring not only to concerts or jam sessions, but to anything that occurs in real time during a performance: the onset of a chord, a hit of the cymbal, the unfolding of a phrase. When musicians at the Terraza scene invite each other to play together in their homes, they do so in order to become more musically reliable to themselves and others. The routine daily practice I heard as I was going up Colis's stairs was meant to make the playing of difficult runs on the saxophone or long notes on the bass more precise, evenly spaced, and sonically familiar. These exercises make musical material available at the precise moment in the performance when it is needed. Similarly, my house session with Colis was meant to make music-making among our small group of musicians more familiar and stable. A musical context that feels like home thus involves musical material and musical relationships that are familiar and reliable.

In the context of the Terraza scene, the question then becomes: What kind of musical material should be made familiar? If a jam session or gig might include both a jazz standard and a bolero, which rhythms or songs should musicians learn on their own? What material should they become familiar with? With respect to musical familiarity and reliability, issues of large-scale monthly or weekly rhythms connect to the rhythms of daily house sessions or the long hours of practice. How long has it been since we last played together? How long since I last played this tune? In deciding what to play next, a musician is making a choice regarding the familiarity of the musical material to all the musicians participating. In the context of the Terraza scene, when musicians of different backgrounds meet for a jam or a house session, jazz serves as the anchor of stability through which new musical material can become familiar and predictable. Consequently, the degree to which jazz "feels like home" can be a delicate question.

In my performances with Colis, Falcón, and Sarnecki and my conversations with Perez, Valera, and Prasanna, all accomplished jazz musicians, the relationship between genre and place of origin was often ambivalent. Prasanna was particularly forceful in his approach:

> When I played jazz, I was so into it. For years and years I would just practice and transcribe Joe Pass solos, Coltrane solos. I did all the things that people are supposed to do. But at the end of the day, that doesn't define you. So at

this point in time, it doesn't matter [to me]. But to get there, you got to walk on your toes. I had to work a lot on jazz but I don't like to talk about it because I think anybody who's good has to do that.

Prasanna's ambivalence is telling: on the one hand, he himself has spent many years practicing and performing jazz, including transcribing and analyzing of great solos. This process, he suggests, is necessary in order to be "good." At the same time, he argues that after putting in all the hard work, he does not like to talk about it because "it doesn't matter." As we continued our conversation, Prasanna's ambivalence toward the connections among genre, instrument, and nationality became even more evident.

> You come from Israel, you play bass, you're into jazz, but you are also into ethnomusicology, so that's the same thing. I am from India, I live in Manhattan now, I am as American as anybody, I am as Indian as anybody, but I think the fact that we play instruments like guitar, and in your case bass, we don't need to associate a nationality with it. If I played sitar forever, people would see me in one way. Like I said, the people before us, the greats, whether it's Coltrane or whether someone from India, they paved the way; the instruments have paved the way. All these things, we are just carrying on.

In arguing against stereotypical associations between instruments and nationality, Prasanna also points to where musical borders are drawn. To him, certain instruments, like the sitar, will always have ethnonational associations, whereas the guitar and bass (perhaps because of their colonial histories) are able to transcend musical borders. For Prasanna, Terraza represents the ability to sustain rather than resolve this tension through the concept of "jazz and immigrant folk." The border between the two, however, remains a contested space.

Manuel Valera expressed a similar sentiment in our conversation. Discussing the degree to which his own music fits in with Terraza's notion of jazz and immigrant folk, he explained:

> My music is in the crease between straight ahead jazz, Cuban music, and contemporary music, so it fits in the middle of all of that. It could actually work anywhere. There's a lot of walking and swinging in the music; there's a lot of rhythmic stuff; it's what jazz is anyway. It's not like jazz today is strictly

Ahmad Jamal and Oscar Peterson. Although I love these guys, that kind of vibe is less and less what jazz is becoming. Modern jazz has become more broad, with different sensibilities. It's not just one thing.

In pointing to aspects of jazz such as swing and walking bass, Valera is reiterating the role jazz plays as a familiar rhythmic foundation to his music. At the same time, however, he is pointing out that this foundation is expanded through the introduction of a variety of sensibilities and approaches. What feels rhythmically at home in jazz is constantly growing.

Our session at Karina Colis's house exemplifies the kind of dynamic Prasanna and Valera described among the neighborhood's network of jazz musicians. While our trio session with Pittsburgh-born guitarist Matt Albeck was not conceived of as "Latin jazz," Karina's presence and her style of playing required that I expand my knowledge and competence to suit her compositions. My sessions with Karina exposed me to the specificity of *tumbao* bass lines associated with the various genres of Afro-Latin music we were playing. Although in jazz performance practice "Latin" is an umbrella term encompassing a wide variety of straight eights and simple skeleton bass lines, the term leaves plenty of room for variation and interpretation (Washburne 2020). When we played Karina's original compositions, she asked me to play the specific *tumbao* line associated with the groove she was playing on the drums, a ternary rhythm with emphasis on the second and third beats. She took the time to instruct me as to what she was after. Our interaction across specific musical competences was communicated and mediated initially through jazz vocabulary.

On another occasion, violinist Leonor Falcón organized a reading session with Trinidadian flautist David Bertrand, Japanese saxophonist Ayumi Ishito, New York–born drummer Carter Bales, and myself on bass. Leonor brought several of her compositions for us to read at the session. One of the pieces, a fast 5/8 tune called "Merenguito," was a particular challenge for all of us. Leonor strummed the rhythm traditionally played on the cuatro (a small string instrument) and played the angular melody of the tune, but the complex harmony and harmonic rhythm of the fast tune sent us over and over to the beginning of the piece and forced us to analyze the problems with the groove and the relationship between the written music and the resulting sound. By bringing her own charts to the session, Leonor created a space where a Venezuelan merengue, played on the violin, was spoken through jazz. Jazz is the musical lingua franca through which Leonor could communicate her composition to us with varying degrees of success and translation.

These sessions, at which Colis and Falcón chose to rehearse their compositions in their own homes, were not meant as simple expressions of Mexican or Venezuelan ethnic identity. Rather, they were intended to create rhythmic familiarity through practice—to ensure that the rest of the ensemble had the ability to play these compositions in future performances. In doing so, they created a musical space in which national markers were inextricably linked to jazz as a familiar musical discourse, not yet a "home" but the repurposing of familiar materials to build the foundations for a musical migrant meeting place. In this way, the long hours of practice and the daily house sessions are a continuation of the sort of interactions created at Terraza through weekly jam sessions and monthly residencies.

Conclusion

Terraza 7, a musicians' hub in Jackson Heights, Queens, is a reflection of the neighborhood's social environment and of the attitudes of the musicians who play there. The conception of "jazz and immigrant folk" promoted by the bar's owner, Freddy Castiblanco, reflects cycles of encounters: monthly, weekly, and daily rhythmic cycles in which jazz serves as a shared musical language. These cycles allow migrants of different backgrounds, whether musicians or audiences, to become acquainted with each other's musics. Thus these social rhythms create the sense of home needed to form a migrant jazz scene.

Rather than seeing jazz as a utopian meta-language that mediates ethnic, national, or folk musics, the chapter argues for a more ambiguous understanding of the realities of migrants' musical worlds. It suggests, on the one hand, that migrant jazz musicians refuse to be limited to the religious, folk, or popular musics of their homeland or to re-creations of them in the "host" country. Instead, they seek familiarity with a variety of musical vocabularies and traditions. Jazz improvisation is one of the ways in which musicians can negotiate the variety of musical identities they encounter. Through its rhythmic familiarity, jazz allows for constant negotiation among musicians, instruments, musics, and memories brought over from the home country and various musics they encounter in New York. As ethnic communities become increasingly dispersed and urban communities become increasingly diverse, the migrant jazz scene at Terraza 7 points up the need to reconsider the methodological coupling of music and ethnicity in music and migration studies. As I show in the next chapter, demonstrating familiarity with jazz as an African American musical tradition is crucial for maintaining these musical interactions.

4
History

August 19, 2012: Kenji Yoshitake and I sit at the bar of Udon West, a small Japanese restaurant in the East Village and our usual spot in the neighborhood. Kenji has been playing in Washington Square Park since that morning, and after several hours under the hot August sun he is quite tired. By the time I turn on my recorder to ask Kenji to tell me his story of arriving in New York, we have already drunk two glasses of beer and eaten two large plates of udon. Kenji is using whatever is left of his energy at the end of the day to tell me his story. He started playing at the age of twelve after seeing an electric bass at the house of a close friend. The two formed a rock band together and began playing at parties. When he was in high school, he took lessons in a music school just across from his house. His teacher was not a famous musician, but he taught him well for three years. After high school, he was accepted to Senzoku Gakuen College of Music in Kawasaki, where he studied jazz and the upright bass, his main instrument today. After three years there, he transferred to Berklee, working with John Lockwood and Greg Osby. He used to transcribe a lot in school, both in Japan and in Boston. He mentions how important piano trios were for him, particularly those of Bill Evans, Oscar Peterson, and Keith Jarrett, as well as Miles Davis's first quintet with John Coltrane, Red Garland, Paul Chambers, and Philly Joe Jones. When I ask if he used to copy the sound of bass players he liked, like Paul Chambers or Ray Brown, he says he did but he doesn't do that anymore. "I am interested," he says, "in finding my own sound."

Japanese jazz musicians have been integral to the New York jazz scene since the arrival of pianist Toshiko Akiyoshi and saxophonist Sadao Watanabe in the late 1950s.[1] In the wake of growing American influence and the increasing popularity of jazz in Japan in the 1960s, Japanese musicians rose to prominence in the New York jazz scene during the 1970s and 1980s. Musicians such as Kiyoshi Kitagawa, Isao Suzuki, Toru "Tiger" Okoshi, Ryo Kawasaki, Kiyoto Fujiwara, and Shunzo Ohno became sought-after sidemen in the bands of Art Blakey, Kenny Barron, Jackie McLean, Woody Shaw, Jaki Byard, and others. Since then, Japanese musicians have made up a significant part of the city's migrant jazz scene, with remarkable representation in straight-ahead, fusion, and avant-garde contexts. While several scholars and jazz writers have discussed the centrality of jazz to contemporary Japanese culture (Moore 1998; Atkins 2001; Minor 2004; Novak 2008) and the role of Asian American musicians, primarily in free and avant-garde jazz (Wong 2004; Asai 2005; Fellezs 2007; Roberts 2016), the musical involvement of Japanese migrant musicians in straight-ahead jazz has received little attention. In fact, considering the significantly higher proportion of successful Japanese migrants in jazz than in avant-garde, the disregard of them in American scholarship is quite striking. I suggest that this disregard results from two interrelated issues: the focus in American scholarship on the position of composer/leader, and the focus on sonic difference, originality, and the liberatory politics of free jazz.

In focusing on Japanese jazz musicians, my primary concern is not to present a comprehensive survey of the influence of these musicians on the New York jazz scene. Rather, I am interested in their conception of jazz history and their way of telling it through performance. While the notion of storytelling has often been used in jazz musicology (and is even considered a cliché by some scholars; see Iyer 2004), it allows for analysis and discussion of sonic difference and similarity in performance. By paying attention to the stories, characters, and places evoked by Japanese migrant musicians in their performances (and those not evoked), I highlight the conflicting demands for authenticity placed on Japanese migrant musicians and their musical responses to these demands.

I begin this chapter with a consideration of the ways in which demands for sonic originality and political freedom have often overlapped with performances reflecting ethnic identity for Japanese musicians. These demands are sometimes at odds with the aesthetic promoted in most New York jazz clubs, where musicians are expected to show their fluency and commitment to the African American history of jazz rather than foregrounding their ethnic identities. Combining interviews with Japanese jazz musicians with in-depth analysis of performances, I show how Japanese musicians create their own history of jazz by negotiating demands for originality and sonic identity while simultaneously evoking the African American history of jazz. In fact, the Japanese musicians I have worked with have not been particularly interested in performing their ethnic identity. Their focus has instead been on integrating into the local New York jazz scene by mastering its musical language, and thereby telling their own history of jazz. As I show next, their approach stands in some contrast to the ways Asian American musicians have been presented in previous scholarship.

Asian American jazz

Among Japanese migrant musicians, demands for an original voice are often heard through an ethnic frame of listening, along with a parallel requirement that they perform and exhibit deep familiarity with the African American jazz tradition (Atkins 2001, 224). In her book *Speak It Louder*, Deborah Wong (2004) listens to jazz improvisation through an Asian American racial framework. Her primary interlocutors are Francis Wong, Jon Jang, and Fred Ho, members of the San Francisco–based Asian Improv aRts organization. Having been born in the United States and come of age during the Civil Rights era, the musicians in Wong's study were deeply influenced by African American cultural nationalism in the early 1970s. Within the discourse of identity politics, they sought to create music that would give voice to their unique experience as Asian Americans. This meant performances that expressed cultural difference—through language, instruments, and stylistic forms. At the same time, these musicians sought anti-essentialist readings of Asian cultural heritage through contemporary treatments of traditional forms and engagement with Black radical practices and alliances.[2] In her book, Wong also discusses traditional music-making practices among first-generation immigrants from Cambodia, Laos, and Vietnam; jazz, hip-hop, and other musical genres associated with the United States are discussed primarily in connection with second- and third-generation musicians. This distinction implies a "linear progression" toward Americanness in which the first generation continues to perform traditional music, while the US-born second generation contributes to "American" musical styles. The implication, whether intended or not, is that jazz continues to be perceived as a birthright, achieved not by first-generation immigrants but primarily by those born in the United States.

Focusing on the marginalization of Asian American jazz musicians, Kevin Fellezs (2007) proffers a definition of "Asian American jazz" suggested by ethnomusicologist and drummer Anthony Brown: "jazz produced with an Asian American sensibility . . . played by Asian Americans, reflecting the Asian American experience [and] involving traditional instruments [as well as] traditional approaches to those instruments." The use of traditional instruments and approaches must be "malleable or open enough to really start to incorporate and . . . take on other influences—in this case, jazz" (Fellezs 2007, 81).[3] Although Brown's groups have almost always been multiracial and multi-ethnic even as they promote a strong Asian American identity, this definition reinforces assumptions about musical and cultural identity. According to Brown and Fellezs, to play "their own" jazz, Asian Americans must mark the music with elements that clearly indicate their own claims to a cultural heritage.

In a biographical essay about composer and bandleader Toshiko Akiyoshi, Fellezs carefully traces the changes in Akiyoshi's musical output, from her focus on bebop performance in Japan and the United States in the 1950s and 1960s to her "mature" period when she infused Japanese elements in her compositions for big band in the 1970s. Although Fellezs explicates the national, racial, and gender boundaries that Akiyoshi had to cross to become a jazz musician in the United States, he goes on to argue that beyond a representation of "Japanese-American-ness," Akiyoshi's music "represents a personal acknowledgement that she will always be, in some way, an outsider, or an alien, to her adopted culture of jazz" (Fellezs 2010, 55). Fellesz is speaking to the reality of perpetual Otherness for Asian Americans (Kim 1999). In some ways, however, the focus on Akiyoshi's "infusion" of jazz and Japanese music, a small fragment of her overall musical output in a sixty-year career, creates a narrative in which her extensive work in straight-ahead jazz, Latin, and Brazilian music are diminished, thus implicitly contributing to her construction as an outsider to jazz (Atkins 2001, 224). Most importantly, it is an affirmation that in order to succeed in jazz (as the 2008 NEA Master certainly has done), one must "be oneself," given "the importance of having an individual voice" (Jackson 2012, 110). As part of her efforts to achieve recognition, Akiyoshi had to first demonstrate her excellence as a bebop pianist and later perform her Japanese heritage, showing her individuality and originality, primarily through her ethnic identity.

Pianist Kei Akagi, who arrived in the United States in the 1970s, shared with me a similar sentiment:

> When one decides to incorporate very clear components of one's culture into the music [jazz], that is not originally your own culture because—face it—it's African American music at its core. You have to be careful. You have to be thoughtful about it. You are always going to be faced with the expectations of other people. "He's Japanese; therefore his music must have Japanese elements to it." I think we have to be careful about that. It's unfortunate that a lot of times it's there. When I do it, I try to make sure I am not just replying, living up to other people's expectations of what a Japanese musician is supposed to do.

Japanese jazz musicians like Akiyoshi have been contending with conflicting demands for authenticity since at least the 1960s. On the one hand, audiences outside of Japan demanded that they perform music that is identifiably Japanese. On the other, Japanese jazz audiences considered jazz to be an African American practice, one that Japanese musicians should master to the best of their ability (Atkins 2001, 243). I further explore these conflicting demands in the next section.

Playing history

If for audiences outside Japan "Japanese jazz" is performed by combining jazz with Japanese folk songs and traditional instruments, what kind of identity is expressed when such influences are absent? What identities are expressed when Japanese migrant musicians perform jazz as it is performed in Japan, attempting to adhere closely to the African American tradition of the music; to its traditional instruments such as the saxophone, drums, and bass; and to central aesthetic elements such as blues and swing?

Scholarship on jazz improvisation has often emphasized the metaphor of "storytelling" and musical narrative (Iyer 2004). Ingrid Monson's seminal work *Saying Something* (1996) explores this metaphor as a way of theorizing communication and interaction on the jazz bandstand. She offers several examples of musicians who have articulated their view of improvised performance as a kind of storytelling (Monson 1996, 86). Paul Berliner (1994) argues that jazz improvisers tell the history of the music by referencing past musicians in their solos. Trumpeter Doc Cheatham, for example, informed Berliner that he sometimes performs "a few little bars from players like Clifford Brown, Clark Terry, and Dizzy that come to me all of a sudden in my solo work" (Berliner 1994, 195). George Coleman remembered concluding one of his improvisations on "You Don't Know What Love Is" by quoting the musical chant from John Coltrane's "A Love Supreme" (Berliner 1994; see also Monson 1996, 97–98). John Murphy similarly suggests that jazz musicians "celebrate their debt to their precursors . . . by invoking and reworking [their] music" (1990, 9). The emphasis on storytelling alongside the creation of new narratives suggests that the stories jazz musicians improvise are themselves archives or chronicles of jazz, curated by the musicians in the course of performance.[4]

João Costa Vargas critically reminds us that invoking the influence of earlier musicians is not without tensions. In his account of a jam session in Los Angeles, Costa Vargas discusses the social, racial, and gendered aspects that influence the narration of a jazz history. Many musicians, he says, "attempt to evoke the mood produced by John Coltrane's latter performances."

> Given the numerical and symbolic dominance of self-described respectable black males in the jam sessions, it should not be surprising that the aesthetic principles guiding these performances and their appreciation derive considerably from this group's raced, classed, gendered, and sexualized shared perspectives. (Costa Vargas 2008, 325–326)

Despite being situated in Los Angeles in the late 1990s, Costa Vargas's analysis can arguably represent a more general status quo in jazz performance as an African American expression. Costa Vargas further notes that "the racial, gender, class, and sexuality character of such statements and performances [suggests] that black males, presumably heterosexual and self-defined as respectable middle- or working-class, seem to have almost a monopoly over the possibility of satisfactorily expressing the spirit of Coltrane" (Costa Vargas 2008, 327). Although Costa Vargas is discussing a context in which Black males are the majority of the musicians present, I suggest that the symbolic importance of Black males continues to shape aesthetic considerations in contexts where Black male musicians are in the minority or entirely absent. It reflects the contribution of specific African American canonical musicians as well as the recognition that jazz music was developed within mostly male, African American contexts.

The practice of telling a jazz history in the course of performance is thus entangled in the tensions involving jazz historiography at large, in particular what Scott DeVeaux describes as the construction of the "core" of the jazz tradition and its boundaries (2005, 16). This narrative follows closely with the monopoly suggested by Costa Vargas: those who are included in the core history and who are permitted to tell a version of that history in sound are bound by the constraints outlined by DeVeaux, namely, that jazz is male, jazz is Black, jazz is art, jazz swings, and—most importantly for our discussion—jazz is American. Jazz musicians who are positioned outside the boundaries of the core tradition are thus faced with the unenviable task of improvising a history of jazz that shows their commitment to a core history while attempting to reflect their own individual voice. As record producer and guitarist Sun Chung told me:

> Jazz is a language that you decide to either incorporate or not. . . . For me jazz means a certain definition of swing, a certain definition of the language. . . . It's a very specific thing. Art Tatum is jazz, Wes Montgomery is jazz, Miles Davis is jazz. Even though I love his music, I don't think it's right to say that Bill Frisell, for example, is a jazz musician. He doesn't use the language, he doesn't swing, he is an incredible musician, but not a jazz musician, even if he is called that.

What I would like to explore here are the specific ways in which Japanese musicians balance these conflicting demands, carefully negotiating their current positioning through the integration of "core" elements into their own improvised histories of jazz. While the definition of "core" musical elements of jazz is highly problematic, I follow the framing of the "musical borders" of jazz proposed in the introduction to this book. I suggest that "core elements" are simply those elements whose degree of belonging to jazz is contested by musicians in the scene. As I show next, the use of swing and specific phrasing, harmonic approaches, and blues by particular "canonical" musicians is crucial to a discussion of what constitutes jazz for Japanese musicians, in particular as they negotiate the expectations placed upon them by both Japanese and non-Japanese listeners.

Ayumi, Webster, and Lester

March 12, 2015: Ayumi Ishito and I are sitting and chatting in my living room. A trumpeter in the mariachi band playing in the restaurant next door occasionally distracts us from our conversation, stealing our attention with some particularly impressive high notes. When I ask how she adapts to different audiences, Ayumi recounts that she felt she was expected to play differently when booked for gigs in Japan. "In Japan," she says, "jazz is more about traditional music. I mean, people like bebop and swing jazz more than modern things, so growing up I only studied about Dexter Gordon, Charlie Parker, Lester Young. But when I went to Berklee, the teacher told me, 'Don't play Parker's lick. You should play your own thing.' I had to be really creative. It was very difficult at first."

As Ishito explained to me in our conversation, in many Japanese jazz clubs, whether in Tokyo or in New York, the accepted way of playing jazz involves a rather strict adherence to straight-ahead jazz. This is done in part through extensive quotations from recordings, primarily of bebop and swing musicians. When she arrived in Boston to study, she was told to quit playing "Lester and Webster licks" (referring to Lester Young and Ben Webster) and to come up with her own approach. "Berklee doesn't really teach you about jazz history," she said. "Their way is to teach you how to improvise. So they just told me to follow the rules, the concept of Berklee." Ishito was told to "follow" Berklee's concept rather than quote licks by famous musicians, but as she explained to me, having to choose one over the other marks precisely the tension between playing "jazz" and creating an original, personal voice. Since she already knew the language of bebop, she now had to find a different sound or language to call her own.

When I asked Ishito to give me an example of Berklee's concept, she mentioned ideas of trombonist Hal Crook. "[Crook] told me: practice not-to-play, practice how to rest when you play. He never told me about jazz vocabulary and stuff." What does it mean, then, to play jazz without recounting its history? Particularly in contexts when playing "more traditional" or straight-ahead jazz is expected? For Ishito this meant taking more liberties with her improvisation, trying to develop melodies and leave more space. "I still play bebop, but I no longer feel it is necessary to play it all the time." Ishito's improvisations have indeed changed greatly since her arrival in the United States twelve years ago. They now involve complex harmonic and metric variations as well as free-jazz and hardcore influences resulting from her work with saxophonist Daniel Carter and various punk and noise bands. When playing outside of Japanese musical contexts, Hal Crook's influence and her work in free jazz became part of her own music history. However, as the examples below show, bebop still plays an important part in her improvisations.

July 2014: During a rehearsal session in Brooklyn with Swiss drummer Michel Maurer and Pennsylvania-born guitarist Matt Albeck, we play through several of Ishito's charts. We play "Since I Was a Kid," a sweeping composition alternating between minimalist melody in 6/4 in the A section and a driving guitar ostinato in the B section. In her solo, set in 5/4 meter, Ishito chooses a pensive, intentionally ambiguous phrasing, fully embracing the concept of "practicing not-to-play" by leaving plenty of space between phrases. Three bars after the beginning of the chorus, Ishito breaks her silence, playing a mellow minor sixth descent from F to A. Then another two-bar break. A short scalar descent on D minor, another full-bar break, another statement on A, a fifth above. Michel and I respond with a light but busy straight eighth-note accompaniment, filling the gap between phrases.

Ishito's solo testified to the musical distances she had traveled since her first days at Berklee. By not-playing, she was inviting the other musicians to respond to her solo statements, leaving plenty of room between phrases for the music to grow. While one could trace Ishito's full, warm sound to her early dedication to the music of tenor saxophonists Ben Webster and Lester Young, these early influences are integrated with her choice to space out her phrases and play rhythmically flowing lines over a dense rhythm section. In her telling, these elements allow her to be "freer." In "Since I Was a Kid" Ishito pursues biographical and nostalgic references in melody and title, alongside uneven meters and ostinato bass lines. Through the composition, Ishito creates her own history of jazz, with a clear reference to her early commitment to swing jazz, through her experiences at Berklee, to her current collaborations in the New York scene.

After a short break, we decide to play some standards to contrast with the changing meters and pensive melodies of Ishito's originals. Unprompted, Albeck starts the opening line of "Oleo," a jam-session favorite written by saxophonist Sonny Rollins. We respond immediately, playing the melody in unison and continuing on to the improvised B part. Albeck takes the first solo, running a string of consecutive swung eighth notes over the driving up-tempo swing Michel and I are holding. As Ayumi begins her solo, her deep familiarity with the musical vocabulary of Charlie Parker is on full display. She focuses on the upper range of the tenor with the smooth, uninterrupted transition between sections and the changes outlined. And yet I cannot help thinking of how different this is from her assured and contemplative playing in her own complex compositions. Here, in a song she has played thousands of times, she feels a need to play out, to never breathe, to fill the space with notes. This uninterrupted phrasing indicates, at least to me, a lack of space for dialogue.

In the example above, the context of a familiar bebop tune left little space for interaction among the musicians. Despite the fact that the "rhythm changes" piece was highly familiar to the musicians and was supposed to provide an opportunity for a break from the more complex original compositions,[5] the commitment to the fast rhythm of bebop, the extended use of arpeggios and scales, and the frequent use of triplet feel meant that our interactions felt predetermined, a dry retelling of history. For one reason or another, the rhythmic "set up and pay off" or call and response so central to bebop was absent from our playing. Even though we were all "speaking" bebop, we were not saying much that was new to one another. In the next section, I explore how paying tribute to non-canonical moments in jazz history can express a critique of the dominance of bebop language both in Japan and in the New York scene.

Hiro's hero

August 18, 2012: I see Hiro waiting for me as I come out of the Long Island City train station. We have a late lunch at a small taco place just under the tracks. Local cable news is blaring as he tells me about his background in jazz. "My first instrument was the guitar," he explains, almost apologetic. "I only started playing drums at age fifteen. But before that I played bass [briefly]. We were forming a band, for the first time, and there was a drummer already, so I was playing the bass. But the drummer sucked, so we switched. Until I got in university, I was playing more rock 'n' roll; I didn't play jazz at all. I didn't even know it existed. . . . Then, when I was 18, I got into university in Japan, I got into a jazz circle, like a club, and I was introduced to [jazz] there. And I didn't like it for some reason. There were many friends who gave me a bunch of jazz records, but they would give me bebop or . . . even older stuff. And now I love bebop, but in those days I didn't. I didn't like drum solos, I still don't like drum solos, but at the time I almost hated [them]. I wanted to be [a] musician. I didn't want to be featured, solo, or whatever. So if you are not interested in [a] soloistic position, it's kind of hard to tell the difference between different drummers, because they are doing kind of the same thing. To me, they were just doing the timekeeping, and so that's why I didn't like it."

Hironori Momoi's introduction to jazz seems almost reluctant. When he arrived in New York in August 2007 to embark on his music studies at CUNY's City College, Hiro had only been playing jazz for three years. He had not cared much for jazz before that. But after hearing drummer Brian Blade, he felt inspired and decided to move to New York to become a jazz musician. He began taking lessons in music theory, composition, and orchestration and playing in the school's ensembles. To maintain his visa and continue developing as a musician, Hiro enrolled in the master's program at Queens College, receiving his degree there in 2012. In our conversation he recalled the difference between hearing Blade and the older bebop records that had been suggested to him by his schoolmates. "I think the first record I got that really struck me was [the] Wayne Shorter Quartet. The drummer was Brian Blade . . . and of course they don't play . . . these thirty-two-bar forms. It's more like the music has a story. And he [Blade] was just burning, so [I thought], Oh, you are allowed to bang! So that was my first jazz record."

Hiro's approach to telling jazz history seems to be a synthesis of the attitudes described by Ishito. Although he initially disliked bebop and swing, his encounter with the playing of contemporary African American drummer Brian Blade served as an entry point and made him realize the music could tell a story. "I checked out almost all the records that he was in. I tried to imitate him just by listening to the drums." Importantly, Hiro's method of developing as a jazz musician was by copying Brian Blade, ostensibly going against the notion of "finding his own voice." But in his telling of his own jazz history, the open song structures used by Brian Blade and the Wayne Shorter Quartet played a crucial role.

Hiro was preparing to record his first album as a leader. He was working out his arrangements and rehearsing his band Identified Strangers. I went to hear the group play at Shapeshifter Lab, a warehouse that had been converted into performance space in the Gowanus neighborhood of Brooklyn. On the piece "Showers," Israeli guitarist Gilad Hekselman took a long beautiful intro, leading the group into the main theme, a sentimental ballad in 6/8 played by Chad Lefkowitz-Brown on tenor saxophone. The groove of the B part, reminiscent of the Pat Metheny Group from the late 1980s, was uplifting and energetic, leading to a subdued bass solo by Sam Minaie accompanied by Julian Shore on piano. For the most part, Hiro's playing stood out for its gentleness, using the crash and ride cymbals extensively to paint different shades and colors. During Minaie's solo, Hiro tailed Minaie's phrasing closely, echoing his rhythmic and melodic movement but always remaining in the background, lower in volume than either the piano or the bass. Even though he was the leader of the band, he took no solo on the piece, faithful to his claim that he did not want to be a featured soloist, just a musician.

What kind of history was Hiro performing in this piece? After our conversation, I could not help but hear an ambivalence about jazz history in Hiro's compositions. While these were some of the best young jazz musicians in the city, Hiro's compositions and playing showed little reference to bebop, the blues, or swing—to jazz's "undisputed" history. Instead, its main references were to jazz's more ambiguous moments: the 1980s, and even more so, the contemporary scene. Admittedly, I did not hear Brian Blade's dense snare and tom-tom work, with the cymbals that never last for more than a few moments. Instead, I heard Paul Motian's sustained cymbals in Hiro's playing, perhaps homage to his work with pianist Geri Allen in the 1980s. The references to the 1980s were also present in his pop-inflected pentatonic melodies and his harmonic simplicity, akin to the pop-fusion sound of the late 1980s. Hiro's music was, in a sense, jazz-rock fusion played with acoustic instruments. True to his desire to be simply a musician, without restrictions of genre or instrument, Hiro's compositions and accompaniment highlight a history of jazz's musical borders—moments in jazz history that are still openly debated by musicians in the scene. In front of a supportive audience of fellow musicians at Shapeshifter Lab, Hiro eschewed explicit performances of Japanese-ness, both by avoiding fusion with Japanese musical elements, as well as by rejecting clear references to bebop and swing. By highlighting the 1980s, a period often neglected in canonic jazz histories, Hiro was able to perform his own perspective on jazz as an evolving, changing, and multifaceted musical tradition. In the next section, I discuss how the "set up and pay off" call-and-response dynamic integral to bebop is used by migrant musicians to express, juxtapose, and evoke different moments in jazz history.

Kenji's trio

June 23, 2012: The scaffolding covering the building facades on 53rd Street makes it difficult to recognize the entrance. After twice accidentally walking past the staircase leading down to Tomi Jazz, a small bar in Japantown, I finally see the heads of Kenji and Nitzan as they come out for a cigarette. We chat for a few moments and then go in to order drinks before they begin their set. The bar is very dimly lit, only a couple of light bulbs hanging from the low ceiling. The place is packed. I sit in the only available seat, at the corner of the bar, right next to the door. A rectangular black column obstructs my view of the niche where the musicians are setting up to play. Nitzan begins improvising an intro on the piano. I feel unfit for this place, underdressed around the men in business suits, as if I had taken some more qualified customer's seat. Following the intro, the trio begins playing the head to "If I Should Lose You." "What did you want again?" the bartender asks while shaking a cocktail. "A whisky. This one." I point to the menu, indicating a $10 glass, the cheapest one there. "OK, give me a sec."

Since 2010, Tomi Jazz has offered New York–based Japanese musicians a stable place to perform and build their reputations. Ken Mukohata, the owner, books the shows personally and hires only a small number of musicians each month, creating informal residencies that enhance the association of certain musicians with the venue. Many of the bandleaders are Japanese, and in many of the bands at least one other musician is Japanese as well. While Mukohata has been increasingly booking non-Japanese headliners, the diversity of the musicians performing at Tomi Jazz results primarily from the hiring practices of the Japanese musicians associated with the place, who invite both Japanese and non-Japanese sidemen and women. This serves to facilitate a more fluid interaction between the performing musicians and the Japanese-speaking restaurant management and staff.

The club is situated in Japantown, a loosely defined area of several blocks on the East Side of midtown Manhattan. Although there is no historically recognized Japanese neighborhood in New York (Inouye 2018), the concentration of Japanese-owned businesses and residents in the area in the last few decades has earned Japantown its reputation as a newly formed immigrant neighborhood, an informal commercial reaction to the nearby Koreatown. Aside from the concentration of Japanese restaurants and bars within a short walking distance, there have been two other Japanese-owned jazz clubs: Jazz at Kitano on 38th Street and the now-defunct Somethin' Jazz Club on 52nd Street. One element that makes Tomi Jazz distinct from other jazz clubs in the city is its audience: the patrons at Tomi Jazz are mostly not musicians. In fact, due to the limited seating, musicians I spoke to said they were asked by the staff to refrain from inviting musician friends to their gigs. For a scene based on the social bonds created through "hangs," this is not a trivial request.

The music performed at Tomi Jazz is culturally Japanese in subtle ways if at all. Most vocal performances are in English, sometimes with a slight accent. Songs are chosen from the classic jazz repertoire: Miles Davis, Duke

Ellington, and the Great American Songbook. Saxophonist Ayumi Ishito told me that at Tomi Jazz, she plays "more standards and straight-ahead than anywhere else." The club serves multiple functions: a place of socialization and commerce for members of the Japanese community, a tourist attraction, and a historical allusion to the midtown bebop clubs on 52nd Street, such as the Onyx and Three Stooges. Significantly, these multiple functions and the alignment of an "ethnic" restaurant and jazz club are possible due to the popularity of American jazz and its history in Japan (Atkins 2001).

Musicians at Tomi Jazz reinforce their multinational community through collaborations with others from different countries and backgrounds. For a performance in December 2013, guitarist Yusuke Yamanouchi invited Chilean drummer Rodrigo Recabarren, Swedish bass player Lars Ekman, Japanese tenor player Yuto Mitomi, and Israeli pianist Nitzan Gavrieli, all of whom had been playing with one another in various contexts around that time. On October 4, 2014, Japanese singer Tak Iwasaki invited Brooklyn-born pianist Alex Clough and Israeli bassist Nadav Lachish to accompany him on his gig. While both American-born and migrant musicians are booked regularly to perform at Tomi Jazz, it is Japanese musicians who create the connection between the diverse community of migrant jazz musicians and the Japanese residents, businessmen, and tourists who patronize Tomi Jazz.

One such "multinational" group is the Kenji Yoshitake Trio. Yoshitake, a Japanese bassist, formed the trio with Alex Wyatt on drums and Nitzan Gavrieli on piano, primarily for gigs he books himself, often through contacts in the Japanese community. The trio performs almost exclusively standards.

The trio plays "Bye Bye Blackbird" (Audio Example 4.1 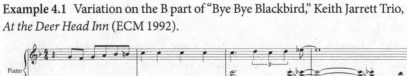). At the beginning of the B part of the first chorus of his solo, Gavrieli alludes to

Example 4.1 Variation on the B part of "Bye Bye Blackbird," Keith Jarrett Trio, *At the Deer Head Inn* (ECM 1992).

a particular version of the song by the Keith Jarrett Trio through a slight alteration of the melody. Yoshitake couches the quote in a short 4/4 walk accompaniment on the descending half-step harmony, pushing towards a "straight-ahead" swing in the B part, but moves back into half-time after two bars. Wyatt responds with syncopated brush accents on the hi-hat cymbal and bass drum, filling in the gaps in the melody variation while maintaining a half-time feel.

When performing their own jazz histories, musicians are not always aware of the origins of a particular song, the first time it was recorded, or its original text and context. Instead, they rely on histories as they are carried on sonically from one musician's narrative to the next. This performance by the Kenji Yoshitake Trio tells the musicians' personal histories of jazz until June 2012, with renditions of "Bye Bye Blackbird" being an important component in these histories, albeit not the only one.

The first chorus of the performance, which outlines the head (melody) and chord changes, is an active construction of the setting against which later musical and historical events and actions can be interpreted. The variation on the melody of the B part takes place soon after Gavrieli begins his solo, after the melody has been played. It is a quote from the Keith Jarrett Trio album *At the Deer Head Inn*, recorded for ECM in 1992, with Gary Peacock on bass and Paul Motian taking the place of the trio's third regular member, drummer Jack DeJohnette (Example 4.1). Gavrieli's quotation gives Jarrett's version of the melody special importance and demonstrates intimate familiarity with Jarrett's trio work (Example 4.2). In this instance, Gavrieli has chosen to chronicle a moment that is personally meaningful to him. When I visited Gavrieli at his home for house sessions during my field work, he would often share with me his latest transcription of a Jarrett performance, whether in notation, on the piano, or simply singing the solo. Through the quotation, Gavrieli is musically implying that the characters, actions, and events recorded that day at the Deer Head Inn are (also) part of his own jazz history.

The ensemble's negotiation of the quote suggests several possibilities. While Gavrieli invokes Keith Jarrett's rendition directly, both Yoshitake and Wyatt support the invocation with common intensification procedures: Yoshitake's momentary move to 4/4 and Wyatt's strong accents on the bass drum. Yoshitake's and Wyatt's moves allude to a moment that is perhaps less intimately familiar but nonetheless transformative in their own histories of jazz. The development of these intensification techniques

Example 4.2 "Bye Bye Blackbird," Kenji Yoshitake Trio, recorded at Tomi Jazz, June 23, 2012, quoted from Keith Jarrett's variation on the B part melody of "Bye Bye Blackbird" (Chorus 2, B, 1:00–1:04).

is attributed to the shared work of bassist Walter Page and drummer "Papa" Jo Jones—part of the All-American Rhythm Section of the Count Basie Orchestra of the late 1930s. "During the swing period, Walter Page's largely stepwise walking bass accompaniment in Count Basie's band epitomized the changing emphasis on the four-beat approach to meter" (Berliner 1994, 315). Through Gavrieli's solo, Yoshitake alternates between scalar motion (using the figure 1-2-3-2) and motion in fifths (using the figure 1-1-5-1). These two figures capture the first important transformation in the harmonic and melodic roles of the bass in jazz, from a New Orleans bass line based largely on the root of the chord and its fifth to a stepwise bass line during the swing era, linking one chord to the next melodically. In effortlessly performing this transition, Yoshitake is showing the significant role of swing in his own musical history.

While it may be difficult to trace their direct influence on Yoshitake's and Wyatt's choice to increase the momentum, the musical innovations of Page and Jones affected generations of bass players and drummers—arguably, all subsequent generations. In his biography, Jo Jones told Albert Murray about the historical importance of the move from half-time to 4/4: "Without Mr. Walter Page, you wouldn't have heard of Basie, Jimmy Rushing, 'Hot-Lips' Page, Lester Young, Charlie Parker, nor myself" (Jones 2011, 90).

Example 4.3 Sparse "Miles Davis" phrasing (Chorus 4, A, 1:47–1:54).

By simultaneously demonstrating their knowledge of these techniques, Yoshitake and Wyatt are alluding to the birth of swing. In discussing the performance, Gavrieli also remarked that "Kenji and Alex have a very comfortable quarter note." It was this sense of comfort and rhythmic familiarity (as discussed in the previous chapter) that allowed Yoshitake, Gavrieli, and Wyatt to juxtapose their own historical references.

The first A of the fourth chorus opens with remarkable clarity. A sparse melodic question is posed in measures 1–4 and answered effortlessly in measures 5–8, with the resolution exploiting the symmetry of this thirty-two-bar form (Example 4.3). In contrast, the last A is among the denser, more convoluted, and more challenging sections of the performance. Responding to a sextuplets call by Wyatt at the end of the B part (measure 22), Gavrieli begins a series of triplet runs that cuts through the last A. The driving forces behind this dramatic increase in energy are Wyatt's rapid stream of bass drum "bombs" and snare accents and Yoshitake's stable quarter notes in the A and B. Yoshitake plays a melodic bass line in the midrange in the first A, but gradually climbs to the upper register in the second A, increasing its intensity.

In our conversation at Udon West, Yoshitake mentioned two bands lead by Miles Davis as being highly important to his musical development, especially through the influence of bassist Paul Chambers. Davis recorded the "canonical" version of "Bye Bye Blackbird" in 1955 with John Coltrane, Red Garland, Paul Chambers, and Philly Joe Jones (not to be confused with Papa Jo Jones mentioned earlier), and it appeared on the album Round about

Example 4.4 Dense "John Coltrane" phrasing (Chorus 4, A2, 2:06–2:13).

Midnight in 1957. A second important version was recorded by Davis's band at the Newport Jazz Festival in 1958, this time with Bill Evans at the piano. Both these versions, and the ways Chambers plays on them, inform Yoshitake response to his trio's rendition of "Bye Bye Blackbird."

The transition from the light swing played in the first half of the chorus to the intensity generated by the rhythm section at the end of the fourth chorus points up some of the complications of interpreting personal sounded histories. Accepting Wyatt's offer to "go beyond" for the entirety of the last A of the fourth chorus, Gavrieli creates a sharp contrast with the temperament of the first A and B parts. Meanwhile, Yoshitake continues to play a stepwise walking bass line but moves up to the upper register. What histories is the trio telling here? One possibility is an invocation of Davis's sparse improvisations in the first part of the chorus juxtaposed with Coltrane's "sheets of sound" technique in the second. Coltrane developed this technique toward the end of his time with the Davis Quintet, and it is a feature of the 1958 recording of "Bye Bye Blackbird" at Newport (Porter 1999, 160). When employing this technique, Coltrane used extremely dense arpeggios and scale patterns played in rapid succession (with smaller subdivisions than sixteenth notes), running from the lowest to the highest registers.[6] In this instance, Gavrieli is showing that both horn men are part of his own jazz history. He creates a synthesis of the two in his solo, playing with Davis's melodic clarity in the first part of the chorus and contrasting it with Coltrane's free-flowing approach in the last A.

In his own playing, Yoshitake beautifully demonstrates his knowledge of bassist Paul Chambers's approach to supporting these two widely different soloists. Following Chambers's example on the 1958 recording, Yoshitake plays a melodic, scalar line under Gavrieli's sparse phrasing—filling up the space Gavrieli left open in the midrange. As Gavrieli's playing intensifies in the second A, Yoshitake moves to the upper register and leaves the midrange clear, making sure not to clash with Gavrieli's flurry of notes, just as Chambers does in his accompaniment of Coltrane.

Griffin and Washington (2008) attribute further significance to this historical moment. They suggest that the tensions between Davis's "lyricism" and Coltrane's "improvisational effusiveness" led Coltrane to leave Davis's band after the release of *Round about Midnight* in 1957 and continue his explorations as a soloist.[7] Coltrane's "sheets of sound" and later free-form explorations, contrasted with Davis's consistent way of playing against changing musical rhythm sections, are emblematic of the different approaches, tensions, and interpretations that would be seen in jazz in the years to come. In his musical recounting of this historical moment, Yoshitake highlights Chambers's crucial but often neglected role in musically mediating the growing tension between the two musicians.

As the trio enters the fifth chorus, Gavrieli leads in with a piercing blues phrase, sustaining a single high F over series of short, syncopated chord blocks in his left hand. In the fourth measure of the chorus, Gavrieli begins a four-bar bebop phrasing (Example 4.5). The arpeggiated chords, swung in eights, are linked together chromatically to imply substitute harmonies. As Gavrieli alternates between blues and bebop phrasing, Yoshitake moves in a largely stepwise chromatic walking bass to support the blues phrasing (under a harmonically open F major). He closely tails the fast-changing harmony of measures 5–8 with half a measure per chord progression. Wyatt responds to the opening blues phrase of the fifth chorus with strong accents on beats 2 and 4 on the hi-hat, which are maintained throughout the A part. The transition between blues and bebop is subtler in his accompaniment. He indicates the beginning of the chorus with syncopated accents on the crash cymbal (in measure 2) following Gavrieli's short chord blocks, and introduces intermittent snare accents in measures 5 and 6.

The trio's seamless flow from blues to bebop and back, and their penultimate deconstruction of bebop techniques mark yet another important

Example 4.5 Transition between blues and bebop phrasing (Chorus 5, A, 2:21–2:25).

moment in their own jazz histories: the passing of the torch to a new generation of musicians with the switch from the fast bebop tunes of the 1940s to the bluesy phrasing and soulful grooves of "hard bop" in the 1950s. While the first part of the chorus fits neatly within bebop, it is in fact the dissolution of the bebop phrasing that preceded the development of the new sound by Davis and Trane in their 1950s recordings of "Bye Bye Blackbird."

In the eleventh measure of the chorus, Gavrieli plays a cadential blues phrasing with a strong accent on the dominant C (Example 4.6). He repeats the phrase in measures 13 and 14. The A ends with yet another bebop phrase, with sequentially descending chromatic lines dissolving from the dominant C to G, Gb, F, Eb, and D. The end of the phrase does not mark the end of the second A part clearly; rather, it continues dissolving into the B part. In fact, without Wyatt's accent on the downbeat, it would be hard to recognize the beginning of the B part. Over the second bebop phrase, Yoshitake intensifies his walk by moving to a higher register, with a faster harmonic rhythm of two chords per measure. As Gavrieli moves out of the harmony in measures 15–16, Yoshitake holds the pedal point on C, occasionally including a neighboring dissonant note to mark the shift. Wyatt signals a new chorus and a new dynamic level by switching from brushes to drumsticks. He plays a series of accented straight eighth notes on the snare to mark the beginning of the sixth chorus.

Example 4.6 Dissolving bebop phrasing (Chorus 5, A to B, 2:28–2:34).

The influence of Davis's quintet on Yoshitake and his trio is thus not limited to their decision to perform "Bye Bye Blackbird." Rather, it is embedded in the ways they sonically negotiate its historical significance—the new sound of Davis, Coltrane, and their bandmates. The trio's performance in the fifth chorus indicates the importance of hard bop in their own musical histories: the continued prominence of the blues, the use of harmonically "out" bebop phrasing (following Trane's explorations of new sonorities), straight-eight hits on the snare drum (alluding to the new, heavy drumming style of Philly Joe Jones), and a strong pedal point in the bass (following Paul Chambers's approach of supporting these new sonorities and rhythms). This confluence of elements suggests that this crucial historical moment holds a privileged place in these musicians' own personal jazz histories.

All of the historical references made in this analysis are contingent and refutable and may have any number of different interpretations. However, I maintain that jazz history reflects in some sense the previous contributions of musicians, and that musicians narrate these moments—through "set up and pay off"—in their improvisations and interactions. The specific references to Jarrett in the second chorus, the pervasive use of bebop and blues phrasing, reflect Gavrieli's own conception of what jazz is and who the characters are who provide the wisdom necessary for performing this music. Yoshitake's and Wyatt's responses and suggestions during Gavrieli's solo indicate that they too were reacting to the historical moments he was invoking, and they responded with events and characters from their own jazz histories.

Conclusion

Despite the importance of Japanese straight-ahead musicians to the New York jazz scene, their contribution has been often overlooked. This is partly because these musicians are not focused on thematizing their ethnic identities (as non-Japanese audiences may expect); instead they focus on certain aspects of jazz history that they find compelling. Using the notion of storytelling as an analytical tool makes it possible to examine these musical narratives as they are told by Japanese migrant musicians. Such narratives go beyond markers of ethnicity and individual solos to ensemble action and interaction. Following these narratives, I have argued that Japanese jazz musicians' performances of their own jazz histories reflect a dual commitment to finding their "own" voice and to jazz as rooted in African American expressive culture. While their degree of comfort with bebop, swing, and blues allows them to perform them in the context of their own histories and as part of their own sound, they might hark back to alternative jazz histories, those of jazz-rock fusion, contemporary jazz, and avant-garde. More than twenty ago, bassist Jerome Harris suggested that "people who live halfway around the world cannot rely on getting the approval of an Art Blakey or Miles Davis or Betty Carter or Wynton Marsalis to confirm the validity of what they do; that validity must, of necessity, be confirmed by the players and audiences in their home areas" (2000, 124). At the time, Harris and other US-born musicians could not fully appreciate the extent of commitment and dedication of contemporary Japanese musicians and audiences to the core jazz narrative. It is precisely this commitment that encourages migrant jazz musicians to travel thousands of miles to play in the places where Bird, Miles, and Trane played before them. Japanese migrant musicians travel to the United States precisely because they are searching for a *living relationship* with jazz in America. As I have shown in the cases of Ishito, Momoi, and Yoshitake, by telling their own histories of jazz in their improvisations, Japanese jazz musicians in New York confront and challenge these conceptions and their own place within jazz history. In the next chapter, I further explore how migrant musicians contend with and respond to expectations that they perform their own nationality in jazz.

5
Home

The word *place* to me can mean two different things. . . . One meaning can be a venue, the place you play—the kind of theater, a small place or a club. But for me a place can also mean a place in my heart, in terms of where I come from, the history of where I've been. I had a lot of—you might call it struggles, or doubts, conflicts, inner questions, you know, just trying to understand the history of jazz, of this music that I really love, Black American music. I've been transcribing and studying since I lived in Argentina, and sometimes feeling a bigger connection to that music than [to] some of the [Argentinian] folklore. Particularly because folklore can become rigid in the style. I realized that I feel more comfortable when there's a place of listening to each other, in the band, and that you have the freedom to bring different things that can flow and be a part of it, and not feel constrained by a style. When it gets too specific, I feel maybe I don't belong. . . . So it's been a search in that sense, of finding a place of comfort.

The previous chapters explored how obtaining knowledge of jazz becomes a motivation and a means for musicians to migrate to New York, how it allows them to enter new scenes in the city, how knowledge of jazz enables new scenes to form around new rhythms and styles, and how migrant musicians communicate their knowledge of jazz in the course of performance. In this chapter, I further explore how migrant musicians use their knowledge of jazz in tandem with other genres, styles, rhythms, and instruments to highlight the constructed nature of performances of national and ethnic identity.

During my fieldwork, one of the most challenging aspects was to capture in writing what migrant musicians experience as a musical and personal home. In the quote above, Argentinian flautist and saxophonist Mariano Gil described to me the ambiguity of home as a place of personal and musical comfort. This is because for migrant musicians, "home" is at once fixed and moving, related to the country of origin but separate from it, pointing to different social relations, physical spaces, personal histories, and musical experiences. A second complication (which I discuss in more detail in the next chapter) comes from listeners' assumptions that migrant jazz musicians reflect their "home" countries in their music, an assumption that some musicians embrace at times and reject at other times. Migration scholars have explored the connections and networks that link migrants' homes in their places of origin to the places to which they move (Glick Schiller 2008; Çağlar 2016). In ethnomusicology, music has long been described as crucial for migrants' processes of home-building and belonging, moving along similar networks (Reyes 1999; Shelemay 2012; Silverman 2012; Rapport 2014; Chávez 2017). Importantly, the meaning of "home" as an affective experience and "home" as performative action do not always coincide.

As discussed in Chapter 3, for some of these musicians "home" can also express a sense of sonic familiarity with a particular style, which is essential for musical communication and improvisation. In highlighting the shifting meanings that migrant musicians attach to home, one important challenge is to conceptualize not only its mobile aspects but also those that are stable. As David Ralph and Lynn A. Staeheli (2011) have shown, there is a tendency in migration studies to "underplay the resilience of stable, bounded and fixed interpretations" of home. But perhaps the complexity of "home" for migrant musicians is embedded in its dual meaning as simultaneously moving and fixed, both felt and performed. Benjamin Piekut has argued that musical sound is an "entity that requires [many] entanglements" to sustain itself (2014, 192). Thinking of the relationship between "home" as affect and "home" as improvised performance brings to mind the similarities of these two concepts—most importantly, the notion that for migrant musicians a feeling of "home" (like musical sound) requires many entanglements, connections, and networks in order to be sustained. Moreover, for migration musicians, jazz—like home—has fixed and mobile dimensions. This chapter explores these dynamics and argues that home is experienced as an affect, a location, and as a set of musical relationships that shape identities and feelings of belonging among migrant musicians.

To trace the ways in which migrant musicians in New York perform multiple regional, national, and ethnic musical identities (home as performance), and the extent to which these performances give rise to a sense of home and belonging for them (home as affect), I begin the chapter with a theoretical discussion of processes of globalization of jazz, in which various jazz styles are constructed as performance of national identity. I then move on to the role of jazz in New York's ethnic art worlds, where immigrant organizations and government institutions from the home country work together to create cultural representation of the immigrant community, creating the diasporic performance of "home" through jazz (Becker 1984; Zheng 2011). After exploring the relationship between performances of nationality and New York's ethnic art worlds, I focus on several performances by South American musicians—primarily from Argentina and Chile—in which the contradictions between the affective and performative aspects "home" are exposed and negotiated. These performances take place in contexts that highlight the moving and fixed senses of home for migrant musicians: the Consulate General of Argentina, a Latin American community center, an evening dedicated to a Spanish-language newspaper, and a CD launch concert by a Chilean saxophone player. Each of these performances represents a case in which movement between genres, histories, and places creates a feeling of home for the participating musicians. Moreover, as they tease out the distinctions between home as expressed and home as felt, South American musicians gesture toward the complex role of music under dictatorial regimes, where performances of "home" and "United States" could simultaneously signify oppression and liberation.

Although "Latin jazz" often refers to the greater Latin Caribbean (including Panama, Colombia, and Venezuela), South American performers are positioned in between jazz and Latin contexts and are often overlooked in scholarly discourse (Karush 2017; Washburne 2020). Analyzing various performances in which national and traditional musical genres are embedded in jazz contexts, I argue that these musicians create a sense (or a feeling) of home through motion, moving along a spectrum from performances as "migrant jazz" musicians to performances as migrant "jazz musicians." By the former I refer to musicians who perform an imagined "national jazz" genre through the choice of sidemen, instrumentation, repertoire, and sonic vocabulary. The latter term, on the other hand, emphasizes an explicit refusal to be bounded by prescribed national attributes. While the same musicians may move from one extreme position to the other or choose intermediary positions between them, it is the possibility of expressive movement that engender "home" as an affective experience. As such, performances of nationality and ethnicity by migrant jazz musicians are highly context-specific, reflecting fluctuating desires and demands to suppress and express ethnicity and national belonging within American multicultural politics and institutions. In order to feel at home, migrant musicians use their diverse musical skill to perform identity and belonging in relation to an art world shaped by and through multiculturalism and identity politics (Becker 1984; Roberts 2016). As I show next, such performances are embedded the history of jazz as global (and in some cases imperial) music in which various jazz styles have been constructed as performance of modern, local national identity.

Nationalizing jazz

In recent years, a growing number of jazz scholars have documented the rich history of jazz scenes around the world (Atkins 2003; Bohlman and Plastino 2016; Johnson 2019). In many of these case studies, scholars have traced musicians' use of specific instrumentation, modal systems, rhythms, and repertoire to ground the music in particular cultural and national contexts. Whether individual musicians in these scenes collectively create what constitutes a national style is bound up in the complexity of genre definitions (Holt 2007) and thus remains an open question. An influential artist may end up inadvertently leading collaborators and other musicians to create within a national framework (Lie 2020; Shelemay 2016), concert promoters may choose to identify the music of a particular artist as representative of a national jazz style (Picaud 2016), and listeners themselves may recognize jazz from their country as a local type of jazz (Lemish 2020). Whether collective or individual, such performances present attempts, however tentative, at imagined national jazz forms throughout the world (Nicholson 2014; Holt 2016; Johnson 2019). As I show next, the division of jazz into ethnic categories within the United States is at once an antecedent globalization process—rooted in racial ideologies of the America music industry (Gazit 2020) and in consequence resurging with the struggles for recognition among ethnic minorities in the 1970s.

Studies on musical representation of ethnic identity within US jazz have emphasized the close relationship between jazz and American national belonging, attempting to map out the ways in which Black, White, Asian, Latin, and Jewish musicians perform racial and ethnic identity through jazz (Monson 1995; Jones 1999; Wong 2004; Sandke 2010; Hersch 2013; Barzel 2015; Murray 2017; Washburne 2020). While scholars of global jazz and American jazz have demonstrated how jazz performances can express national or ethnic identity, these studies underplay how contingent, contextual, and malleable they can be. Musical performances of one ethnic or national identity do not prevent a performer from presenting multiple and at times conflicting identities in other performance contexts (Gazit 2020). Such multiple representations have a long history as survival strategies among migrant jazz musicians. For example, in discussing the life of saxophonist Sidney Bechet in France, Rashida Braggs (2016) convincingly shows how Bechet negotiated his multiple subjectivities as an American, as a Frenchman, and as a person of African descent depending on the context in which he was performing. At times he would stress his roots as a Black American and at others as a French Creole; on some occasions he would be a Parisian and on others a New Orleans native (Braggs 2016, 31). Matthew Karush (2017) similarly shows that Argentinian musicians Lalo Schifrin and Gato Barbieri adapted their musical identities (as young bebop "purists" in 1950s Buenos Aires) to fit North American and European notions of "Latin" musical and ethnic identity. By assuming that migrant jazz musicians perform a single musical-cultural identity upon arrival in the United States, whether to distinguish themselves from American musicians, to "avoid" competition with them, or as part of their pursuit of jazz's individual voice (Lemish 2020), we risk diminishing the agency of migrant jazz musicians to make strategic aesthetic, economic, and political choices about how, when, and whether to express cultural and national identity in their music. In the following section, I discuss the ways in which such nationalized jazz discourses are expressed in performance.

Performing nationality

The notion that musicians perform a fixed national identity in their music has often been discussed with regard to the relationship between American and European jazz musicians abroad. George Lewis argues that in the 1970s, European musicians sought to "liberate" themselves from comparisons to African American musicians but, in an ironic turn, created their own cultural nationalism deeply influenced by the ideas circulating among African American musicians at the time. He quotes German jazz journalist Joachim-Ernst Berendt as writing that "the creative European musician has ceased to imitate American musicians. He has ceased to compete with him in areas—above all in swing and in the field of black traditions—in which he cannot catch him" (Lewis 2004). As the careers of Joe Zawinul, George Mraz, Miroslav Vitous, and many other European migrant musicians testify, both the notion that migrant musicians "naturally" express their own cultural background (due to cultural distance from the United States) and the idea that they do so in order to distinguish themselves and avoid competition with African American musicians run counter to the fact that many migrant musicians play both straight-ahead and "nationally" marked jazz with equal proficiency, frequently collaborating across ethnic and racial lines.

Focusing on jazz musicians in Paris, David Ake (2010) explores how they express their nationality in performance and in composition. He identifies two dominant groups among the musicians with whom he worked. The first group is the *Americanists*, who believe that "those born in the US enjoy certain cultural, historical, perhaps even biological advantages and claims to jazz authenticity" (Ake 2010, 123). A subgroup, the *African-Americanists*, maintain that "black Americans play more authentically than nonblack Americans" (Ake 2010, 123). On the other side are *assimilationists*, who "make no special claims of authenticity due to the circumstances of nationality or ethnicity." Ake further claims that musically, "Americanist players uphold . . . bop- or postbop-based linearity, and they employ more blues inflections," while "assimilationist musicians tend to incorporate a relatively greater range of stylistic sources" (Ake 2010, 132). Following Ingrid Monson, Ake is quick to mention that this seemingly inclusive stance of the assimilationist can have racial undertones: White musicians may adopt universalist rhetoric as a way of countering an African-Americanist position regarding jazz, understating the central role of African Americans in the creation and development of jazz to preserve their legitimacy (Monson 1995). In an attempt to adapt Ake's framework to migrant musicians in New York, one may reverse the roles, claiming that assimilationists are those who maintain a "purist" attitude toward bebop, whereas nationalists are those who maintain a purist attitude toward their own "national jazz," playing only Cuban, Brazilian, or "Israeli" jazz. As I suggested in the introduction to this book, such a stance may be an individual choice made by some musicians, but it is hardly the norm. More commonly, as I emphasize in this chapter, musicians hold neither of these purist attitudes, but rather aim for versatility, responding and reacting to the conditions and requirements of different performance contexts.

These various modes of expressing national identity assume congruence between sonic representation and the national or ethnic identity of the performer. Roberts argues that such assumptions can amount to sonic identity politics, "a hegemonic discourse in which singular sounds come to stand in for entire groups of people through fixed and essential representations of race and culture" (2016, 123). Roberts articulates how multiculturalism evolved in jazz from a radical practice in the 1990s (through the work of Fred Ho, John Zorn, and others) into a dominant political agenda, part of jazz's growing attraction for the neoliberal marketplace (Chapman 2018). This change entailed the use of musical sounds, instruments, repertoires, and renowned composers as national or ethnic markers, part of a political project of diversity. As I show next, musicians negotiate demands for sonic and ethnic cohesion while pursuing the economic and infrastructural resources afforded to them by the "ethnic art world."

New York's ethnic art worlds

Ethnic institutions, immigrant associations, and governmental entities are central to New York's multicultural economy. As part of their public cultural programs, these institutions sponsor the production of cultural events, presentations, and festivals (Rapport 2014, 16). Over the last two decades, and with increasing momentum since UNESCO's declaration of International Jazz Day in 2011, jazz has become increasingly central to these cultural programs. As part of the nationalization of global jazz, concert halls, jazz clubs, churches, museums, and outdoor venues are temporarily transformed into "migrant jazz" venues. Several jazz clubs, including Dizzy's Club at Lincoln Center, Smoke Jazz and Supper Club in Harlem, and the now-defunct Cornelia Street Café, have been hosting annual nationality-themed jazz festivals, including Italian Jazz Days, the Japanese Jazz Festival, and Israeli Jazz Spotlight.

Occasionally, migrant jazz musicians would elicit the help of private and governmental organizations associated with their home country in order to obtain sponsorships and subsidies for international tours, produce recordings, or take part in nationally themed jazz events and festivals in the city (Oakes 2003). The musical repertoire, title, and personnel chosen for such concerts are neither coincidental nor "natural," but must clearly express the performer's national identity. In order to obtain governmental support for such concerts, band leaders must recruit musicians from their home country and play music that is clearly associated with the home country (whether original or an interpretation of an existing piece). They may also frame the concert as a tribute to national cultural icons. In other words, to perform jazz within New York's ethnic art worlds requires a specialized skill set, part of a highly sophisticated improvisational and compositional vocabulary musicians develop expressly for such performances. It is within this complex economic, political, and aesthetic matrix that migrant jazz musicians make decisions about how, when, and where to perform national and ethnic identity in jazz. As the next discussion suggests, the degree to which migrants experience as sense of home in these different contexts may be affected by their performance of national identity, but this is neither restricted to nor predetermined by their country of origin.

Mariano Gil at the Argentinian Consulate

October 30, 2014: Mariano Gil, an Argentinian flautist and painter, has invited me to hear his trio perform at the Consulate General of Argentina. The trio, with fellow Argentinians Leo Genovese on piano and Lautaro Burgos on drums, plays Gil's original compositions as well as arrangements of Argentinian folk songs. The concert is billed as a "jazz concert" on the consulate's promotional material and is entitled "Cronopios Sin Fama," an allusion to the short-story collection *Historias de cronopios y de famas* by Argentinian author and jazz aficionado Julio Cortázar. On the wall behind the band are the colorfully painted faces of Dizzy Gillespie and Thelonious Monk, part of Gil's series of jazz portraits. Over the past year and a half, I have heard Gil, Genovese, and Burgos play in various musical contexts in the city, and I have even played with them on a couple of occasions, but I have never heard any of them give such an overtly Argentinian performance. It seems like the perfect way to represent Argentinian jazz musicians in New York City. A bit too perfect perhaps? I have seen Gil masterfully perform bebop, Balkan music, free jazz, and Brazilian music. But there is nothing disingenuous about this particular performance; the particular venue requires a national kind of music, Argentinian jazz. Nevertheless, to describe these people as "Argentinian jazz" musicians gives more weight to their nationally distinctive performances than to their musical projects that would define them as Argentinian "jazz musicians."

When I interviewed him for this book, Gil explained that for that particular performance, the questions of whom to play with, what music to play, and how to interpret it were directly related to the national context of the performance:

> It was pretty deliberate; it was a trio of all Argentinian musicians. We played mostly my original music, and my original music is definitely informed by my love for jazz, but I come from Argentina and there's a lot of music from Argentina I used to play, both ... folklore and ... tango. We did a traditional chacarera, then we did an original of mine with that same rhythm—you know, the 6/8 Argentinian-type rhythm. And I think Leo suggested one of the chacareras, one of the traditional ones. Lautaro played bombo, and he is from Chaco, one of the provinces where the folklore is a little heavier. There were a few of my songs that have a little bit of a tango flavor.

As Gil makes clear, playing Argentinian music in the context of a performance at the Argentinian consulate was a deliberate act, a choice the trio made to explore certain aspects of their musical histories, which include Argentinian folklore and tango. But the show was also an opportunity to explore a relationship among music, art, and poetry that they found interesting, compelling, and relevant. For example, they incorporated a text by the great Argentinian author and jazz critic Julio Cortázar. Cortázar had been an important influence on Gil's music and art, not only because many of Cortázar's writings deal with the lives of Argentinian expatriates but also because jazz holds a prominent place in his protagonists' lives. The term *cronopio* was initially used by Cortázar in a Louis Armstrong concert review entitled "Louis, Enormísimo Cronopio" (1968), and subsequently in his stories. *Famas*, too, are characters in Cortázar's stories, but *sin fama* can also be interpreted ironically, as in "jazz musicians without fame."

> In the show, I did a reading of some of Cortázar's text, and we did an improvisation over that. So there was a very deliberate [approach]. We're Argentinian, we love a lot of music, we're going to bring something [from that experience], but how *we* feel it, *now, here*, without being tied down to being "correct" in terms of tradition. There's something both in the rhythm and melody that I feel a big connection to, in tango and in folkloric music in Argentina.

In this quote, Gil makes an explicit distinction between home as performed and home as felt. It was the freedom to play—"without being tied down to being correct"—enabled in part through jazz, that opened the possibility for feeling in the context of performing "home." While Argentinian music, ranging from the tangos of Ciriaco Ortiz to the songs of Atahualpa Yupanqui and the rock music of Luis Alberto Spinetta, has left an indelible mark on Gil's musical development, it was jazz that brought him to the United States and made the most profound impact on his life:

> I love . . . jazz. It was the main reason I came to this country. It's hard to explain why. Words are always of limited use in explaining something that is best understood through pure sound: the essence of African rhythm (polyrhythm), the spontaneity that allows a unique interpersonal chemistry between individuals, the harmonic richness, and the variety of expressions that have emerged in its short history. The sound! The sonic beauty of Elvin Jones's drums, Monk or McCoy Tyner's piano, Coltrane's sax, Miles's trumpet has changed me and affected my worldview. In that sense, my portraits also serve as tribute and expressions of gratitude. (Gil 2014)

Gil's commitment to jazz is modeled on both his literary and his musical heroes. Like Cortázar, who attempted to give a sense of musical improvisation to his prose about the life and music of Charlie Parker (García 2003), many of Gil's compositions and paintings are about jazz musicians and their legacy. Part of that legacy is the ability to adapt to a particular musical context and to create in response to a specific audience, both aesthetically and commercially. It requires the ability to be an "Argentinian jazz" musician as well as an Argentinian "jazz musician." Gil's concert represents his background as a performer, composer, and improviser—his experience playing tango and Argentinian folkloric music, his love of Argentinian poetry and prose, and his decades-long experience playing jazz on the New York scene. His own sense of home, however, as he describes it, comes not from a musical representation of a particular home country but from specific musical relationships and dynamics in the course of performance.

For Gil, being constrained by genre categories meant giving up part of his history in jazz, Argentinian music, Brazilian music, and other genres he has been involved in. In our conversation, he expressed this sense of unease regarding specific genres as expressions of "home." "I love bebop," he said, "but when it gets too specific, I feel maybe I don't belong. . . . Whereas when I go too much into tango or folklore, I feel, likewise, I am not playing myself." To Gil, a sense of belonging comes from collective listening on the bandstand.

As I show next, listening enables migrant jazz musicians to share their own musical histories and experience those of others, ultimately creating a shared sense of belonging.

Remembering Arauco at Whynot Jazz

July 2014: I am at a show at the Whynot Jazz Room, a small cellar club in the West Village. The room is crowded. I lean back against the glass door, holding my audio recorder high in the air. The back of the room is packed with musicians. Leading the band is Francisco "Pancho" Molina, one of the most successful Chilean musicians of the 1990s as a member of the band Los Tres, who has been playing jazz in the city for almost twenty years. We have played together at several house sessions, and I always appreciate his wise advice about "making" it in the scene: "It takes ten years, man," he says. "Once you have the sound, now it's only a matter of time." On bass is Peter Slavov from Bulgaria, who received his green card just a month ago after fifteen years in New York. On the Fender Rhodes and keyboards is Leo Genovese; Uri Gurvich from Israel is playing saxophone; Oscar Peñas from Spain is playing guitar. Singing and playing a second guitar is Pancho's compatriot, Chilean guitarist and vocalist Camila Meza.

Perhaps more than any other club in Manhattan, Whynot Jazz captured the diversity of the migrant jazz scene in New York, if only for a brief moment. Located at the heart of Greenwich Village, Manhattan's preeminent "jazz neighborhood" (Jackson 2012, 52), it continually challenged national borders and social boundaries by bringing together migrants and natives of diverse cultures and legal statuses in close musical and social relationships. The musicians performing at Whynot attributed this to the collaborative work of the booking managers: Macedonian-born Aleksandar Petrov and African American Solonje Burnett. Gathering a tightly knit community of musicians around the club, organizing jam sessions, concert series, and curated collaborations, the two helped musicians realize their potential to shift from performances as "migrant jazz" musicians to performances as migrant "jazz musicians." In doing so, they diversified the audiences that attended Whynot Jazz and the very notion of migrant music.

The group has already performed several of Molina's original compositions before one song, a rendition of Violeta Parra's "Arauco Tiene una Pena," captivates the audience completely. Parra's legacy as one of Chile's most important folk singers and originators of Chilean nueva canción looms large over the small club, packed with South American musicians and listeners. Meza's voice, performing Parra's 6/8 cueca protest against the subjugation of the indigenous Mapuche people of Chile, cuts through the thick textures produced on bass, Fender Rhodes, and guitar. On acoustic guitar, Parra's signature instrument, Meza plays chopped high chords, octaves, and tremolos, revealing only fragments of her hard-earned and impressive technical ability as a jazz guitarist. At the end of the second verse, Genovese begins his solo. The Fender Rhodes keyboard is plugged into a distortion effect, creating a sharp, fuzzy timbre. Fast lines run in and (mostly) out of the harmony, pushing, creating a dense mass of sound. The solo ends, and the dynamics are lowered to a new starting point. A hand reaches from behind and gives something to Camila. It is Slavov's hand, returning the music for the song.

Arauco is the historic homeland of the indigenous Mapuche people of Chile and was a war zone for centuries. But the song is also a critique of modern Chile, calling on its people to reconnect with their roots, to listen to the cry of the land beyond the noise of modernity. The *cueca*, the 6/8 dance that serves as the rhythmic foundation for the song, is Chile's quintessential national dance and a marker of its rural countryside. What does it mean for Chileans in New York to sing for Arauco, for the forgotten homeland of the Mapuche?

Arauco tiene una pena	Arauco is filled with pain,
que no la puedo callar.	That I cannot assuage.
Son injusticias de siglos	For centuries, injustices
que todos ven aplicar.	Have been committed for all to see.
Nadie le ha puesto remedio	No one has found a solution
Pudiéndolo remediar.	If there even is one.
Levántate, Huenchullán.	Rise up, Huenchullán!
Un día llega de lejos	One day the conquistador thief
Huescufe conquistador,	Comes from afar,
buscando montañas de oro	Looking for mountains of gold
que el indio nunca buscó.	That the Indian never sought.
Al indio le basta el oro	The Indian is content with the gold
que le relumbra del sol.	That shines from the sun.
Levántate, Curimón.	Rise up, Curimón!

(Parra 1985, 156–157)

By drumming and singing about Arauco, both Molina and Meza were sonically marking their identity as "Chilean jazz" musicians in New York. What was the role of the other musicians in this context? What identities were they expressing? Despite having never played, or perhaps even heard, the song before, after two verses and a keyboard solo Slavov had already committed the song to memory. This is how, quite matter-of-factly, a Chilean historical landmark found its way into the hands and ears of a Bulgarian jazz bassist. It was a moment of higher musical learning, where a song saturated with cultural meaning and Chilean history was placed in front of musicians who could not fully grasp it in all its significance, and yet contributed immensely to its performance. The sense of "home" experienced in Molina and Meza's performance of Arauco came from the intimate dynamic of listening created among the musicians and audience at Whynot. By committing the song to memory, Slavov became equally important in creating this shared sense of belonging, not only responding to the music in the moment, but carrying Arauco and a sense of musical home with him. In the next section, I show how an experience of "home" can be created in contexts where multiple national belonging are performed simultaneously.

Performing migrancy: Legal Aliens at El Taller Latino Americano

June 2013: I am going to Leo Genovese's birthday party at El Taller Latino Americano on the Upper West Side of Manhattan. There is no sign to indicate the venue, only a white glass door. I enter and walk up the stairs to the second floor. The walls of the stairwell are adorned floor to ceiling with paintings, flyers, and posters in Spanish and English. As I walk into the room, I see a large assortment of musical instruments to my right: a piano, several keyboards, an electric guitar, two upright basses and an electric one, a cello, various hand drums and percussion instruments, a drum kit, a long row of woodwinds (flutes, saxophones of various registers), trombones, and trumpets. There are close to thirty different instruments on the stage.

After proposing a toast to the many guests who fill the room, Leo sits down at the piano. Argentinian drummer Franco Pinna takes his place at a modified drum set, which includes a bombo legüero instead of the floor tom-tom (Figure 5.1). Argentinian singer Sofia Rei (Koutsovitis) approaches the front of the stage and adjusts her microphone, which is routed to a

Figure 5.1 Franco Pinna's modified drum set (photograph by Pinna, reproduced with permission).

multi-effects unit. She checks the volume, flipping quickly between presets. Exchanging a quick glance with Genovese, who is already playing an introduction, she begins to sing "El Silbador," a 6/8 zamba by Argentinian composer Gustavo "Cuchi" Leguizamón. Manipulating her voice, she distorts, loops, and sustains certain sounds while using the multi-effects to improvise new melodies on top of them. Rising from their seats in the front row, three Uruguayan candombe drummers join in: Arturo Prendez, Sergio Camaran, and Claudio Altesor, playing low (piano), medium (repique), and small (chico) drums, respectively. Drumsticks in their right hands, they softly strike a clave on the side of the drum. Genovese reaches far to his left to play heavy bass lines on a small Korg synthesizer; with his right hand he interjects fast melodic lines and chopped chords on the piano. After the second verse, Argentinian flautist Mariano Gil and Israeli saxophonist Uri Gurvich join in, adding rapid high lines in unison on piccolo and soprano saxophone over the percussion, synthesizers, and electronically modified voice. As the melodic and harmonic instruments gradually fade out, the percussion instruments hold a steady groove. Genovese stands up and lifts a huge piano drum from behind the piano. The rhythm intensifies. A dancer goes onstage, then another, then another. The audience shouts encouragement, rising from their seats. The room begins to move, listeners becoming performers, performers becoming dancers, clapping, singing, smiling. By the time the music ends some two hours later, many more instruments have been added to the stage, and everyone in attendance, including myself, has been playing, singing, and dancing. At the end, I am embraced by the crowd of musicians around me. We shake hands, hug, and exchange compliments: "We should play together; we should play together sometime."

Legal Aliens, as I later learned the group was called, is a rotating ensemble of musicians assembled and orchestrated by and around Genovese. Their performances often involve dense, thickly textured harmonies, along with infectious grooves, furiously improvised solos, and spectacular, virtuosic melodic failures. Taking inspiration from the various vocabularies of the participating musicians, including free improvisation (its distinctive sound used as composed melodic material), Balkan melodies and rhythms, and Afro-Latin grooves from Brazil, Argentina, and Uruguay, Genovese's Legal Aliens turn performances of nationality into a heaving musical mess. As Gurvich told me, the participating musicians jokingly describe the music through various metaphors of public humiliation, all intended to reflect the extreme difficulty of executing the music, with eventual release in the form of a big dance party. Using the very skills that allow them to perform free and straight-ahead jazz, traditional wedding music, and highly complex new music scores, the Aliens dismantle the conceptual separation between these sorts of performances. For them, these are musical skill sets, not national identities that need to be kept separate.

The woodwind and string sections, consisting fairly regularly of Dan Blake, Uri Gurvich, and Mariano Gil on saxophones and flutes, with Entcho Todorov on violin, and Agustin Uriburu on cello, struggle to keep the tangle of musical threads together. At a first listening, they might sound like the playful melodies of a Bulgarian hora, but soon enough, through a musical bait-and-switch, something goes astray. Unlike in the hora, the melodies do not repeat themselves but continue to change, ever permuting in new directions, never landing on a strong downbeat. During the performance of a particularly challenging composition, Blake or Gurvich will quickly remove his hand from the saxophone, giving a sudden poke to the score in front of them to mark their position—desperately trying to stay in unison. Genovese, guiding the group, insistently plays the angular melody on the Korg synthesizer, pushing forward, onward, marking the way for the other melodic instruments. With his left hand, he punctuates thickly textured chords and clusters on the Fender Rhodes, leading and conducting the rhythm section. Barely visible to the audience behind the front row of musicians, Italian bassist Francesco Marcocci, Macedonian tapan drummer Aleksandar Petrov, Georgian drummer George Mel, and the three Uruguayan candombe players hold on to Genovese's groove. Eventually, when the seemingly endless melodic line comes to an abrupt close, the drums take over, continuing the percussive clashing of meters and traditions.

El Taller Latino Americano, where I first saw Legal Aliens, is a community center located on 99th Street between Broadway and Amsterdam Avenue. El Taller ("The Workshop") is dedicated to the promotion and conservation of Latin American culture in New York and to bridging the gap between Latin Americans and North Americans through art, dance, and music. While the Latin American presence is undoubtedly dominant, the range of musics and languages I heard in the course of the evening extended far beyond Latin America. The performance charted a uniquely New York migrant experience, clearly referenced in the name "Legal Aliens." On July 9, 2015, Legal Aliens performed at Bard College as part of Argentina's Independence Day celebrations. The concert was billed as "An evening of Latino Art and Culture" featuring Genovese's "prolific brand of contemporary Latin Jazz." But the mix of themes, rhythms, and influences was as eclectic as ever.

In what way do Legal Aliens represent "Latin American culture"? In what sense are Genovese and Legal Aliens making Latin jazz? Or even Argentinian jazz for that matter? It is at these moments—when a tapan drum is playing clave and a candombe drum is playing a hora—that the gaps between the economic practices of multiculturalism and the musics that accompany them create sonic ironies and paradoxes, much like Genovese's intentionally failing unisons and polyrhythmic, polynational grooves. Legal Aliens sonically juxtapose musical markers of nationality to challenge performances of ethnicity and national identity in jazz. They foreground issues of power connecting national borders, social boundaries, and musical categories, but also demonstrate their malleability and their creative potential. To be a Legal Alien is to navigate between identities, between borders, and between categories of musical belonging. In the next, concluding section, I show how performances of home can critique its association with national identify, addressing instead on home as an affective musical experience.

Conclusion: Melissa Aldana at Birdland

March 2016: I am meeting Nitzan at Jazz at Kitano, a small club on the first floor of the Kitano Hotel in midtown. I only manage to hear the last few seconds of his gig with Valentina Marino, an Italian jazz singer. Hearing our conversation in Hebrew, the amused bartender cracks a dry joke: "This is America! You should speak Spanish!" We head out to the rainy street and take a quick cab across town, catching the tail end of Chilean saxophonist Melissa Aldana's CD release show at Birdland. Nitzan often plays with the group in their quartet format, but the album and this performance feature only the trio, with Pablo Menares on bass and Jochen Rueckert on drums.

We pick up our tickets at the door and sit at the bar, doing our best to remain inconspicuous. Aldana leans toward the microphone to introduce the next song. "This next song is called 'Back Home,' and it's dedicated to Sonny Rollins. . . . Well, the whole album is dedicated to Sonny Rollins, and this is the title piece." "Home," she continues, "'doesn't mean Chile in this case. It means the first time I heard Sonny Rollins." At the end of the show, I go over to say hello to Melissa and congratulate her on her new CD. She and her manager are talking to a journalist and promoter about the new project. After I introduce myself, the journalist recognizes me and asks, "So what ever happened to those Bulgarian musicians you promised for my global jazz column? We never had Bulgarians."

In this chapter, I have argued that the performance of nationality by migrant jazz musicians in New York is neither a natural nor a neutral expression of their identity, nor is it linked directly to home as a felt experience. The artistry and musical competence of migrant jazz musicians in New York allow them to immerse themselves fully in the innermost private cultural moments of their fellow musicians, whether African Americans, Cubans, Balkans, or Chileans, and to become part of these musical cultures, if only for the duration of a song, or perhaps long afterward. The ability to move from one musical culture to another, to perform one's own "nationality" one moment and another nationality the next, is at the heart of migrant jazz musical experience and the sense of belonging.

This ability is directly related to migrant jazz musicians' engagement with cultural institutions as resources of public exposure and income. Performances in government institutions (such as embassies) or immigrant cultural centers come with an obligation: they require the construction of a set of musical markers that communicate to insiders and outsiders alike the national identity of the performer. This entails verbally prefacing a song with a comment on its relationship to their home country; playing a cover of a renowned national composer or a famous folk song; applying specific dance rhythms, melodic lines, timbres, and instruments associated with the national tradition; and even wearing traditional costumes. Few "migrant jazz" concerts will include all of these devices. But some will require the construction of a program geared toward expression of national markers, and even a nationally homogenous ensemble of musicians.

As Melissa Aldana's performance at Birdland demonstrates, a migrant "jazz performance" can easily have none of these markers, and may even play with the audience's expectations that a migrant's musical home is always the home country. In their performance of "Back Home," Aldana, Menares, and German-born Jochen Rueckert demonstrate that for a migrant jazz musician, home can be experienced through the music of Sonny Rollins, McCoy Tyner, or Violeta Parra.

The nationalist jazz discourse and the emerging global jazz literature may suggest that migrant jazz musicians perform national markers of identity in order to distinguish themselves from American musicians, developing their own aesthetic criteria that enable them to avoid competition with the exceptional "swing" or "blues" of American musicians. But all of the musicians mentioned in this study are hired regularly by White and Black American musicians to perform straight-ahead jazz. Rather than "naturally" performing their identity, the musicians whose stories I share in this chapter deliberately play jazz as both fixed and moving: a Black American music, a musical competency that requires lifelong study and dedication, a particular scene that connects sounds, people, and places. Yet their sense of belonging comes not from expressing a fixed identity, but from creating a place for listening—from allowing different sounds to flow in and become part of the music without the constraints of style. Without that place of listening, we would not be able to hear the seamless transition between "migrant jazz" music and migrant "jazz music" that is the daily bread (and butter) of many of New York's musicians today. It is within this movement that migrant jazz takes place.

6
The Village

September 7, 2014: The Uri Gurvich Quartet, with Leo Genovese, Peter Slavov, and Francisco Mela, is playing the closing show of "Angels at the Vanguard," a week-long celebration of John Zorn's music at the legendary club. As I walk down Seventh Avenue toward the familiar red door, I see Kate, Uri's wife, standing in line. I join her and three of her friends. Uri and Kate were married several months earlier, and as we stand there, friends and fellow musicians come to congratulate her, constantly referring to both the wedding and the Vanguard performance. At some point, with more and more people arriving, the line begins to coil around itself and stretch around the corner, a visual representation of Gurvich's success: the show is sold out.

Our tickets are waiting at the door, and we are lucky to find seats just a few feet from the stage. On the wall around us are pictures of the musicians who made this venue legendary: Rollins, Coltrane, Monk, Evans. I begin to test myself: Can I recognize the pictures of all of the musicians on the wall? Would I recognize them if instead of pictures, there were sounds? Each look triggers a memory of a song, a solo, a piano intro. Will Uri's sound be that recognizable some day? Will a quick glimpse of a picture be enough to conjure Uri's playing in listeners' minds?

How do migrant jazz musicians navigate their performance in view of the conflicting demands of the key listeners who make up the New York scene: bookers, venue owners, musical mentors, and journalists? While improvising musicians are often said to surprise, subvert, and "play with" listeners' expectations as part of their performance practice (Berliner 1994, 264), some expectations are more easily subverted than others, and some listeners are harder to surprise. In the previous chapters, I have discussed moments in which musicians chose to actively perform their histories of jazz as African American music, and ways in which musicians actively perform their own cultural background through references to traditional, popular, or religious musics of their homeland or ethnic group. In this chapter, I look at the choices musicians make with regard to the performance of ethnic identity and at the extent to which these choices clash or correspond with the expectations of key listeners on the scene: veteran musicians and music professionals (Greenland 2016, 6). Drawing on the work of Nina Eidsheim, Tamara Roberts, and Jennifer Stoever, I consider how performances are shaped by power relations between performers and key listeners as well as by perceived ethnonational identity. While musicians actively attempt to attach and decouple ethnonational identity from genre, their ability to do so is ultimately dependent on the interpretations of listeners of diverse racial, cultural, and national backgrounds and positions. Working within a sociomusical scene that codes genre along ethnoracial lines in what Roberts refers to as "sonic identity politics" (2016, 122), I inquire into the ways migrant musicians negotiate, challenge, and attempt to reinscribe systems of sonic-ethnic signification, aiming to maintain artistic freedom of movement between different musical contexts while being dependent on key listeners to make these moves. I also explore the risks that artists who wish to challenge the sonic-ethnic frame and cross "musical borders" take in being heard as "inauthentic," or alienated from their own presumed identity.

Retracing the sonic expectations of listeners is difficult even in controlled laboratory settings (Huron 2008), and even more so in live musical contexts. Without the benefit of hindsight, accessing the expectations of a diverse group of key listeners remains imprecise. Here I focus on indications of how musicians react to key listeners—how they plan and frame their performances in relation to these expectations. I also ask how the presence of these listeners shapes interactions among musicians during a performance. Focusing on two performances at the Village Vanguard, the most prestigious continuously operating club in New York City and a contemporary symbol of the jazz tradition (Teal 2021), I examine the different ways in which migrant musicians work to assemble and disassemble key listeners' expectations regarding the relationship among sound, jazz, and ethnic identity. I analyze how the relationship among embodied knowledge of the jazz tradition, the historical significance of the Village Vanguard, and markers of Jewish identity is entangled in the booking and promotion of these concerts, and how musicians attempt to control these frames of listening with the tools at their disposal: the choice of sidemen, interactions on the bandstand, and use or rejection of ethnic musical markers. Finally, I argue that these choices can function as subtle resistance to the musical border.

Power differentials in ethnic listening

In recent years, a growing number of scholars have focused on the ways in which listeners construct interpretations of musical sound based on the perceived racial identity or gender of the performer. Nina Eidsheim has shown that "when listeners connect a singer with a particular community, their listening is filtered through assumptions about that community and the music and vocal genres with which its people are most commonly associated" (2019, 23). In Eidsheim's analysis, the voices of opera singer Marian Anderson, jazz singer Jimmy Scott, and others are replaced by identities created for them in the listener's mind. While Eidsheim's focus is on how White listeners can only hear Black voices as Other, creating what she calls "sonic blackness" (2019, 61), she categorizes listening as social and cultural (2019, 177). Yet it is important to note the substantial power differentials that exist within cultural groups, and the influence of diverse key listeners on how a musician is heard.

Jennifer Stoever focuses on the agency of Black listeners, and particularly Black women, to show how racialized and gendered frameworks create different ways of hearing particular sounds. She argues that listeners are able to "construct and discern racial identities based on voices, sounds, and particular soundscapes ... assigning them differential cultural, social, and political value" (Stoever 2016, 11). Stoever emphasizes the key role played by White journalists in the antebellum North in shaping the listening of their White readers, and W. E. B. Du Bois's role as a consultant to CBS Radio a century later in achieving a "racial realignment" of Black audiences' listening, hinting at the disproportionate power of certain key listeners to shape understandings of sound for a broader audience.

While both Eidsheim and Stoever are primarily interested in listeners' racial transformation of human voices, Roberts (2016) makes an important contribution to understanding how listeners encode racial meaning in musical instruments. In discussing Fred Ho's work with his Afro Asian Music Ensemble, Roberts argues that the "physical characteristics of instruments ... the tonality and timbre ... are the substance of sonoracialization" (2016, 139). Instrumental timbres are partially embedded in the physical features of instruments, but they have as much to do with the specific bodies that produce the sound. Sounds are produced by both bodies and instruments, but as Roberts argues, "because race is assumed to be of the body, racialized sound retains a link to its attributed producer or whom it is supposed to represent, even if it has nothing to do with the actual cultural expressions of those bodies" (2016, 4). Engaging in what Roberts terms "sonic identity politics" thus creates an a priori definition of a unified sonic racial identity—in other words, a musical border.

Musical instruments, timbres, and ways of playing signify racial and ethnic identity for listeners. As Siv Lie (2020) recently argued, listeners interpret certain instrumental sonic qualities as carrying racial or ethnic "feeling." Lie uses the term *ethnorace* to call attention to "the mutability and interchangeability of ethnic and racial categories in formal and everyday discourse" (2020, 371). While Lie correctly claims that distinctions between the two are historically contingent, in the US historical context the notion of ethnicity was embedded in the creation of hierarchies between ethnic groups later identified as White and racial minorities (Omi and Winant 2015). In the context of the contemporary United States, race and ethnicity are not interchangeable, nor are their meanings shared across different speakers and communities. While listeners are equally likely to attribute a certain racial or ethnic "feeling" to a musician's sound, conflating the two categories will fail to account for the reasons that Afro-Latin, Anglo-Caribbean, and African American musicians are heard differently when performing in jazz contexts (Gazit 2020; Washburne 2020).

Within American (multi)cultural industries, such musical borders are often the prism through which public and private funding is obtained, events are curated and publicized, and venues are selected (see Chapter 5). They are thus crucially dependent on the listening frames employed by those who book, curate, promote, and critique musical performances. It is no coincidence that musical borders have been employed not only by concert producers, publicists, booking agents, and journalists as a marketing strategy, but also by musicians themselves, creating what might be called an ethnic art world. The ethnic frame of such influential art-world listeners becomes disproportionately significant in determining musicians' careers, livelihoods, and public image. In other words, we cannot discuss the racial color line, the race of sound, sonoracialization, or the musical border without accounting for the crucial position of gatekeepers and influential listeners—musical mentors, record producers, radio broadcasters, journalists, curators, and booking agents.

Tamar Barzel's study of Jewish American identity in the New York "downtown scene" (2015) demonstrates that the rise of multiculturalism and identity politics in the 1990s motivated Jewish musicians involved in experimental music and jazz to look for inspiration and compositional material in the Jewish liturgy, klezmer music, and other musical resources of the Ashkenazi Jewish tradition. Initially, funding and support for such projects was found not in the United States but in Europe, particularly in Germany, where alternative culture and Jewish revival were received enthusiastically (Barzel 2015, 81). It was the organizers of the Munich Art Projekt who heard Zorn's experimental Jewish music as noteworthy art and entrusted him with the resources to curate a two-day Festival for Radical New Jewish Culture. Able to identify the potential resonance of experimental Jewish music in Germany, Zorn targeted the ethnic listening framework of specific powerful listeners, and only later, if at all, of German concertgoers.

Barzel shows how Zorn's music communicated "Jewishness" to these influential listeners. Zorn's group Masada, for example, used specific musical material to signal Jewishness to its audience. This included specific "Jewish" modes, such as "Mi Shebberakh" and "Ahavah Rabbah," in which the instrumental timbres of the clarinet are imitated as markers of Jewish identity, and Hebrew (or Hebrew-sounding) song titles. Also significant are the musicians Zorn recruited for the project: Masada is made up entirely of Jewish musicians steeped in experimental music.

Barzel argues that Zorn's adaptation of explicit Jewish elements to create improvised and avant-garde practices was indicative of a "modern" Jewish American identity. In the case of Masada, listeners' expectations about the producers' ethnic identity are reinforced and made readily evident within the format and performance context of an avant-garde piano-less quartet (following the format of Ornette Coleman's early recordings). Using sonic markers of "Jewishness," the musicians communicate an identity that is coherent to key listeners—critics, curators, academics, and the paying audience. Similarly, Barzel shows that the manifesto that Zorn wrote to accompany his piece "Kristallnacht" (1992) communicated his intentions and identity to an audience of "traumatized captive German intellectuals" (Barzel 2015, 75). The Jewishness implied in "Kristallnacht" is expressed relationally: second-generation German intellectuals were willing to subject themselves to Zorn's painful and piercing sounds in recognition of their own culpability in their parents' (in)actions during the Jewish Holocaust. Implicit in Barzel's argument is the notion that these listeners heard Jewishness in ear-shattering noises through Zorn's mediation.

Zorn uses Jewish sonic signs, sounds that are "nameable" and have a specific reference or association, to direct listeners' attention to the music's ethnic identity. Jewish sonic signs such as klezmer scales or the "weeping" glissando effect as used by Zorn are easily recognizable to listeners because they stand out in the context of a free-jazz quartet. This free-jazz musical "context" or setting is created through Zorn's and trumpet player Dave Douglas's improvised interactions with the rhythm section—bassist Greg Cohen and drummer Joey Barron. As David Borgo (2005) suggests, the interactions between soloist and rhythm section in a free improvisation give meaning to the music that is intrinsic—without signifying beyond itself. The emotional and dramatic content of the music is communicated through the dynamic level, melodic contours, shifting tonalities, rhythm, and synchronization. To these features of the music, Zorn and Douglas add a layer of Jewish musical signification. This mode of signification allows key listeners to clearly perceive a congruence between the identity of the musicians and the Jewish identity they assign to the music.

While musical ethnic signification has been an invaluable musical tool for jazz and free improvisation projects such as Zorn's Radical Jewish Culture (Barzel 2015), Fred Ho's Afro Asian Music Ensemble (Roberts 2016), or Jon Jang and Francis Wong's Asian Improv aRts (Wong 2004), their explicit association with specific ethnic identities risks reifying the connection between the ethnic identity of the performer and the perceived ethnic identity of the music. As tools for resisting assimilation, musical expressions of ethnic identity by minority performers in the late 1980s and 1990s constituted important political and musical action. But as diversification and "tokenism" became embedded in the New York cultural economy over the last two decades, economic and social pressure to perform one's "own" identity musically became integral to musicians' work life. For migrant musicians, exercising the freedom not to perform one's own ethnic identity or to perform in musical settings that represent other musical traditions became its own form of political and musical resistance.

Listening in the Village

Because of its singular position, the Village Vanguard is an important focal point for key listeners in the New York jazz scene. As such, it provides a valuable context for examining how ethnic frames of listening shape the relationships between migrant musicians and key listeners on the scene.

The significance of the Village Vanguard as a listening space has been at the heart of several recent studies (Jackson 2012; Greenland 2016; Teal 2021). In these accounts, scholars have emphasized the club's historical legacy as a performance venue and a recording space. Kimberly Teal explains that the Vanguard is recognized by musicians and listeners as the "core" of the genre because it connects the music's past to its present "without taking on the role of the direct reaction or revival" (2021, 26). In an interview with Vanguard owner Lorraine Gordon, Teal discusses pianist Ethan Iverson's first booking at the club. She cites Gordon's importance as a key listener on the scene: "I heard him as a sideman," Gordon recalled, "and fell in love with his playing." Iverson described Gordon's continued impact on his career. "I was [sitting in] with Mark Turner . . . and Lorraine heard it, and then she encouraged Kurt Rosenwinkel to take me on piano, and that was the first time I played at the Vanguard" (Teal 2021, 34). More than a decade passed before Iverson performed at the Vanguard with his own group, but it was Gordon's listening that put the process in motion.

Reflecting on the audience's behavior at a Joshua Redman concert at the Village Vanguard in the mid-1990s, Travis Jackson commented that "uninformed" audience members, tourists, or "spectators" responded enthusiastically to the playing of the melody "in the form of whoops and 'yeahs'" and subsequently "seemed to respond primarily to Redman's playing of high notes, squeals, and repeated phrases" (Jackson 2012, 192). Jackson was at the show with *New York Times* jazz critic Peter Watrous, who had previously written a review accusing Redman of pandering to the audience. "Redman, who had been playing with his eyes either closed or downcast, seemed at that moment to look directly at Watrous, back at the crowd, and then again at Watrous. I guessed that he was wondering whether Watrous would again accuse him of playing to the crowd; alternatively, he might have been playing a game with the critic" (Jackson 2012, 194). As Jackson's description makes clear, the presence of the journalist as a listener had a considerably different impact on Redman than did the young, enthusiastic audience. While Redman certainly appreciated the audience response and depended on it for future invitations to the Vanguard, Watrous's reflections on what he had heard would have a crucial impact on Redman's career.

Greenland points out "the presence of distinguished musicians" (2016, 153) as key listeners on the scene, particularly at the Village Vanguard. He cites jazz critic David Adler, who claims that when important "musicians turn out for shows . . . that changes the dynamic . . . [Y]ou've got people who are listening on another level. It changes the experience of the show to know who's there listening" (Greenland 2016, 152). I have observed similar recognition by musicians during performances. For example, at a show at SEEDS in Brooklyn in 2015, along with his band introductions, drummer Jonathan Blake acknowledged pianist Kenny Barron (who was sitting next to me) and publicly thanked him for attending the concert. Thus he identified Barron as a contributor to the sound of the performance, along with the musicians on the bandstand. Mentors and respected musicians, as key listeners to their mentees' performances, affect the sound of the performance.

To identify the subtle ways in which the ethnic frame impacts performers' engagement with key listeners in the New York scene, I analyze two performances at the Village Vanguard. Both concerts were influenced by aspects of Jewish identity, but also by the performing musicians' implicit rejection of the idea of producing a Jewish performance. By analyzing how key listeners impact musicians' framing, preparations, and interactions on the bandstand, I demonstrate how musicians actively respond to expectations of key listeners on the scene.

Uri Gurvich at the Village Vanguard

When Israeli-born saxophonist Uri Gurvich was first invited to perform with his quartet at the Village Vanguard, where John Coltrane, Sonny Rollins, and many others had made music history, it was a special occasion for him and his group. The Village Vanguard, "the most prestigious basement in the city," is the oldest remaining club in Greenwich Village. It is a musical temple for generations of musicians and a spatial representation of the New York jazz tradition (Teal 2021, 16). To receive the invitation to this "home" of jazz, Gurvich had to follow certain musical contours of New York multicultural politics.

Part of a week of performances called "Angels at the Vanguard," dedicated to John Zorn's composition cycle *Masada Book II: The Book of Angels*, Gurvich's booking depended on various factors. As a recording artist for John Zorn's label, Tzadik, and his Radical Jewish Culture imprint, Gurvich was first invited to perform in a concert entitled "Newish Jewish Music" at the Town Hall in New York City on March 19, 2014. The concert featured twenty different ensembles performing the premiere of Zorn's new composition cycle *Masada Book III: The Book Beri'ah*. In the audience were Deborah Gordon, the daughter of Lorraine and Max Gordon and part-owner of the Vanguard, and Vanguard general manager and booker, Jed Eisenman. Though he had been a fixture in the New York scene since the late 1970s, Zorn had never performed at the Vanguard before. This is not surprising considering the club's commitment to booking "mainstream jazz" (Teal 2021, 24). In an unusual move (perhaps motivated by the commercial success of the concert at the 1,500-seat Town Hall), Gordon decided that it was time for Zorn's music to be featured at the famous club.

Zorn and Gordon, who have known each other since high school, came up with a unique presentation for Zorn's music: a kind of residency that would mirror the booking practices of Zorn's own venue, the Stone. Rather than playing only with his own group, Zorn would become the Vanguard's "booking manager" for a week, choosing twelve of his favorite groups to perform his new composition cycle on various nights. Zorn himself would perform on Saturday night with his group Masada and would occasionally join other ensembles as a guest. (In fact, the week-long marathon of concerts had been planned for the Stone before Zorn received the invitation to present his music at the Vanguard.) As Gurvich later told me, Zorn may have seen this invitation as an important sign of acceptance by the jazz mainstream.

Established in the mid-1990s, Zorn's imprint Radical Jewish Culture was part of a multicultural strategy to promote "Great Jewish Music," a tongue-in-cheek reference to the Association for the Advancement of Creative Musicians' motto "Great Black Music" (Zorn 2006). Gurvich released two albums with the label: *The Storyteller* in 2009 and *BabEl* in 2013. Both reference Israeli and Jewish themes in both sound and text. For Gurvich, Zorn's label was a prestigious avenue for distributing his music. This meant clearly marking his music as Jewish, rather than emphasizing, for example, the influence of Cannonball Adderley and John Coltrane on his playing, or the equally important musical influences of Mela, Slavov, and Genovese, hailing from Cuba, Bulgaria, and Argentina, respectively. Gurvich's second album *BabEl* frames the multinational background of his quartet within a Jewish context by recounting the biblical story of the Tower of Babel, in which the world's plurality of languages was ordained as a divine punishment.

When Zorn asked Gurvich to perform the Village Vanguard show, he gave him a list of about fifteen compositions from which to choose. They all had a melody and some rhythmic indications, but little else. Some were simple while others were more intricate and complex. None of them resembled Gurvich's original style of composition, with its infectious bass lines and drum grooves so well suited to Slavov's and Mela's playing. Zorn's pieces were fragmented, skeletal, bare—"sketches to inspire creativity," as Zorn described them. From this small selection, Gurvich had to choose those most suitable for arranging for his quartet, whose strengths he knew well, and ones that would allow him to communicate his own sound and aesthetics. "I thought of myself kind of as a 'sideman' in the performance, since I was playing his music... as if I had been commissioned to perform the piece," he told me.

As the performance begins, it is clear that Gurvich's arrangements of Zorn's compositions require flawless communication. Using his saxophone as a baton, he cues each new part, pointing to timed and untimed sections, odd and even time signatures. Genovese, sitting on the left side of the stage, looks intently at Gurvich for musical instructions, making sure not to miss a move while glancing quickly at the chart in front of him. Slavov and Mela, relying on years of collaboration (as part of Joe Lovano's and Kenny Barron's groups, among others), seem more focused on listening to each other than on following the chart. On "Katzfiel," a ballad alternating between a 4/4 ostinato and a 5/4 swing, the quartet demonstrates the importance of their familiarity with each other's playing, particularly when performing relatively unfamiliar music (Audio Example 6.1 ▶). Gurvich cues the intro, signaling the opening meter, 4/4. Slavov, following with a repeating bass line, enters at the half-measure rather than playing in unison, creating a polyrhythmic feel. In these few bars, the downbeat of the measure is unclear. Did Slavov come in late? Was this part of Gurvich's arrangement? As the ballad enters its main melodic section, changing the time signature to 5/4, their familiarity becomes evident—there was no mistake. Knowing Gurvich's use of ostinato bass lines, the musicians are able to communicate this ambiguity to the audience. Gurvich begins his solo, balancing the asymmetric ten-measure form with pensive melodies in the A part and rhythmically urgent scalar runs in the vamp-based B part. Genovese, taking the second solo, manipulates the scalar melody, chopping it up and inserting sweeping passages between melody fragments. Mela, his snare and tom-tom tuned a fourth and a fifth above the floor tom-tom, superimposes various subdivisions and little drum melodies over the groove while keeping syncopated accents on the cymbal's bell. As the performance unfolds, a constant question remains open: will Zorn come onto the stage? Standing at the back of the room, wearing his famous tallit katan under his shirt, Zorn is listening intently, sometimes closing his eyes and other times looking straight at the band.

Example 6.1 Jewish melodic markers in "Katzfiel," *Masada Book of Angels*, piece no. 86, recorded at the Village Vanguard, September 7, 2014. Ornamented sextuplets (Chorus 3, B, 1:51–1:52), marked with boxes.

Despite being framed as a marker of Jewish identity by its composer, "Katzfiel" as performed by the Uri Gurvich Quartet has surprisingly few Jewish references. One such marker was a short squeak followed by sequences of ornamented sextuplets that Gurvich used on the ostinato groove-based B part. These appeared twice in Gurvich's solo, once at the beginning (1:51; Example 6.1) and once in the middle (2:44; Example 6.2). A second Jewish sonic marker appeared in the A part: an upper neighbor appoggiatura to B♭, taken from the theme, followed by a trill on E♭, an octave and a fourth above (3:03–3:07). Surprisingly, the pensive A section in 5/4 afforded more freedom of interaction for the group, allowing Slavov and Mela to respond freely to Gurvich's playing. For example, at the beginning of the fifth chorus, they doubled each other in triplets to support one of Gurvich's more expansive fast runs. The vamp-based 4/4 B parts tended to jolt the musicians into a more restrictive position, largely following the accompaniment of the opening bass line. For the most part, Gurvich kept his identifiable clear and

Example 6.2 Jewish melodic markers in "Katzfiel," Ornamented sextuplets (Chorus 6, B, 2:44), marked with boxes.

direct sound, using symmetric scales and gradual motivic development to highlight the contrasting shades of the short melody.

For Genovese, the constant shifting between grooves seemed to pose both an obstacle and an opportunity. The two rhythmic feels were so diametrically opposed that at first he marked the transition by playing impressionist scale sequences on the A, followed by a flurry of atonal runs with large intervals on the B, repeatedly referring to the original melody to mark the transitions between parts. But by the second half of his solo, Genovese was no longer contrasting impressionism with atonality. Instead he settled firmly on a lyrical reference, perhaps to famed pianist Bill Evans, whose iconic picture was looking down at him from the wall. Bulgarian bassist Peter Slavov, the last to solo on the piece, eschewed musical markers altogether. Instead, he chose the development of clear motivic lines, chromatic phrasing, and an occasional reference to the main melody. All in all, the use of Jewish markers in the performance was thus restricted to Zorn's title and composition and to three short statements in Gurvich's solo.

In our conversation, Gurvich emphasized that at the top of his mind throughout the performance was the hope that Zorn would be happy with his arrangements and execution of the pieces. Although he considered it important for Vanguard manager Jed Eisenman to enjoy it, too, because of the potential for securing future bookings, Zorn was *the* key listener. In fact, Zorn sent him an email right after the show to schedule a lunch meeting for the next day to discuss the performance. At the meeting, Zorn encouraged him and commented on various musical aspects. When I asked Gurvich if Zorn had expected a more extreme or aggressive performance in terms of energy and dynamic range, akin to his own *Masada*, he responded that he actually thought it was Zorn's intention to have a more "jazz, post-Coltrane"–type quartet to close a week at the Vanguard, connecting Gurvich's group sound to the legacy of the club. "There is no point in being an imitation of him. We're completely different players. But he did tell me when there were things he didn't like."

Gurvich's relationship with Zorn was important to his development as a leader and inextricably linked to his Jewish identity. Zorn has mentored him as a composer, as a saxophonist, and as the musical producer of his albums. Without Zorn's support and without his assuring booking managers, radio broadcasters, and jazz critics of the quality of Gurvich's music, Gurvich's first two albums would not have received as wide a listenership as they deservingly achieved. By performing pieces from Zorn's *Book of Angels*, with their Hebrew-sounding names and their association with Jewish mysticism, Gurvich became an actor in Zorn's larger Jewish multicultural project. Zorn's wearing of a *tallit katan*—the undergarment of Orthodox Jewish men, visible due to long tassels hanging below the hem of the shirt—is another visual aspect of this project. But what do these Jewish markers mean to Gurvich? In our conversations, Gurvich mentioned that he sometimes used such embellishments while playing at Hasidic weddings and occasionally when improvising on his own compositions, but that he rarely used them in other jazz contexts.

In response to Gurvich's performance, several fans of Zorn's music said that while they enjoyed aspects of it, it had not risen to the level of dissonance and loudness they were accustomed to from projects associated with Zorn's label. Sarah—an avid Zorn fan who attended all twelve of the week's performances—said that the "the style of jazz they played is not really [her] favorite—a little too mainstream and tame. They will probably be a lot more popular than the stuff I usually listen to" (Vallee 2014). A second Zorn fan, Rodrigo Sanchez, who attended the concert while visiting from Spain, similarly expressed a desire for a more aggressive performance (Sanchez 2016).

Both audience members reflected a lack of congruence between their expectations of a performance of Zorn's music and the musical choices made by Gurvich and the other musicians. This is not surprising. Discussing the disdain expressed by free-jazz fans toward the Vanguard's conservatism, Greenland (2016) mentioned avid free-jazz fan Irving Stone (the namesake of John Zorn's East Village performance venue) as saying that he was "uninterested . . . in 'Village Vanguard music' sort of post-bebop, fucking with the rhythm a little bit." He wanted to hear something much louder and more dissonant. While none of the fans at Gurvich's concert mentioned the lack of "Jewishness" in the music, their responses share important similarities with Stone's earlier remark regarding the conventionality of "Village Vanguard music." Despite Zorn's claim to disavow purists, Gurvich's reserved use of extended saxophone techniques (often associated with Zorn) such as shrieks, multiphones, and vocalizations and his minimal use of explicit Jewish signs placed him at odds with the audience's conception of Jewish avant-garde.

In considering how ethnic frames of listening shaped Gurvich's performance, various perspectives and hierarchies emerge. While Zorn's fans heard Gurvich's music as "Village Vanguard music," lacking the kind of intensity they were expecting, their response seems to have had little effect on Gurvich during the performance. Listeners like myself who came specifically to hear Gurvich's quartet likely heard the performance in the context of the Village Vanguard as a historic venue, or in relation to previous performances they had heard by Gurvich. Hearing Gurvich's performance in relation to performances by John Coltrane and Bill Evans gave it an additional aura of significance: it carried the sound of the room, as well as the gravity of its legacy. Although Gurvich later recalled having been preoccupied with attracting a large enough audience before the show, the presence of supportive listeners was not on his mind during the performance itself. Moreover, he intimated that during the sound check "the room sounded like those (classic) albums," but he was not conscious of it during the concert itself.

One's first Village Vanguard performance is an important event in any jazz musician's career because of the legendary performances that have taken place there and the meaning that generations of jazz musicians, journalists, and audiences have invested in it. In order to enter the hallowed triangular hall of the Village Vanguard, Gurvich had to walk through the door that Zorn's "Jewish" compositions had opened for him, so to speak. This created an imbalance: on the one hand, Gurvich's music is firmly anchored in the contemporary jazz scene, integrating straight-ahead jazz with various other musical skill sets reflecting Gurvich's musical biography as an Israeli of Argentinian descent. His work thus aligns with Stone's term "Village Vanguard music." The audience at "Angels at the Vanguard," on the other hand, was divided between those who expected Gurvich to perform "radical Jewish" avant-garde music and those who expected Gurvich's rhythmically sweeping quartet (and perhaps a few listeners who had no knowledge of either Zorn or Gurvich). Creating a "radical Jewish" space at the Vanguard was a matter of explicitly marking it as such, something Gurvich chose not to do.[1]

For Gurvich, Zorn's focused listening from the back of the room was by far the most important influence, as Zorn was a mentor, a record producer, and the composer of the pieces they were playing. To Gurvich, Zorn was assessing whether the quartet's rendering of *The Book of Angels* was in keeping with his own vision of "radical Jewish music." The influence was intensified by the ramifications of Zorn's approval in the short and long run: from the likelihood that he would sit in during the performance, thereby giving it a stamp of approval in real time, to his recording the group as part of the *Masada* series. To be heard and receive wider public recognition, Gurvich had to sound radically Jewish—first and foremost—to Zorn.

Anat Cohen at the Village Vanguard

When Anat Cohen walked down the stairs of the Village Vanguard in late June 2009, she was already quite familiar with the famed venue. She had performed there the previous year and was slotted for another weeklong residency before the year's end. But this week of concerts was a special occasion. Some months earlier, Vanguard owner Lorraine Gordon had approached Cohen with an idea: it would be the hundredth birthday of Benny Goodman, one of the most celebrated clarinets in jazz history, and she proposed a week-long residency to celebrate his music. "I knew Lorraine Gordon really loved Benny Goodman," Cohen told me. "She was actually in love with him, wanted to marry him, but it didn't happen of course. So when she pitched me the idea, I said, OK, a week at the Vanguard!"

By then, Cohen had become the darling of the New York trad jazz scene through her work with the Diva Jazz Orchestra, David Ostwald's Louis Armstrong Eternity Band, and her involvement in Arbor Records jazz parties in Clearwater, Florida, where she performed alongside some of the best clarinetists of the swing era, including Kenny Davern, Buddy DeFranco, and Bob Wilber. The show was symbolic in yet another important way: it would be recorded for her first live album—*Clarinetwork: Live at the Village Vanguard* (2010). As such, it would follow in the footsteps of many landmark live recordings made at the club. As Kimberly Teal and others have noted, "Live at the Village Vanguard" albums "function not only as musical sound but as objects defining both a heritage and a place" (Teal 2021, 29). "I'm very honored that [Lorraine] let me come in and play," Cohen later recalled,

> that she allowed me to make a live record there and become part of that tradition.... When I first came to the Vanguard with my quartet, I was playing more of my own compositions, they're a bit more "world music," more jazz, more modern maybe, but this time was really an opportunity to pay tribute to the [jazz] tradition. (Cohen 2010)

In a way, Gordon's booking of Cohen for a tribute to Benny Goodman became Cohen's tribute to the Village Vanguard itself as a bearer of the jazz tradition. This decision was reflected on several levels, from the type of repertoire selected for the performance to Cohen's choice of sidemen to the style of playing and interactions among the musicians.

For the recording, Cohen did not select Goodman's signature songs or those associated with his orchestra, such as "Sing, Sing, Sing" or "Flying Home." These songs did not suit the quartet format she wanted, although she did play big-band arrangements during her Vanguard residency with a guest five-piece horn section. Instead, she selected standards from the 1920s and 1930s that have been widely recorded and performed by generations of musicians, including Goodman. "Choosing the repertoire was very easy because Benny Goodman recorded almost every possible standard," she later recalled (Cohen 2010). The idea was to showcase her own clarinet playing within a straight-ahead, standard jazz context but in a way that stood out.

In our conversation, Cohen recalled the process of forming the ensemble for the performance and recording. One of her first decisions was not to book her regular quartet, which at the time consisted of pianist Jason Linder, bassist Joe Martin, and drummer Daniel Freedman, but instead to choose a more conservative group of players. I said, "Benny Goodman, OK, so I'll take swing musicians." By swing musicians, Cohen was not referring to colleagues who played big-band swing or trad jazz, but rather musicians who swung—who played straight-ahead contemporary hard bop. Her choice reflected a desire to not only connect Benny Goodman to the present, but to play with musicians who maintain the "tradition" in their own contemporary style of playing. She was after a particular sound that was not associated with Benny Goodman, but that placed his music in dialogue with the Young Lions movement of the 1990s. In the end, Cohen chose Benny Green, Lewis Nash, and Peter Washington, three musicians she barely knew, but who knew each other well. "A friend suggested Benny Green to me," she recalled. "I had never imagined myself playing with Benny Green, but I said, 'Let's ask him,' and he said yes." Following Green's acceptance, Cohen researched his musical relationships in order to construct the rest of the rhythm section. The negotiation process that she describes highlights the delicate process of forging new, almost "instant" musical relationships on a tight schedule.

> I had to see who he played with, what kind of music he played with them. I knew he played a lot with Lewis Nash, and I knew Nash from a session we had played with Ann Hampton Callaway, a recording session for a song. There are people you meet but have never *really* played with before. I played a few bars of solo on a song. But when I called him, he also asked around— "What do you think? Do you know her? Can she play?" That's how it is when you don't know each other.

Finally, once trust and familiarity with the musician's network had been established, it became easier to recruit bassist Peter Washington. Choosing an entirely new ensemble for her recording was a risky move, but Cohen's gamble paid off. The rhythm section's familiarity with one another and her own vision of Goodman's music created the kind of layering she was after— swing within hard bop, within modern jazz. "These are people I never played with before," she said, "but when we started playing it was just amazing. Obviously for me it was amazing, because they are amazing, but there was something there.... There was a chemistry, and I don't separate the personal side from the musical."

Although by this time Cohen was already a seasoned musician, with ample performance experience, she considered her new collaborators valuable guides to follow into the tradition, with expertise and insights she could learn from. As she told me:

> I never have the feeling that I'm there [at the Village Vanguard] so I can play with these people. The amount of stuff I can learn from these people just from their passion for swing, and how much they talk about it, how

the quarter note feels when they play . . . hours! They can talk about albums, about Blue Note Records, for hours, just about how the music feels. Suddenly you say, OK, this is the difference between the older guys and the younger guys, and the approach. The young guys, a lot of them are dismissive of playing straight-ahead, or playing swing, and it's so hard to play it well. It's the hardest.

Despite Cohen's concerted effort to choose a repertoire and rhythm section that would express a particular aesthetic, listeners often heard the way she related to the clarinet and the way she related to Benny Goodman as reflecting a Jewish jazz identity. In an interview with Terry Gross in 2013, Cohen was asked if cantors have an influence on her music. Cohen answered diplomatically, in explicitly general terms, sidestepping being reduced to or pigeonholed as a Jewish token:

Cantors have an influence on anybody that listens, that is there. Because here is someone that is speaking out of their hearts and using one single melody, and all they do is express it in the most heartfelt way. And as a jazz musician—or as any musician—of course it would have an influence. I mean, that's what I try to do when I play music, when I play any music: When I play a cadence at the end of a song, you want to take one note and make it meaningful. And if you hear a cantor and they're doing it right, you're going to be so moved. (Cohen 2013a)

The relationship between Cohen and Goodman is set up as a generational passing on of the clarinet tradition, with the clarinet serving as a marker of their shared Jewish identity. As Nate Chinen wrote:

Jazz has long had its share of what you could, with tongue in cheek, describe as "the Jewish tinge." The clarinet players Benny Goodman and Artie Shaw both drew from cantorial traditions, however obliquely, and there are many other examples past the swing era, including the sprawling Masada project initiated by the avant-garde saxophonist and composer John Zorn in the early 1990s. (Chinen 2012)

A line running through Goodman, Shaw, and Zorn sets up the Jewish frame through which Cohen is heard—with the overwhelming emphasis on her clarinet playing over her performance on the soprano and tenor saxophone.

Example 6.3 Lewis Nash drum call, "Sweet Georgia Brown," (Chorus 2, B, 0:54). Anat Cohen, *Clarinetwork: Live at the Village Vanguard* (Anzic Records, ANZ-1203, recorded July 5, 2009).

Despite this ethnic listening frame, Cohen's tribute to Goodman uses virtually no Jewish markers. Instead, the ensemble displays tightly knit sequences of communication, mimicking the shape and timing of each player's phrasing. As Cohen later recalled, this was a gradual process: "Each night, we learned about each other—what we like, what we like to play, what kind of support we look for" (Cohen 2010). On "Sweet Georgia Brown," a 1925 standard with ABAC form, the group lays down the familiar melody with a light, effortless swing (Audio Example 6.2 ▶). At the beginning of the first B of Cohen's solo, at 0:54, Nash marks a short drum call on the snare and repeats it (Example 6.3). By the second iteration of the call, he is joined by Green with an off-beat chord. Just eight bars later, at the end of the second A (1:05–1:06), the two double each other's syncopation virtually simultaneously, as Green plays a series of chord tensions and resolutions outlining the B♭7 harmony (Example 6.4).

Throughout the solo, Green closely follows the harmonies outlined by Cohen. In the B part of the second chorus of her solo, Cohen begins to outline an E♭7 chord, approaching a G from below with an F♯ (1:23). Green harmonizes the F♯ with a sustained Asus chord, creating bitonal sonority over the Eb. Both Cohen and Washington immediately react and adjust, playing an A over the Eb, the tritone substitution leading back to an E♭7 chord. Green continues the sequences, playing a Bsus over Cohen's C♯ (or D♭, the seventh of E♭) leading to a D♮ major chord, which Washington supports with a bass line of F♯ to A (Example 6.5).

The kind of meaningful interaction created by the group is perhaps most evident at the first A of the fifth chorus (2:18–2:26), where the ensemble marks an internal division of three over the 4/4 swing rhythm (Example 6.6). Cohen's flurry of triplet notes emphasizes the new grouping, and the rhythm section responds with a clear demarcation every three beats to close the eight-bar cycle. Green supports Cohen's line with a sequence of chromatically ascending minor chords (E♭7, A♭m7, Am7[11], B♭m7[11], Bm7 resolving to B♭7) and then repeats the sequence again. Washington supports this rhythmic modulation with a chromatic line in the opposite direction, descending from B♭ to A♮ to A♭.

Example 6.4 Lewis Nash and Benny Green, simultaneous syncopation (Chorus 2, A2, 1:05–1:06).

Example 6.5 Benny Green closely following and altering the harmony outlined by Cohen (Chorus 3, B, 1:23).

Example 6.6 The quartet marks divisions of three against the $\frac{4}{4}$ meter (Chorus 5, A1, 2:18–2:26).

To conclude their virtuosic display of ensemble communication, the group produces one last synchronized movement (2:47–2:48). Using A♭ as the upper anchor, Cohen constructs a chromatic figure beneath it (D, E♭, D, D♭). Green and Washington quickly tail the direction of her line with a sequence of breaks over descending chords (B♭, A, A♭), leading into the final cadence of Cohen's solo (Example 6.7). In short, the most active type of signification that occurs on the bandstand is not the symbolic type, despite ample references to the blues, but the kind that involves intimate communication and proximity in musical time and shape: setup and payoff, call and response.

Example 6.7 Final cadence of Cohen's solo, simultaneous marking of chromatic line (Chorus 5, C, 2:47–2:48).

In her performance at the Vanguard, Cohen avoided easy references to Jewish music, although these were clearly on the mind of certain key listeners in the scene at the time of her concert. This was a deliberate choice. It was her desire to "learn from these people," "from their passion for swing," that framed her tribute to Benny Goodman, to the Village Vanguard, and to straight-ahead jazz. As a point of comparison, consider Cohen's performance of the Tin Pan Alley hit "Bei Mir Bist Du Schoen" at a Jazz at Lincoln Center Orchestra tribute to Benny Goodman in 2018, with a full klezmer section as in Goodman's 1938 arrangement of the song. At the Vanguard, Cohen deliberately addressed veteran straight-ahead musicians, including her own new bandmates, as key listeners, but she was also addressing those listeners who expected her to perform "Jewish jazz," to draw on cantorial traditions or to highlight Goodman's Jewish-tinged numbers. As the 2018 performance demonstrates, she is more than capable of doing so. But this time she chose not to. Not on her own "Live at the Village Vanguard." In deciding to not perform Jewishness, Cohen was making a statement about musical borders—about the freedom to choose when, where, and how she wants to cross them.

Conclusion

Nina Eidsheim pointedly narrates countless moments in jazz history in which sound, and more specifically voice, were assigned particular racial, gender, and age characteristics. While these attributes seem to be grounded in the physicality and materiality of sound, they are in fact, as Eidsheim (2019) shows, frames of listening, shaped by culture, collective assumptions, and the interpretation of listeners at specific times. These attributes are thus symbolic, nameable elements that enable listeners to label and discuss music. It is no coincidence, then, that genre categories and subcategories like jazz, Jewish music, or hard bop, as Holt (2007) and Brackett (2016) have shown, have more to do with the identifiable, nameable attributes of the performer and his or her instrument than with any dynamic musical properties. This is in no way an argument for analyzing the "music itself" and forsaking social analysis for the relationship among band members, notes, and sections. Quite the contrary. It is an argument for analysis of the musical relationships between musicians and key listeners that pays close attention to elements that go beyond established symbols or markers of ethnic identity. It argues for the dynamic relationships and identities expressed by musicians in preparation for the execution of a given performance and on the bandstand.

Gurvich's and Cohen's performances were both marked by a variety of symbolic elements: the historical significance of Greenwich Village for jazz, the role of the Village Vanguard in making that history, the rare introduction of avant-garde and swing—Zorn and Goodman—into this sanctuary of hard bop jazz aesthetics, and the significance of the first concert and first live recording in a jazz musician's career. But to glean these meanings, one need not be at these concerts or even listen to them. What is captured in the performances by Gurvich and Cohen are choices that are important for a different reason altogether. These are choices regarding the musicians onstage, their ways of acting and communicating, and what they mean to one another in time and in form. Gurvich chose to play Zorn's Jewishly labeled music with his own trusted quartet, a group whose trained intimacy was honed over a decade of friendship, and whose members eschew performances of a single musical identity and affiliation. Perhaps because their music captures the multiple belongings of New York migrant musicians, it did not meet the expectations of Zorn's avid fans. Perhaps it was their choice to remain restrained, away from the extremes of Zorn's Masada ensemble.

On the other hand, Cohen's choice to select an ensemble unfamiliar to her was grounded in both symbolic and interactive calculations. While she also wanted to cement her position as a gifted straight-ahead player, she understood that nothing but a "purist" ensemble of bona fide Young Lions would do. She was quite explicitly going against her designation by journalists and critics as a player of "modern jazz, world music." The towering figure of Benny Goodman, though providing the impetus for the show with its connotations of Jewish jazz passing the torch, was a foil for a different tribute. It was a tribute to a musical establishment she was now part of as a mainstream jazz musician recognized by institutions, media, and other musicians, but also a rebuke—a demonstration that one can be musically "both," a choro player, a sentimental ballad tenorist, and a trad jazz and modern jazz clarinetist. It was her choice to focus on the kind of figurative and temporal interaction that a swinging rhythm section can provide that allowed her to show, once again, that she belongs.

Conclusion

Places that Move

In this book, I set out to think about migrant music anew. I focused on a multinational movement of musicians, instruments, rhythms, and repertoire whose visibility in New York City has reshaped the meaning of jazz since the 1990s. Joining this migratory movement allowed me to tackle some of the foundational questions of US cultural politics over the last century: the impact of migration on American music, the simultaneous denial of this impact through practices of exclusion and Othering, and most powerfully, the tethering of national and ethnic meanings to sound, inextricably entangling musical genre, place, and ethnoracial identity. Responding to recent scholarship that explores the relationship between sound and US racial ideologies, I argued that the meanings of jazz as American music is powerfully shaped by these sonic ideologies, and that over the last thirty years, migrant musicians have been redrawing, reshaping, and expanding the meanings of jazz in the United States by playing with and against listeners' expectations of jazz on one hand and migrant music on the other.

I used two interrelated concepts to analyze this process; the first is epistemic and perceptual: using the term "ethnic frames of listening," I sought to explain the ways ideas about ethnicity and race shape listeners' attention and aesthetic judgment in the course of performance. These frames of listening are embedded in the historization of jazz in New York, in the canonization of African American musicians as bearers of the jazz tradition, and in perceptions about the relationship between jazz and racial formation in the United States. The intersection of race and ethnicity with gender and sexuality also serve as an important listening framework in jazz, visually predetermining the sounds of female and queer bodies. Posing these ways of listening as historic and constructed, yet deeply embedded in American epistemologies of gender, race, ethnicity, and national distinction, I argued for the persistent dominance of these frames of listening as they continue to restrict expressions that challenge widely held beliefs about difference and authenticity. I used a second concept to describe the discursive and active manifestations of these restrictions.

Where ethnic frames of listening are perceptual, the musical border is social and enacted. It represents discourses and actions of inclusion and exclusion that seek to privilege the possibility of certain individuals to practice a wide array of musics while restricting such musical possibilities for others. As with any social boundary-making process, musical borders have both protective and political functions. They assert a special relationship to specific musics through discourse, economic incentives, and public recognition but also create inequalities in access to musical genres perceived as incongruent with the ethnoracial and gender identity of the performer. As such, musical borders are bound up in legacies of colonial disposition in American cultural industries. Through the various case studies analyzed in this book, I examined the ways in which national borders and social boundaries in the United States are maintained through musical borders, and how migrants and minorities negotiate and cross these borders.

Framing the colonial and racial legacies of sonic segregation as borders allowed me to detail the various strategies that migrant jazz musicians use to cross the physical borders of the United States and the social and musical borders of American society with its particular histories of race, gender, religion, and national structures of domination. By highlighting these strategic crossings, I emphasize one of the central aspects of the New York jazz scene, one that has resonances in various US cultural spaces, namely, the ways in which migrant and minority cultures are reconstituted, not only in relation to a dominant culture, but crucially in relation to one another. Addressing the mutual constitution of minority cultures and the negotiation of ethnic boundaries, I sought to expand on and challenge extant discourse on music and migration in which the ethnic community is privileged as a unit of analysis, and ethnic music is heard as the predominant expression of the group in the United States. Rather than analyzing the lives of migrant musicians as collectively organized around a transnational split between cultural affinities to the home country and the demands of the dominant host society, I examined the ways in which musicians manage these expressive expectations by building networks across and beyond ethnonational affiliations.

Exploring the ways such networks form allowed me to trace how the unique conditions of the New York jazz scene—its legacy, vibrancy, and diversity—provide a motivation for migration, a sense of belonging, and a sonic and affective home for a diverse group of migrant musicians. Some aspects of the scene, such as the inclusive politics of house sessions and (most) jam sessions, the ethics of listening, and the possibility of interacting across racial, gender, generational, genre, and language boundaries support a view of a utopian space, one that is sustained and promoted by the musicians themselves. But the image of New York as a musical inter-migrant meeting place—a borderland—has also been romanticized and fetishized by institutions who benefit, economically or otherwise, from commodifying access to this mytho-musical reality. Focusing on the economic relationships between academic jazz programs and jazz clubs, and between students and teachers, I showed how dreams of migration to New York as a utopian music city contribute to unsustainable conditions on the scene, slowly leading to a decline in the number of lower- and middle-class minorities that can support themselves as active professional musicians on the scene.

The paths of migrant jazz musicians in New York City begin and end with this dream: The possibility of encountering, hearing, and playing with one's heroes; of making a living doing what one loves; of being part of a diverse, like-minded, merit-driven musical community. Realizing this dream entails a whole host of practicalities: enquiring competence in jazz as a musical lingua franca, embodying and distributing this knowledge with other musicians, finding the economic means to complete its first steps: visa fees, air fare, tuition, rent. It also entails more abstract aspects, like that insistent, nagging feeling—kindled by myth and market—that something is amiss; that aspects of one's musical knowledge are incomplete, not without the social and cultural contexts of New York City, where this musical knowledge was created. Or that feeling that this music can only be truly shared with audiences, with other musicians—even with oneself—in the spaces where it was formed, in the places *"it"* calls home.

These gaps—and the possibility of closing them—are embedded in New York's migrant jazz experience. Through far-reaching international programs, academic jazz programs transform this myth of the New York scene into a procedural, and logistical, undertaking: they quantify the musical gaps through audition scores, they appraise their monetary value through scholarships, and they provide the necessary documentation required to close the musical gaps resulting—as legend has it—from mere distance from New York City. Migrant musicians take stock of the practical and economic hurdles of fulfilling these musical gaps, of satisfying that mytho-musi-capitalist sense of incompleteness. They may decide to audition to academic jazz programs, to earn a scholarship and facilitate a visa, to make contacts in one's home country or already in the

United States. Or they otherwise may decide to learn in the course of doing, to move without long-term documents and the financial assistance and obligations that schools afford. Whatever their choice may be, the paths that migrant jazz musicians take lead them into established entry points of the New York Jazz scene: hanging out in clubs for extended periods of time, playing in jam sessions and house sessions, getting to know the scene's guardians and gatekeepers. In the process and along these lines, migrants create their utopia: they build networks, associations, and meaningful attachments through the people with whom they play: compatriots, schoolmates, and fellow musicians striding the scene's paths. They become acquainted with those whose listening has the power to grant access and recognition: experienced musicians, venue owners, booking agents and critics.

With and through time, migrant musicians acquire familiarity in various scenes. They earn a place of recognition in venues and with the people, instruments, rhythms, and repertoires that furnish them. The musical events that make up these scenes become predictable to them. Scenes of guessed education, of knowing who, where, and what to expect at a given musical moment. The ability to predict and rely on people, places, and times turns scenes into homes to the migrant musicians that frequent them. For these migrants, hourly, daily, weekly, and monthly performances map on to the spatial dimensions of the city's boroughs: apartments set up as studios, bars with weekly performances and jam sessions, jazz clubs with nightly gigs. They become regulars in performance venues where month-long residencies seem to detach art from economic considerations, in cultural institutions hosting annual jazz festivals, in major jazz clubs with decades-long legacies.

As they move along the paths of New York's jazz scenes, migrant jazz musicians soon discover that their listeners—other musicians, booking agents, venues owners, and fans—have divergent ideas about their music, where it comes from, what it sounds like, and what it should sound like. These ideas would change, depending on the event, the venue, and the listener. They would get a feeling for what "works," what they should and should not play. They might discover that certain clubs do not really tolerate—to take an example—Brazilian music. Except, on some occasions, when they compose and improvise their own Brazilian music in a certain way, with that precise combination of rhythms, with the right sidemen and the right instruments, that what they play—and who they are—is suddenly permitted.

Throughout the book, I have argued that ideas, expectations, and aesthetic judgment that listeners hold in their head about music made by migrant musicians—their ethnic frames of listening—intersect powerfully with gender. This intersection is particularly significant when expressed by key listeners on the scene: club owners, booking managers, journalists, and esteemed musicians. A conversation with Cuban pianist, singer, and composer Ariacne Trujillo Duran highlighted for me just how powerful are the musical borders created by the intersection of gender boundaries and ethnic frames of listening:

> I was born in Cuba, in Havana. I came [here] in 2002, when I was twenty years old. I came to the city on a composition scholarship. Do you know [the] Tropicana club [in Havana]? I worked there for two years, so that made me be a little bit more into popular music. I played a little bit of [jazz] there but nothing like what I do now. I was going to study classical composition, but I came here and I was by myself, so it was really hard and I couldn't make it to school. I wanted to [continue] my career as a classical pianist, but Latin and classical pianists don't really [mix], so I started working with Pedrito Martinez. I played with Johnny Pacheco, [I] played with Paquito D'Rivera, I sang with Paul Simon. I play Cuban music, but I have a big thing for gospel music and jazz.

Cuban timba, classical composition, jazz, salsa, gospel, popular music: Trujillo's musical worlds overlapped with her performance of Cuban music, but her freedom to move among them—to crossover—was limited. In her experiences, despite her credentials, Latina (and Latino) pianists and classical piano "don't really mix." There it was, a musical border, once again.

During my research for this book, I was working with people who were playing outside of their traditional music, outside of their "ethnic community." I also interviewed people who had a strong commitment, if not active engagement, with straight-ahead jazz in one way or another. But of course, in framing the project that way, I was the one being exclusionary. I was making assumptions about what is and is not jazz, drawing the lines between American jazz, Cuban jazz, Cuban jazz in America, and so forth. As our conversation progressed, it became clear to me that Trujillo and I were not part of separate scenes: I was the one drawing the boundaries between Cuban music and jazz. We knew the same people, played in similar venues, and struggled with similar challenges relating to family, relationships, and employment. We were living on different sides of the same scene. There was no actual separation between the music Trujillo was playing every Wednesday at the Guantanamera restaurant in midtown Manhattan and the music I was playing in bars in Brooklyn. Her music reflected her choices and options in life, just as my music reflected mine.

As we discussed her experiences in New York, the impact of gender as a musical border came to the fore. Most clearly, it highlighted the challenges she experienced in separating her position as a Latina migrant single mother from her career as a composer, bandleader, pianist, and singer. She had recently "gone solo," left the Pedrito Martinez Quartet, but was also recovering from a breakup and raising her child on her own. These experiences informed her interactions with other musicians. "You have to set up the line and the respect; that's the first thing. Once they see you are able to do what they do, they respect you and they kind of take you like another musician. I am a musician, and they respect that. You get used to being with men." Considering my conversation with Trujillo, I cannot help but wonder about the degree to which the exclusionary historiography (and ethnography) of jazz is the result of a preoccupation with stable categories, labels, taxonomies, and boundaries. But jazz is equally invested in breaking boundaries—in transgressing, in trespassing, and in heroic acts of refusal to comply with established norms. Both of those modes of interaction seemed inadequate to represent the kinds of creative engagements that migrant musicians have with the boundaries they face.

In my conversation with Trujillo, she did not seem interested in breaking the boundaries of jazz, nor in challenging its gender norms. She was interested in finding ways to make music her life and her livelihood—an amalgam of the experiences, sounds, people, and places she had lived through and with. Like the many thousands of migrants crossing borders around the world at that very moment, she could not afford to stay where she was, but neither was she interested in breaking down the walls that blocked her way. Rather, she developed skills to get past them, to navigate around them, to skip over them. In their path, migrant jazz musicians move between highly divergent social and musical spaces: from city parks to concert halls, from restaurants to museums, from academic institutions to embassies. When we spoke after her weekly gig at Guantanamera, Trujillo recounted to me that "never in [her] life" had she imagined being nominated for a Grammy, attending the ceremony in a shimmering blue gown, immersed in a sea of camera flashes. The social spaces of the red carpet and the restaurant bar are not mutually exclusive, but simultaneous and co-constitutive in migrant musicians' lives.

Such simultaneity is reflected in musical performance as well. Migrant musicians move between stylistic and genre categories, playing straight-ahead one day and free jazz another, leading a big band in the evening and teaching piano in the morning. Moroccan pianist Amino Belyamani tours with his acoustic piano trio Dawn of Midi as well as with his Gnawa ensemble Innov-Gnawa. Grammy winner Leo Genovese tours with Wayne Shorter, Jack DeJohnette, and Esperanza Spalding but also with Puerto Rican singer Residente of the group Calle 13, with the prog-rock group The Mars Volta, and with and his own group, Legal Aliens. These musicians make radical musical moves as part of their everyday work lives. Such stylistic movements have financial, aesthetic, and social significance, allowing musicians to balance musical skills, performance opportunities, economic considerations, social prestige, and aesthetic-experimental ambitions. Movement along migratory routes and musical competencies while following touring schedules allows migrant musicians to keep themselves connected, vital, afloat.

Over the last two decades, the entanglements of migrant musicians with New York Artworlds have been further strengthened by audiences, patrons, public and private institutions, venues, media outlets, record labels, and new technologies of circulation. This is attested by Dafnis Prieto's receipt of the MacArthur "genius grant"; the naming of Abdullah Ibrahim, Dave Holland, Candido Cámero, and Toshiko Akiyoshi as NEA Jazz Masters; the awarding of a Guggenheim Fellowship to Manuel Valera; and a long list of Ivy League professorships, Grammys, and *DownBeat* accolades. If, as Benjamin Piekut argues, musical sound is "a weak entity that requires entanglements" (2014, 192), then migrant jazz musicians in New York aim at strengthening themselves and one another by connecting as many sounds as possible, entangling themselves in as many contexts as they find themselves. To these musicians, movement—as well as the connections it creates—is the place to be.

Notes

Introduction

1. I discuss Kun's notion of an "audiotopia" (2005), its potentials and limitations in "A dream" below.
2. Here and throughout the book I use the term *migrant musicians* as shorthand for transnational migrant musicians. These individuals were born outside of the United States, were not American citizens at the time of their arrival, and came to the United States in order to perform music. The term *immigrant* is retrospectively applied to those migrants who settle permanently in the new country. Although a significant number of the musicians discussed in this book eventually became green-card holders or citizens, the stable citizenship status implied by the term *immigrant* would not accurately represent their position at the time I conducted my research. Although I do discuss musicians who came to the United States as the children of immigrant families and American citizens who grew up abroad, they are not the main focus of this book.
3. Zheng argues that Chinese American musical culture is influenced and shaped by a triangular motion involving the Chinese immigrant/ethnic society, the host country, and the homeland (2012, 14). This risks diminishing the specificity of interactions between immigrant groups, both those that are racialized as Asian and those that are not.
4. Beyond scholarly interest in transnational migrant exchanges, applied ethnomusicological projects working with migrants remain hesitant to foster explicit intercommunity musical exchanges. The Center for Traditional Music and Dance in New York, for example, recognizes immigrant musics as the product of distinct ethnonational communities and traditions but has no programs dedicated to advancing transmigrant musical projects.
5. The intersection of race, nationality, and gender is similarly addressed by Picaud (2016). Discussing the representation of women in jazz festivals in France, Picaud shows that a musician's country of origin is often used as a veiled reference to her race. In addition, female musicians are often compared to important "diva" figures, informing perceptions of them through canonical, but also stereotypical, images. An extensive study of the representation of women in the National Public Radio (NPR) Jazz Critics Poll, Pellegrinelli et al. (2021) found that between 2017 and 2019, the majority of albums surveyed (48% in 2019) had no women in the core ensemble, and within those that included women, women made up only 16% overall. The study also showed no significant increase in the number of projects led by women between 2007 and 2019 (with the highest share being 6% in two of the years surveyed).

Of the musicians repeatedly represented in the poll, four women were US-born Black Americans, four were US-born White Americans, and one was White and foreign-born.

6. A recent strand in the literature has also complicated and reframed histories of the origins of jazz in the United States, placing them in a broader perspective of Caribbean urban dance music (Gebhardt 2012; Madrid and Moore 2013; Washburne 2020; Gazit 2020).

7. The current literature in migration studies on music as an act of cultural citizenship and form of resistance to nation-state boundaries is vast. Here, I will briefly mention Aoileann Ní Mhurchú's work (2016) on music-making as an ambiguous and unfamiliar act of citizenship.

8. On the role of instruments as markers of inside/outside position, see Chapters 2 and 3.

9. Although selecting a range of years as a way to measure a long-term historical processes is always a subjective decision to some degree, several events set the late 1980s apart from previous periods in the canonization and internationalization of jazz and in the role of immigrants within it. In the late 1980s, Dizzy Gillespie established his United Nations Orchestra giving a formal structure to his decades-long promotion of immigrant jazz musicians. The year 1986 saw the opening of the New School for Jazz by saxophonist Arnie Lawrence and the establishment of the Thelonious Monk Institute of Jazz, both of which would become crucial for attracting and boosting the careers of immigrant jazz musicians. Finally, 1986 marked a renewed dominance of bebop and hard bop, with the massive reissue on CD of recordings from the 1940s, 1950s, and 1960s, Lincoln Center's first concert series devoted exclusively to jazz, and Wynton Marsalis's recording of "Marsalis Standard Time, Vol. 1." While this period ushered in what is referred to as "neoclassical jazz," it simultaneously disseminated the educational materials (CDs and books) for studying it, attracting unprecedented global interest in bebop.

10. For example, in the 1980s and 1990s, avant-garde composer and saxophonist John Zorn played frequently at venues like the Kitchen, the Knitting Factory, and Tonic. Zorn made his debut at the Village Vanguard, considered a straight-ahead mainstay, in 2014, along with other musicians associated with the downtown avant-garde scene (see Chapter 6).

11. The reason for the change is not entirely clear, since jazz musicians have long been interested in diverse musical cultures. One potential explanation is the growing importance of self-released albums. While albums recorded under commercial labels were beholden to certain standards of marketability and cohesion, by the late 2000s and early 2010s the decline of the jazz recording industry gave artists greater artistic liberty in the conception and production of their albums. Among the first things to fall by the wayside was the traditional jazz album format, in which a fixed ensemble runs through a series of standard songs with a common theme (ballads, x meets y, the music of x, etc.), and a more eclectic approach took its place (see Beuttler 2019, 15).

12. See Chapter 1 for an extended discussion of the economics of the jazz scene.

13. Carrying on Dizzy Gillespie's legacy in the internationalization of the New York jazz scene, D'Rivera led the United Nations Orchestra after Gillespie's passing in 1993.

Chapter 1

1. The COVID-19 pandemic has had a disastrous impact on New York jazz clubs, one whose magnitude is not yet fully clear. Suffice it to say that at the time of this writing, fundraising campaigns are in progress for all major clubs, including Birdland, the Village Vanguard, and Smalls.
2. Pianist Kenny Werner has memorably claimed that jazz musicians "multiply like coat hangers in your closet" (1996, 46).
3. For a recent discussion of the relationship between "college jazz," employment, and class in the Cleveland jazz scene, see Blake 2021. For a discussion of precarity in the work lives of professional musicians in the context of Greek popular music, see Tsioulakis 2020.
4. See, for example, Berliner 1994; Monson 1996. For ethnographic and musicological writing about jazz education, see Ake 2002, 2010; Murphy 2009; Wilf 2014; Prouty 2012.
5. For comparison, other prestigious programs such as the New School for Jazz and the University of North Texas produce around fifty graduates in jazz performance/composition a year.
6. For a discussion of the confluence of jazz and Karnatic music in Chennai, India, see Kalmanovitch 2005, 2008.
7. At Berklee, the incorporation of non-Western musics can also be attributed to the promotion of jazz-rock fusion and psychedelic rock. Indian classical music served as an important influence on these genres (Fellezs 2011).
8. Not to be confused with the US state of the same name.
9. The term "O-1" refers to Section 1101(O)(i) of the Immigration Act of 1990, which provides for the admission of "aliens of extraordinary ability." Together with the growing academization of jazz, the O-1 visa has been an important contributor to the rise of migrant musicians in the United States since the 1990s, allowing many of them to remain in the country and build their careers.
10. This account was corroborated repeatedly in additional interviews. I am refraining from using the musician's name and origin per their request, in part because it might jeopardize their current immigration status.
11. Being hired by one's own teacher is considered a coveted achievement for migrant musicians, the best possible start to a career in jazz. While the list of musicians who have been hired to go on the road with their former teachers is too long to consider here, even that achievement is far from a guarantee of stable employment.
12. One might say that children of musicians often begin their training as toddlers as well (regardless of economic status). The number of jazz musicians I encountered during my work who are children and siblings of jazz musicians seems to confirm this.
13. WeBop website, https://2021.jazz.org/webop, accessed January 10, 2021.
14. Musicians figure the loss of teaching income in their touring expenses. A more active student roster means a greater loss of income.
15. Some of the teachers, however, commute from as far as Queens or Brooklyn.
16. International student data was not available for LaGuardia.

17. There is a dearth of up-to-date quantitative data on the number of musicians in the New York scene. However, Local 802 of the American Federation of Musicians (AFM) showed a steady decrease in membership from 9,335 in 2002 to 6,612 in 2019. The yearly number of jazz-school graduates between 2012 and 2019, including from the New School, Julliard, and Berklee, stayed the same.
18. It is important to note that experimental music is not new to the New School. Henry Cowell, John Cage, and many others composers who were on faculty at the New School performed their pieces there. I am interested here specifically in the relationship between independent performance venues and academic institutions.

Chapter 2

1. This is hardly an exhaustive list of jazz musicians who lived in the neighborhood, many of them migrants from the US South and Midwest. On the transformation of the cultural scene in Bedford-Stuyvesant between the 1960s and 1980s, see Konadu 2009 and the recent documentary *The Sun Rises in the East* (2022).
2. For a discussion of similar situations in a Javanese gamelan context where a lead musician's choice of repertoire is based on his assessment of others musicians' competence, see Brinner 1995, 170–171. For a discussion of repertoire selection and knowledge in a jam session context, see Doffman 2011, 2013.

Chapter 4

1. Here and throughout the chapter I am discussing Japanese musicians who immigrated to the United States themselves, or *Issei* (first generation).
2. For discussions of the political framing of Asian American jazz, see Asai 2005; Ho 2009; Kajikawa 2012.
3. See also Ho 1999 for a similar definition of "Asian American jazz."
4. For a notion of storytelling as embodied practice, see Iyer 2004.
5. "Rhythm changes" refers to a common chord progression based on George Gershwin's "I Got Rhythm." This progression is used as the harmonic foundation for many later songs, including "Oleo."
6. In Coltrane's biography, Lewis Porter cites Coltrane's own explanation of the potential of the new approach: "In fact, due to the direct and free-flowing lines of his [Davis's] music, I found it easy to apply the harmonic ideas that I had. I could stack up chords—say, on a C7, I sometimes superimposed an E♭7, up to an F♯7, [resolving] down to an F. That way I could play three chords on one" (Porter 1999, 160).
7. Davis apparently complained that "Trane liked to ask all these motherfucking questions back then about what he should or shouldn't play.... So my silence and evil looks probably turned him off" (Griffin and Washington 2008, 144). Coltrane himself

claimed that "if you ask him [Davis] something about music, you never know how he's going to take it" (Griffin and Washington 2008, 145).

Chapter 6

1. Several of the compositions debuted by Gurvich at the Vanguard were first recorded by a trio consisting of Craig Taborn, Christian McBride, and Tyshawn Sorey under the title *Flaga: Book of Angels Volume 27*. Like Gurvich, the three African American musicians—and particularly McBride—chose to reject the association between genre and ethnoracial identity. In their recording, the three emphasize Jewish music as an acquired skill set by performing Jewish musical markers extensively throughout, including the use of quarter tones, klezmer scales, and quotations of Jewish melodies.

References

Ake, David. 2002. *Jazz Cultures*. Berkeley: University of California Press.
Ake, David. 2010. *Jazz Matters: Sound, Place, and Time since Bebop*. Berkeley: University of California Press.
Akiyoshi, Toshiko. 2008. "Smithsonian Jazz Oral History Program NEA Jazz Master Interview." Interview by Anthony Brown, June 29. https://amhistory.si.edu/jazz/Akiyoshi-Toshiko/Toshiko_Akiyoshi_Transcript.pdf. Accessed March 3, 2020.
Alba, Richard, and Victor Nee. 2009. *Remaking the American Mainstream: Assimilation and Contemporary Immigration*. Cambridge, MA: Harvard University Press.
Aldana, Melissa. 2018. "Interview w/ USA Teacher Melissa Aldana." Prince Claus Conservatoire website, December 20. https://www.hanze.nl/nld/onderwijs/kunst/prins-claus-conservatorium/organisatie/overzichten/nieuws/interview-w-usa-teacher-melissa-aldana?r=. Accessed January 8, 2020.
Allen, Ray. 2019. *Jump Up! Caribbean Carnival Music in New York*. New York: Oxford University Press.
Anzaldúa, Gloria. 1987. *Borderlands: The New Mestiza*. San Francisco: Aunt Lute Books.
Asai, Susan M. 2005. "Cultural Politics: The African American Connection in Asian American Jazz-Based Music." *Asian Music* 36 (1): 87–108.
Atkins, E. Taylor. 2001. *Blue Nippon: Authenticating Jazz in Japan*. Durham, NC and London: Duke University Press.
Atkins, E. Taylor. 2003. *Jazz Planet*. Jackson: University Press of Mississippi.
Atkinson, Rowland, and Gary Bridge. 2005. *Gentrification in a Global Context: The New Urban Colonialism*. London and New York: Routledge.
Banks, Rachel. 2023. "NAFSA International Student Economic Value Tool." https://www.nafsa.org/policy-and-advocacy/policy-resources/nafsa-international-student-economic-value-tool-v2. Accessed December 13, 2023.
Barzel, Tamar. 2015. *New York Noise: Radical Jewish Music and the Downtown Scene*. Bloomington: Indiana University Press.
Beck, Ulrich. 2007. "The Cosmopolitan Condition: Why Methodological Nationalism Fails." *Theory, Culture & Society* 24 (7–8): 286–290.
Becker, Howard. 1984. *Art Worlds*. Berkeley: University of California Press.
Bennett, Andy, and Richard A. Peterson. 2004. *Music Scenes: Local, Translocal and Virtual*. Nashville: Vanderbilt University Press.
Berliner, Paul F. 1994. *Thinking in Jazz: The Infinite Art of Improvisation*. Chicago: University of Chicago Press.
Bertrand, David. 2020. "David Bertrand's Hope of Fellowship." *DownBeat*, September 15. https://downbeat.com/news/detail/david-bertrand-hope. Accessed September 15, 2020.
Beuttler, Bill. 2019. *Make It New: Reshaping Jazz in the 21st Century*. Amherst, MA: Lever Press.

Blake, George. 2021. "A Tale of Two Cities (and Two Ways of Being Inauthentic): The Politics of College Jazz in 'Official Cleveland' and in the 'Other Cleveland.'" *Ethnomusicology* 65 (3): 549–573.

Bohlman, Philip V., and Otto Holzapfel, eds. 2002. *Land without Nightingales: Music in the Making of German America*. Madison: Max Kade Institute, University of Wisconsin–Madison.

Bohlman, Philip V., and Goffredo Plastino. 2016. *Jazz Worlds/World Jazz*. Chicago: University of Chicago Press.

Borgo, David. 2005. *Sync or Swarm: Improvising Music in a Complex Age*. New York: Continuum.

Born, Georgina. 2005. "On Musical Mediation: Ontology, Technology and Creativity." *Twentieth-Century Music* 2 (1): 7–36.

Brackett, David. 2016. *Categorizing Sound: Genre and Twentieth-Century Popular Music*. Berkeley: University of California Press.

Braggs, Rashida K. 2016. *Jazz Diasporas: Race, Music, and Migration in Post-World War II Paris*. Berkeley: University of California Press.

Brinner, Benjamin. 1995. *Knowing Music, Making Music*. Chicago: Chicago University Press.

Brinner, Benjamin. 2009. *Playing Across a Divide: Israeli-Palestinian Musical Encounters*. New York: Oxford University Press.

Byrd, Samuel K. 2015. *The Sounds of Latinidad: Immigrants Making Music and Creating Culture in a Southern City*. New York: NYU Press.

Çağlar, Ayse. 2016. "Still 'Migrants' after All Those Years: Foundational Mobilities, Temporal Frames and Emplacement of Migrants." *Journal of Ethnic and Migration Studies* 42 (6): 952–969.

Chapman, Dale. 2018. *The Jazz Bubble: Neoclassical Jazz in Neoliberal Culture*. Berkeley: University of California Press.

Chávez, Alex E. 2017. *Sounds of Crossing: Music, Migration, and the Aural Poetics of Huapango Arribeño*. Durham, NC: Duke University Press.

Chinen, Nate. 2012. "From Israel, a United Nations of Jazz." *New York Times*, May 4. https://www.nytimes.com/2012/05/05/arts/music/jazzrael-festival-in-new-york.html. Accessed April 5, 2021.

Chinen, Nate. 2014. "Fabian Almazan's Rhizome Project." *New York Times*, March 20. https://www.nytimes.com/2014/03/21/arts/music/jazz-listings-for-march-21-27.html. Accessed September 3, 2014.

Clifford, James. 1997. *Routes: Travel and Translation in the Late Twentieth Century*. Cambridge, MA: Harvard University Press.

Clifford-Napoleone, Amber R. 2018. *Queering Kansas City Jazz: Gender, Performance, and the History of a Scene*. Lincoln: University of Nebraska Press.

Cohen, Anat. 2010. "Anat Cohen Brings Her Benny Goodman Tribute to the Dakota." *Minnpost*, April 22. https://www.minnpost.com/arts-arena/2010/04/anat-cohen-brings-her-benny-goodman-tribute-dakota/. Accessed May 5, 2020.

Cohen, Anat. 2013a. "Anat Cohen: Bringing the Clarinet To The World." A Blog Supreme, February 6. https://www.npr.org/2013/02/06/171334048/anat-cohen-bringing-the-clarinet-to-the-world. Accessed May 5, 2020.

Cohen, Anat. 2013b. "Jazz Is a Blessing: An Interview with Paquito D'Rivera." *JazzTimes*, updated April 25, 2019. https://jazztimes.com/features/interviews/jazz-is-a-blessing-an-interview-with-paquito-drivera/. Accessed May 5, 2020.

Cohen, Brigid. 2022. *Musical Migration and Imperial New York: Early Cold War Scenes*. Chicago: University of Chicago Press.

Cortázar, Julio. 1968. "Louis, Enormísimo Cronopio." In *La vuelta al día en ochenta mundos*, 121–125. Madrid: Siglo Veintiuno.

Costa Vargas, João H. 2008. "Exclusion, Openness, and Utopia in Black Male Performance at the World Stage Jazz Jam Sessions." In *Big Ears: Listening for Gender in Jazz Studies*, edited by Nichole T. Rustin and Sherrie Tucker, 320–347. Durham, NC and London: Duke University Press.

Davenport, Lisa E. 2010. *Jazz Diplomacy: Promoting America in the Cold War Era*. Jackson: University Press of Mississippi.

DeSena, Judith N. 2009. *Gentrification and Inequality in Brooklyn: The New Kids on the Block*. Lanham, MD: Lexington Books.

DeVeaux, Scott. 1991. "Constructing the Jazz Tradition: Jazz Historiography." *Black American Literature Forum* 25 (3): 525–560.

DeVeaux, Scott. 2005. "Core and Boundaries." *Jazz Research Journal* 2 (1): 15–30.

DiCola, Peter. 2013. "Money from Music: Survey Evidence on Musicians' Revenue and Lessons about Copyright Incentives." *Arizona Law Review* 55 (2): 301–370.

Doffman, Mark. 2011. "Jammin' an Ending: Creativity, Knowledge, and Conduct among Jazz Musicians." *Twentieth-Century Music* 8 (2): 203–225.

Doffman, Mark. 2013. "The Tomorrow's Warriors Jam Sessions: Repertoires of Transmission and Hospitality." *Black Music Research Journal* 33 (1): 71–89.

Drott, Eric. 2013. "The End(s) of Genre." *Journal of Music Theory* 57 (1): 1–45.

Early, Gerald. 1991. "Three Notes toward a Cultural Definition of the Harlem Renaissance." *Callaloo* 14 (1): 136–149.

Early, Gerald, and Ingrid Monson. 2019. "Why Jazz Still Matters." *Daedalus* 148 (2): 5–12.

Eidsheim, Nina Sun. 2019. *The Race of Sound: Listening, Timbre, and Vocality in African American Music*. Durham, NC: Duke University Press.

Ellison, Ralph. 2011. *Shadow and Act*. New York: Random House. (Orig. pub. 1964.)

Enstice, Wayne, and Janis Stockhouse. 2004. *Jazzwomen: Conversations with Twenty-One Musicians*. Indianapolis: Indiana University Press.

Faulkner, Robert R., and Howard S. Becker. 2009. *Do You Know . . . ? The Jazz Repertoire in Action*. Chicago: University of Chicago Press.

Feld, Steven. 2012. *Jazz Cosmopolitanism in Accra: Five Musical Years in Ghana*. Durham, NC: Duke University Press.

Fellezs, Kevin. 2007. "Silenced but Not Silent: Asian Americans and Jazz." In *Alien Encounters: Popular Culture in Asian America*, edited by Mimi Thi Nguyen and Thuy Linh Nguyen Tu, 69–106. Durham, NC and London: Duke University Press.

Fellezs, Kevin. 2010. "Deracinated Flower: Toshiko Akiyoshi's 'Trace in Jazz History.'" *Jazz Perspectives* 4 (1): 35–57.

Fellezs, Kevin. 2011. *Birds of Fire: Jazz, Rock, Funk, and the Creation of Fusion*. Durham, NC: Duke University Press.

Foner, Nancy. 2013. *One Out of Three: Immigrant New York in the 21st Century*. New York: Columbia University Press.

Freeman, Lance. 2006. *There Goes the Hood: Views of Gentrification from the Ground Up*. Philadelphia: Temple University Press.

Garcia, David F. 2017. *Listening for Africa: Freedom, Modernity, and the Logic of Black Music's African Origins*. Durham, NC: Duke University Press.

García, Graciela. 2003. "Time, Language, Desire: Julio Cortázar's 'The Pursuer.'" *Pacific Coast Philology* 38: 33–39.

Gazit, Ofer. 2020. "Passing Tones: Shifting National, Social, and Musical Borders in Jazz-Age Harlem." *Jazz & Culture* 3 (1): 1–21.

Gebhardt, Nicholas. 2012. "When Jazz Was Foreign: Rethinking Jazz History." *Jazzforschung* 44: 185–198.

Gebhardt, Nicholas, and Tony Whyton. 2015. *This Is Our Music: The Cultural Politics of Jazz Collectives*. London: Routledge.

Gil, Mariano. 2014. "Mariano Gil: El Arte de Pintar la Música." Interview with Ximena Hidalgo-Ayala. *Impacto Latino*, August 14. https://impactolatino.com/mariano-gil-el-arte-de-pintar-la-musica/. Accessed May 17, 2015.

Glasser, Ruth. 1995. *My Music Is My Flag: Puerto Rican Musicians and Their New York Communities, 1917–1940*. Berkeley: University of California Press.

Glick Schiller, Nina. 2008. "Beyond Methodological Ethnicity: Local and Transnational Pathways of Immigrant Incorporation." Willy Brandt Series of Working Papers in International Migration and Ethnic Relations 2. Malmö University, Sweden.

Gluck, Bob. 2016. *The Miles Davis Lost Quintet and Other Revolutionary Ensembles*. Chicago: University of Chicago Press.

Gray, Herman. 2005. *Cultural Moves: African Americans and the Politics of Representation*. Berkeley: University of California Press.

Greenland, Thomas H. 2016. *Jazzing: New York City's Unseen Scene*. Urbana: University of Illinois Press.

Griffin, Farah Jasmine, and Salim Washington. 2008. *Clawing at the Limits of Cool*. New York: St. Martin's Press.

Haenni, Sabine. 2008. *The Immigrant Scene: Ethnic Amusements in New York, 1880–1920*. Minneapolis: University of Minnesota Press.

Harris, Jerome. 2000. "Jazz on the Global Stage." In *The African Diaspora: A Musical Perspective*, edited by Ingrid Monson, 101–135. London and New York: Routledge.

Heller, Michael C. 2017. *Loft Jazz: Improvising New York in the 1970s*. Berkeley: University of California Press.

Hersch, Charles. 2013. "'Every Time I Try to Play Black, It Comes Out Sounding Jewish': Jewish Jazz Musicians and Racial Identity." *American Jewish History* 97 (3): 259–282.

Hesmondhalgh, David. 2017. *The Cultural Industries*. London: Sage.

Hiroshi Garrett, Charles. 2004. "Chinatown, Whose Chinatown? Defining America's Borders with Musical Orientalism." *Journal of the American Musicological Society* 57 (1): 119–174.

Ho, Fred. 1999. "Beyond Asian American Jazz: My Musical and Political Changes in the Asian American Movement." *Leonardo Music Journal* 9: 45–51.

Ho, Fred. 2009. *Wicked Theory, Naked Practice: A Fred Ho Reader*, edited by Diane C. Fujino. Minneapolis: University of Minnesota Press.

Holt, Fabian. 2007. *Genre in Popular Music*. Chicago: University of Chicago Press.

Holt, Fabian. 2016. "Jazz and the Politics of Home in Scandinavia." In *Jazz Worlds/World Jazz*, edited by Philip Bohlman and Goffredo Plastino, 51–78. Chicago: University of Chicago Press.

Huron, David. 2006. *Sweet Anticipation*. Cambridge, MA: MIT Press.

Inouye, Daniel H. 2018. *Distant Islands: The Japanese American Community in New York City, 1876–1930s*. Louisville: University Press of Colorado.

Integrated Postsecondary Education Data System (IPEDS), National Center for Education Statistics. 2019. https://nces.ed.gov/ipeds/. Accessed June 12, 2020.

Iyer, Vijay. 2004. "Exploding the Narrative in Jazz Improvisation." In *Uptown Conversation: The New Jazz Studies*, edited by Robert G. O'Meally and Farah Jasmine Griffin, 393–403. New York: Columbia University Press.

Iyer, Vijay. 2016. "Improvisation, Action Understanding, and Music Cognition with and without Bodies." In *The Oxford Handbook of Critical Improvisation Studies*, edited by George Lewis and Benjamin Piekut, vol. 1, 74–90. New York: Oxford University Press.

Jackson, Jeffrey H. 2003. *Making Jazz French: Music and Modern Life in Interwar Paris*. Durham, NC: Duke University Press.

Jackson, Travis A. 2012. *Blowin' the Blues Away: Performance and Meaning on the New York Jazz Scene*. Berkeley: University of California Press.

Jeffri, Joan. 2003. *Changing the Beat: A Study of the Worklife of Jazz Musicians*, vol. 1: *Executive Summary*. Washington, DC: National Endowment for the Arts.

Johnson, Bruce. 2019. *Jazz Diaspora*. London: Routledge.

Jones, Jo. 2011. *Rifftide: The Life and Opinions of Papa Jo Jones, as told to Albert Murray*. Minneapolis: University of Minnesota Press.

Jones, LeRoi (Amiri Baraka). 1999. *Blues People: Negro Music in White America*. New York: Harper Collins. (Orig. pub. 1963.)

Kajikawa, Loren. 2012. "The Sound of Struggle: Black Revolutionary Nationalism and Asian American Jazz." In *Jazz/Not Jazz: The Music and Its Boundaries*, edited by David Andrew Ake, Charles Hiroshi Garrett, and Daniel Goldmark, 190–217. Berkeley: University of California Press.

Kalmanovitch, Tanya. 2005. "Jazz and Karnatic Music: Intercultural Collaboration in Pedagogical Perspective." *The World of Music* 47 (3): 135–160.

Kalmanovitch, Tanya. 2008. "'Indo-Jazz Fusion': Jazz and Karnatak Music in Contact." PhD diss., University of Alberta.

Karush, Matthew B. 2017. *Musicians in Transit: Argentina and the Globalization of Popular Music*. Durham, NC: Duke University Press.

Kasinitz, Philip, John Mollenkopf, and Mary C. Waters. 2002. "Becoming American/ Becoming New Yorkers: Immigrant Incorporation in a Majority Minority City." *International Migration Review* 36 (4): 1020–1036.

Kelley, Robin D. G. 2004. "Brooklyn's Jazz Renaissance." *Institute for Studies in American Music Newsletter* 33 (2): 4–5. http://www.brooklyn.cuny.edu/web/aca_centers_hitchcock/NewsS04.pdf. Accessed September 2, 2014.

Kelley, Robin D. G. 2012. *Africa Speaks, America Answers: Modern Jazz in Revolutionary Times*. Cambridge, MA: Harvard University Press.

Kim, Claire J. 1999. "The Racial Triangulation of Asian Americans." *Politics & Society* 27 (1): 105–138.

King, Cece. 2019. "A Missionary of Jazz." *Our Town*, December 27. http://www.ourtownny.com/news/a-missionary-of-jazz-EY760042. Accessed July 20, 2020.

Konadu, Kwasi. 2009. *A View from the East: Black Cultural Nationalism and Education in New York City*. Syracuse, NY: Syracuse University Press.

Kubik, Gerhard. 2017. *Jazz Transatlantic*, vol. 1: *The African Undercurrent in Twentieth-Century Jazz Culture*. Jackson: University Press of Mississippi.

Kun, Josh. 2005. *Audiotopia: Music, Race, and America*. Berkeley: University of California Press.

Lasky, Kevin. 2015. "Jason Lindner Big Band." *Jazz Speaks*. April 30. https://soundcloud.com/thejazzgallery/jazz-speaks-vol-1-ed-3-jason-lindner-big-band?utm_source=clipboard&utm_medium=text&utm_campaign=social_sharing.

Lassauze, Raphael. 2019. "Live from Riverdale, Here Is the Belgrade Jazz Duo." *Riverdale Press*, December 15. https://riverdalepress.com/stories/live-from-riverdale-here-is-the-belgrade-jazz-duo,70751. Accessed March 5, 2020.

Lefebvre, Henri. 2004. *Rhythmanalysis: Space, Time and Everyday Life*, translated by Stuart Elden and Gerald Moore. London and New York: Continuum.

Leland, John. 2020. "He Was a Rising Jazz Pianist. Then His N.Y.C. Dreams Were Shattered." *New York Times*, October 22. https://www.nytimes.com/2020/10/22/nyregion/jazz-pianist-attack-racism.html. Accessed November 4, 2021.

Lemish, Noam. 2020. "Audiotopias of the Multi-Local Musician: Israeli Jazz Musicians, Transcultural Jazz and the Polyphony of Style." *Jazz Perspectives* 12 (2): 227–245.

Lewis, George E. 2004. "Gittin' to Know Y'all: Improvised Music, Interculturalism and the Racial Imagination." *Critical Studies in Improvisation/Études Critiques en Improvisation* 1 (1): 1–33. https://www.criticalimprov.com/index.php/csieci/article/view/6/15. Accessed July 6, 2022.

Lewis, George E. 2008. *A Power Stronger than Itself: The AACM and American Experimental Music*. Chicago: University of Chicago Press.

Lie, Siv. 2020. "Music That Tears You Apart: Jazz Manouche and the Qualia of Ethnorace." *Ethnomusicology* 64 (3): 369–393.

Lipsitz, George. 2004. "Songs of the Unsung: The Darby Hicks History of Jazz." In *Uptown Conversation: The New Jazz Studies*, edited by Robert G. O'Meally and Farah Jasmine Griffin, 9–26. New York: Columbia University Press.

Madrid, Alejandro L., and Robin D. Moore. 2013. *Danzón: Circum-Caribbean Dialogues in Music and Dance*. New York: Oxford University Press.

Marlow, Eugene. 2018. *Jazz in China: From Dance Hall Music to Individual Freedom of Expression*. Jackson: University Press of Mississippi.

Marshall, Paula. 1985. "Rising Islanders of Bed-Stuy." *New York Times*, November 3. https://www.nytimes.com/1985/11/03/magazine/rising-islanders-of-bed-stuy.html. Accessed August 22, 2014.

Marshall, Tim. 2012. New School Fact Book. http://www.newschool.edu/WorkArea/linkit.aspx?LinkIdentifier=id&ItemID=94325. Accessed August 22, 2014.

Mastin, Mathieu, Christoph Winckel, and Jeremiah (directors). 2011. *New York Jazzed Out*. Kidam Productions.

McGee, Kristin A. 2011a. "New York Comes to Groningen." In *Migrating Music*, edited by Jason Toynbee and Byron Dueck, 202–217. New York: Routledge.

McGee, Kristin A. 2011b. *Some Liked It Hot: Jazz Women in Film and Television, 1928–1959*. Middletown, CT: Wesleyan University Press.

Minor, William. 2004. *Jazz Journeys to Japan*. Ann Arbor: University of Michigan Press.

Monson, Ingrid. 1995. "The Problem with White Hipness: Race, Gender and Cultural Conceptions." *Journal of the American Musicological Society* 48 (3): 396–422.

Monson, Ingrid. 1996. *Saying Something: Jazz Improvisation and Interaction*. Chicago: University of Chicago Press.

Monson, Ingrid. 2007. *Freedom Sounds: Civil Rights Call Out to Jazz and Africa*. New York: Oxford University Press.

Moore, Joe B. 1998. "Studying Jazz in Postwar Japan: Where to Begin?" *Japanese Studies* 18 (3): 265–280.

Morganstern, Dan. 2001. "European Immigrants." PBS. Accompanying website for the film Jazz, by Ken Burns. http://www.pbs.org/jazz/places/faces_immigration.htm. Accessed October 10, 2013. Available at http://web.archive.org/web/20130421060501/http://www.pbs.org/jazz/places/faces_immigration.htm.

Murphy, John. 1990. "Jazz Improvisation: The Joy of Influence." *The Black Perspective in Music* 18 (1–2): 7–19.

Murphy, John. 2009. "Beyond the Improvisation Class: Learning to Improvise in a University Jazz Studies Program." In *Musical Improvisation: Art, Education, and Society*, edited by Gabriel Solis and Bruno Nettl, 171–184. Urbana: University of Illinois Press.

Murray, Albert. 2017. *Stomping the Blues*. Minneapolis: University of Minnesota Press. (Orig. pub. 1976.)

National Endowment for the Arts (NEA). 2019. "US Patterns of Public Participation in the Arts." https://www.arts.gov/sites/default/files/US_Patterns_of_Arts_Participation Revised.pdf. Accessed April 23, 2021.

Navarro, Mike. 1997. "Trumpeter Arturo Sandoval Is Denied US Citizenship." *Los Angeles Times*, April 23. https://www.latimes.com/archives/la-xpm-1997-04-23-ca-51420-story.html. Accessed April 14, 2020.

New York City Council. N.d. "School Diversity in NYC." https://council.nyc.gov/data/school-diversity-in-nyc/. Accessed April 20, 2020.

Nicholson, Stuart. 2014. *Jazz and Culture in a Global Age*. Boston: Northeastern University Press.

Ní Mhurchú, Aoileann. 2016. "Unfamiliar Acts of Citizenship: Enacting Citizenship in Vernacular Music and Language from the Space of Marginalised Intergenerational Migration." *Citizenship Studies* 20 (2): 156–172.

Novak, David. 2008. "2.5 x 6 Metres of Space: Japanese Music Coffeehouses and Experimental Practices of Listening." *Popular Music* 27 (1): 15–34.

Oakes, Steve. 2003. "Demographic and Sponsorship Considerations for Jazz and Classical Music Festivals." *Service Industries Journal* 23 (3): 165–178.

Omi, Michael, and Howard Winant. 2015. *Racial Formation in the United States*. London and New York: Routledge.

Owens, Thomas. 1996. *Bebop: The Music and Its Players*. New York: Oxford University Press.

Parra, Isabel. 1985. *El libro mayor de Violeta Parra*. Madrid: Ediciones Michay.

Pellegrinelli, Lara, Shannon J. Effinger, Jordannah Elizabeth, Kira Grunenberg, Rachel Horn, Georgia Sebesky, and Natalie Weiner. 2021. "Equal at Last? Women in Jazz, by the Numbers." NPR, January 12. https://www.npr.org/2021/01/12/953964352/equal-at-last-women-in-jazz-by-the- numbers. Accessed January 12, 2022.

Picaud, Myrtille. 2016. "'We Try to Have the Best': How Nationality, Race and Gender Structure Artists' Circulations in the Paris Jazz Scene." *Jazz Research Journal* 10 (1–2): 126–152.

Piekut, Benjamin. 2014. "Actor-Networks in Music History: Clarifications and Critiques." *Twentieth-Century Music* 11 (2): 191–215.

Porter, Eric. 2012. "Incorporation and Distinction in Jazz History and Jazz Historiography." In *Jazz/Not Jazz: The Music and Its Boundaries*, edited by David Andrew Ake, Charles Hiroshi Garrett, and Daniel Goldmark, 13–30. Berkeley: University of California Press.

Porter, Lewis. 1999. *John Coltrane: His Life and Music*. Ann Arbor: University of Michigan Press.

Prouty, Ken. 2012. *Knowing Jazz: Community, Pedagogy, and Canon in the Information Age*. Jackson: University Press of Mississippi.

Quirino, Richie C. 2008. *Mabuhay Jazz: Jazz in Postwar Philippines*. Pasig City, Philippines: Anvil Press.

Radice, Martha. 2015. "Micro-Cosmopolitanisms at the Urban Scale." *Identities* 22 (5): 588–602.

Ralph, David, and Staeheli, Lynn A. 2011. "Home and Migration: Mobilities, Belongings and Identities." *Geography Compass* 5 (7): 517–530.

Ramsey, Guthrie P., Jr. 1996. "Cosmopolitan or Provincial? Ideology in Early Black Music Historiography, 1867–1940." *Black Music Research Journal* 16 (1): 11–42.

Ramsey, Guthrie P., Jr. 2001. "Who Hears Here? Black Music, Critical Bias, and the Musicological Skin Trade." *Musical Quarterly* 85 (1): 1–52.

Randall, Mac. 2017. "Francisco Mela: Tricky but Catchy." *JazzTimes*, January 9. https://jazztimes.com/features/profiles/francisco-mela-tricky-but-catchy/. Accessed April 4, 2020.

Rapport, Evan. 2014. *Greeted with Smiles: Bukharian Jewish Music and Musicians in New York*. New York: Oxford University Press.

Ratliff, Ben. 1997. "No Label, No Marketers, Just Room to Grow." *New York Times*, March 9. https://www.nytimes.com/1997/03/09/arts/no-label-no-marketers-just-room-to-grow.html. Accessed April 14, 2018.

Reyes, Adelaida. 1999. *Songs of the Caged, Songs of the Free*. Philadelphia: Temple University Press.

Roberts, Tamara (T. Carlis). 2016. *Resounding Afro Asia: Interracial Music and the Politics of Collaboration*. New York: Oxford University Press.

Sanchez, Rodrigo. 2016. Comment on Masada World's Facebook post, July 14. https://www.facebook.com/MasadaWorld/posts/pfbid02na6BfZAKb38rbpUnLvSfcJSNM9V4yFa4kKquJRAWxrsnSbN9L1GHXreNxPf1TwCrl.

Sandke, Randall. 2010. *Where the Dark and the Light Folks Meet: Race and the Mythology, Politics, and Business of Jazz*. Lanham, MD: Scarecrow Press.

Sardinha, João, and Ricardo Campos, eds. 2016. *Transglobal Sounds: Music, Youth and Migration*. London: Bloomsbury.

Scherbenske, Amanda L. 2018. "On the Production of Alternative Music Places: Immateriality, Labor, and Meaning." *Popular Music and Society* 41 (4): 408–423.

Shank, Barry. 2011. *Dissonant Identities: The Rock'n'Roll Scene in Austin, Texas*. Middletown, CT: Wesleyan University Press.

Shelemay, Kay Kaufman. 1998. *Let Jasmine Rain Down: Song and Remembrance among Syrian Jews*. Chicago: University of Chicago Press.

Shelemay, Kay Kaufman. 2012. "Rethinking the Urban Community." *Urban People/Lidé Města*. 14 (2): 207–226.

Shelemay, Kay Kaufman. 2016. "Traveling Music: Mulatu Astatke and the Genesis of Ethiopian Jazz." In *Jazz Worlds/World Jazz*, edited by Philip V. Bohlman and Goffredo Plastino, 239–257. Chicago: University of Chicago Press.

Sidran, Leo. 2017. Interview with Spike Wilner. *The Third Story*, January 5. http://www.third-story.com/listen/spike-wilner. Accessed July 20, 2020.

Silverman, Carol. 2012. *Romani Routes: Cultural Politics and Balkan Music in Diaspora*. New York: Oxford University Press.

Slobin, Mark. 1995. *Tenement Songs: The Popular Music of the Jewish Immigrants*. Urbana: University of Illinois Press.

Starr, S. Frederick. 1994. *Red and Hot: The Fate of Jazz in the Soviet Union 1917–1991.* New York: Limelight Editions.

Stoever, Jennifer Lynn. 2016. *The Sonic Color Line: Race and the Cultural Politics of Listening.* New York: New York University Press.

Straw, Will. 1991. "Systems of Articulation, Logics of Change: Communities and Scenes in Popular Music." *Cultural Studies* 5 (3): 368–388.

Suzuki, Yoko. 2013. "Two Strikes and the Double Negative: The Intersections of Gender and Race in the Cases of Female Jazz Saxophonists." *Black Music Research Journal* 33 (2): 207–226.

Teal, Kimberly Hannon. 2021. *Jazz Places: How Performance Spaces Shape Jazz History.* Berkeley: University of California Press.

Tesler, Michael. 2018. "Islamophobia in the 2016 Election." *Journal of Race, Ethnicity and Politics* 3 (1): 153–155.

Toynbee, Jason, and Byron Dueck. 2011. *Migrating Music.* London: Taylor & Francis.

Tsioulakis, Ioannis. 2020. *Musicians in Crisis: Working and Playing in the Greek Popular Music Industry.* London: Routledge.

Tucker, Sherrie. 1999. "Telling Performances: Jazz History Remembered and Remade by the Women in the Band." *Oral History Review* 26 (1): 67–84.

Tucker, Sherrie. 2001. *Swing Shift: "All-Girl" Bands of the 1940s.* Durham, NC, and London: Duke University Press.

Tucker, Sherrie. 2008. "When Did Jazz Go Straight? A Queer Question for Jazz Studies." *Critical Studies in Improvisation / Études critiques en improvisation* 4 (2): 1–16.

Turenne, Ella, and Jesse Villa Lobos. 2009. "Desegregating Diversity: From Myth to Mandate." Unpublished report to the provost. The New School, New York.

Vallee, Sarah. 2014. Review of John Zorn's "Angels at the Vanguard" (part 2). Concert Manic blog, September 12. https://www.concertmanic.com/2014/09/12/review-john-zorns-angels-at-the-vanguard-part-two/.

Von Eschen, Penny. 2004. *Satchmo Blows Up the World: Jazz Ambassadors Play the Cold War.* Cambridge, MA: Harvard University Press.

Walker, Katherine. 2010. "Cut, Carved, and Served: Competitive Jamming in the 1930s and 1940s." *Jazz Perspectives* 4 (2): 183–208.

Washburne, Christopher. 2004. "Does Kenny G Play Bad Jazz?" In *Bad Music: The Music We Love to Hate,* edited by Christopher Washburne and Maiken Demo, 123–147. London: Routledge.

Washburne, Christopher. 2020. *Latin Jazz: The Other Jazz.* New York: Oxford University Press.

Watrous, Peter. 1996. "A Cultivator of Jazz Talent Who Operates on the Edge." *New York Times,* September 14. https://www.nytimes.com/1996/09/14/arts/a-cultivator-of-jazz-talent-who-operates-on-the-edge.html?searchResultPosition=7. Accessed April 14, 2018.

Werner, Kenny. 1996. *Effortless Mastery: Liberating the Master Musician Within.* New Albany, IN: Jamey Aebersold Jazz.

Wilder, Craig Steven. 2013. *A Covenant with Color: Race and Social Power in Brooklyn.* New York: Columbia University Press.

Wilf, Eitan Y. 2014. *School for Cool: The Academic Jazz Program and the Paradox of Institutionalized Creativity.* Chicago: University of Chicago Press.

Williams, David Leander. 2014. *Indianapolis Jazz: The Masters, Legends and Legacy of Indiana Avenue.* Charleston, SC: Arcadia.

Williamson, Emily. 2018. "The Son Jarocho Revival: Reinvention and Community Building in a Mexican Music Scene in New York City." PhD diss., City University of New York.

Wong, Deborah. 2004. *Speak It Louder: Asian Americans Making Music*. London and New York: Routledge.

Woolfe, Zachary. 2017. "The Stone, an Influential Music Space, to Move to the New School." *New York Times*, March 1. https://www.nytimes.com/2017/03/01/arts/music/the-stone-music-space-to-the-new-school-john-zorn.html. Accessed July 20, 2020.

Zheng, Su. 2012. *Claiming Diaspora: Music, Transnationalism, and Cultural Politics in Asian/Chinese America*. New York: Oxford University Press.

Zorn, John. 2006. "Radical Jewish Culture." http://www.tzadik.com. Accessed September 12, 2014.

Selected Discography

This brief discography consists mainly of recordings by the artists featured in the book, along with recordings by other musicians to whom I refer in the book. The list is by no means comprehensive, nor is it intended to represent the vast output of migrant jazz music made over the last three decades. Most of the recordings included here have been issued on CD, but many are also available on various streaming platforms. For most entries, I have provided the name of the label; however, many of the recordings are available for purchase directly through the artist's profile on bandcamp.com.

Anat Cohen. 2010. *Clarinetwork*. Anzic. CD.
Anat Cohen 2012. *Claroscuro*. Anzic. CD.
Ayumi Ishito. 2016. *View from a Little Cave*. Self-produced. Streaming.
Common Quartet. 2016. *The Hive*. Self-produced. Streaming.
Cocomama. 2022. *Woman's World*. Self-produced. Streaming.
David Bertrand. 2017. *Palmyra and Other Places*. Self-produced. Streaming.
Francisco Mela and Cuban Safari. 2011. *Tree of Life*. Half Note. CD.
Francisco Mela Trio. 2016. *Fe*. Self-produced. Streaming.
Hironori Momoi. 2015. *Liquid Knots*. Apollo Sounds. CD.
Keith Jarrett Trio. 1992. *At the Deer Head Inn*. ECM.
Leo Genovese and Legal Aliens. 2021. Self-produced. Streaming.
Leonor Falcón. 2017. *Imaga Mondo*. Falcon Gumba Records. Streaming.
Manuel Valera and the New Cuban Express Big Band. 2022. *Distancia*. Greenleaf Music. CD.
Melissa Aldana. 2016. *Back Home*. Wommusic. CD.
Rafał Sarnecki. 2018. *Climbing Trees*. Outside in Music. Streaming.
Prasanna. 2016. *All Terrain Guitar*. Susila Music. CD.
Sofia Rei. 2005. *Ojalá*. Cascabelera. CD.
Uri Gurvich Quartet. 2009. *The Storyteller*. Tzadik. CD.
Uri Gurvich Quartet. 2013. *BabEl*. Tzadik. CD.
Vanderlei Pereira and the Blindfold Test. 2020. *Vision for Rhythm*. Jazzheads. CD.

Interviews and Conversations

Kei Akagi, August 18, 2021, online.
David Bertrand, November 20, 2013, New York.
Carlton Brown, November 2, 2014, New York.
Freddy Castiblanco, January 22, 2016, New York.
Matan Chapnizky, December 12, 2019, Tel Aviv, Israel.
Sun Chung, July 12, 2021, Venice, Italy.
Anat Cohen, October 20, 2015, New York.
Ori Dakari, December 22, 2015, New York.
Vasko Dukovski, November 25, 2019, online.
Leonor Falcón, November 25, 2015, New York.
Nitzan Gavrieli, January 16, 2016, New York.
Mariano Gil, August 8, 2022, online.
Uri Gurvich, April 13, 2014, New York.
Uri Gurvich, September 22, 2021, online.
Ayumi Ishito, March 13, 2015, New York.
Ayumi Ishito, August 19, 2021, online.
George Mel, August 3, 2014, New York.
Juan Lázaro Méndolas, November 20, 2017, Tel Aviv.
Hironori Momoi, August 18, 2012, New York.
Vanderlei Pereira, September 23, 2016, New York.
Edward Perez, January 27, 2016, New York.
Prasanna Ramaswamy. February 5, 2016, New York.
Rafał Sarnecki, November 25, 2015, New York.
Manuel Valera, July 6, 2021, online.
Kenji Yoshitake, August 19, 2012, New York.

For Further Listening

Acuña, Claudia—https://claudiaacuna.bandcamp.com/
Aldana, Melisa—https://melissaaldana.bandcamp.com/album/visions
Akiyoshi, Toshiko—https://open.spotify.com/artist/3HnrKwN3HT9BXwyrDWQCFx
Avital, Omer—https://omeravital.bandcamp.com/
Báez, Aquiles—https://aquilesbaez.net/
Bertrand, David—https://davidbertrandjazz.bandcamp.com/
Cohen, Anat—https://anatcohen.bandcamp.com/
Common Quartet—https://music.apple.com/us/album/the-hive/1115779475
D'Rivera, Paquito—https://paquitodrivera.com/recent-recordings-of-paquito-drivera/
Falcón, Leonor—https://falcongumbarecords.bandcamp.com/
Gavrieli, Nitzan—https://www.nitzangavrieli.com/discography
Genovese, Leo—https://bandcamp.com/tag/leo-genovese
Gil, Mariano—https://www.marianogilart.com/music
González, Benito—https://rainydaysrecords.bandcamp.com/album/sing-to-the-world
Gurvich, Uri—https://www.urigurvich.com/music
Ishito, Ayumi—https://ayumiishito.bandcamp.com/
Juárez, Yuri—https://yurijuarez.bandcamp.com/album/lima
Legal Aliens—https://www.twitinrecords.com/el-sello/catalogo/item/131-leo-genovese-legal-aliens-legal-aliens-2021
Mel, George—https://soundcloud.com/georgemel
Mela, Francisco—https://franciscomela.bandcamp.com/album/fe
Méndolas, Juan—https://open.spotify.com/artist/4QLRuTFOHO2d39SUodsiRk
Menares, Pablo—https://open.spotify.com/artist/0rA6KQCzurSNu3x8PAEj3C
Meza, Camila—https://camilameza.bandcamp.com/album/traces
Micic, Alma—https://almamicic.bandcamp.com/album/tonight
Micic, Rale—https://bandcamp.com/ralemicic
Momoi, Hironori—https://fanlink.to/HironoriMomoi
Perdomo, Luis—https://luisperdomojazz.com/twenty-two
Pereira, Vanderlei—https://vanderleipereira.com/music
Perez, Edward—http://www.edwardperez.com/tracks
Rei, Sofia (Koutsovitis)—https://www.sofiamusic.com/recordings
Slavov, Peter—https://www.peterslavov.com/discography.html
Trujillo Duran, Ariacne –https://www.youtube.com/watch?v=AK6fusMDww4&ab_channel=congahead
Valera, Manuel—https://manuelvalera.bandcamp.com/
Yoshitake, Kenji—https://www.kenjiyoshitake.com/

Index

For the benefit of digital users, indexed terms that span two pages (e.g., 52–53) may, on occasion, appear on only one of those pages.

Figures are indicated by *f* following the page number

academic jazz programs, 33–39
  global extensions of, 38
  private vs. public, 37
  as visa, 39–43
academization of jazz, 17–18, 32–33
acoustic memories, 80, 83
Akiyoshi, Toshiko, 39–40, 92–93, 95, 96, 162
Aldana, Melisa, 45, 63, 130–31
Arauco Tiene una Pena, 124–26
Argentina, 19–20, 21, 26, 58–59, 114, 115–16, 121–24, 126–29
Armstrong Louis, 25, 78, 122, 134–35, 137
Art Worlds, 115–16, 120–21, 162
Asian American musicians, 11–12, 36–37, 39, 47, 58–59, 62, 92–93, 94–96, 134–35, 163n.3
assimilation, 8, 119, 137
audiences, 17, 145–46, 158, 162. *See also* listeners
  decline of jazz, 22, 23–24, 32, 36
  diversity of, 61, 77, 83–84, 90, 124
  expectations of, 79–80, 96, 98–99, 113, 144–45
  inequality of, 32–33, 51
  interaction of musicians with, 77, 98–99
  listening of, 6, 11–12
  musicians as, 79, 90
audiotopia, 9–10, 23. *See also* utopia
avant garde, 92–93, 136
  audiences, 144–45
  in institutions, 52, 53
  as not jazz, 14
Avital Omer, 2, 25, 49, 52

Báez, Aquiles, 2, 22–23
bandleading, 26, 41, 102–3, 104, 120–21, 144, 147–48, 161

Baraka, Amiri, 18
Barron, Kenny, 26, 92–93, 138–39, 141
bebop, 21, 80, 101–2, 110–12, 113, 119
  in Argentina, 117–18
  as jazz history, 103
  as lingua franca, 17–18, 56–57, 101
  as musical border, 25, 26–27, 52, 123–24
  as text, 17–18, 58
  in Japan, 95, 98–99
Becker Howard, 16, 115–17
Bedford-Stuyvesant (neighborhood), 60–62
belonging, 64–68, 77, 115–17
  and ethnicity, 66–67, 73, 114–15, 117–18
  expression and repression in performance, 116–17
  and genre, 8–9
  and movement, 130, 131
  as multiple, 126, 129, 154
  of musical elements, 30, 98
  listening as, 123–24, 126, 131
  and scenes, 5, 6, 21–22, 67, 157–58
Berklee College of Music, 5, 32, 34, 36–39, 40–41, 45–46, 47, 48, 49, 54, 63, 92, 98–99, 100, 165n.7
Bertrand, David, 43, 55, 62, 89–90
Birdland, 21–22, 25, 30, 130–31
Blake Dan, 72, 128–29
Blue Note (venue), 2, 7, 21–22
blues, 56, 98, 103, 110–113, 131
  aesthetic, 96
  as core, 98
booking practices, 21–22, 49–50, 52, 79–80, 81–82, 104, 124, 133–34, 135, 137–38, 139–40, 143–44, 147, 158–59
  impact on visa, 41–42
Borden Mitch, 49, 51

INDEX

borderlands
  jazz as, 5–6, 9–10, 157–58
boundaries, 14–15, 29, 54, 157–58, 161
  vs. core, 13–14, 20–21, 97–98
  crossing of, 6, 13, 83–84, 124, 129
  in jam sessions, 28, 57, 58–59, 60, 62–64, 65, 66–67, 68, 72–73, 84–85
  in jazz (as practice), 18
  between migrant communities, 7, 8, 61, 74–75, 76
  between performers and audiences, 79
  as protective, 13, 157
  between scenes, 22
  social, 12, 55, 57, 95, 157, 159–60
borders, 8–9, 11, 12, 129
  conceptual, 6, 61, 72–73, 124
  in discussions of genre, 10–12, 13, 14, 88, 103, 132–34
  and gender, 9, 12–13, 40, 63–64, 95, 97, 159–60, 161
  in migrant life, 8, 13, 124–13
  musical, 6, 10–15, 27–28, 30, 98, 103, 133–35, 153, 157
  in relation to instruments, 62, 88
  and race, 11–12, 13, 15, 40, 47–48, 55, 57, 58–59, 157
Brazilian music/musicians, 1, 2–5, 6–7, 20–21, 22, 24, 25, 52, 95, 119, 121, 123–24, 128, 159
Brooklyn, 2, 8, 29, 47–48, 55, 61, 100, 102–3, 138–39
Bye Bye Blackbird, 103–13

canon/canonization, 6, 13, 14, 27, 97, 98, 103, 108–9, 156–57, 163–64n.5
  as musical border, 30
  in performance, 103–13
Carter, Daniel, 5, 26, 99
Castiblanco, Freddy, 5, 29, 77–84, 90
Chambers, Paul, 92, 108–9, 110–12
citizenship, 7, 39, 163n.2, 164n.7
clubs, 7, 32–33, 38–39, 61, 93–94, 99, 114, 137–38
  as educational sites, 34, 49–53, 157–58
  as formative of scenes, 21–22, 74, 76, 124, 159
  immigrant-owned, 41, 56, 77, 104–5
  and jam sessions, 57–58

  as sites of national-themed jazz festivals, 120
  transformation in booking practices, 22, 52, 139–40
Cohen, Anat, 5, 22–25, 49, 77, 146–53, 154–55
Cohen, Avishai (bass player), 49, 68
Coleman, Ornette, 136
Colis, Karina, 86–87, 90
Coltrane, John, 27, 32, 61, 64–65, 87–88, 92, 96–97, 108–10, 109f, 112, 123, 132, 139, 140, 143–44, 145, 166n.6
Common Quartet, 56, 66
communities
  critiques of the concept, 9, 75–76, 134, 135, 157
  interaction between diverse, 61, 66–67, 78–79, 80, 83, 124, 163n.4
  in jazz, 14, 37, 57, 59–60, 115–16, 158
  migrant, 8, 104–5
  in New York City, 8, 78
  vs. scenes, 76–77
competence, 59–158
  in interactions, 89, 130
  in jam sessions, 57, 67–68, 69–70, 73, 84–85
  limits of, 37–38, 63, 67, 72, 73
  as social "armor," 62–63
  as tool for border/boundary crossing, 60, 65
  in various genres, 5, 22–23, 26, 89, 121, 128
connections. *See also* networks
  with the home country, 114–15
  with faculty and peers in academic programs, 42, 49, 55
  formation in jam sessions, 65–66, 67–68, 85
  between musicians, 25, 65–66, 67
  as reflected in composition, 25, 162
core. *See also* boundaries; canon
  DeVeaux concept, 13–14, 97–98
  instruments, 67–68
  in telling jazz history, 6, 96, 97–98, 113
  values in jazz, 14
  village vanguard as, 137–38
critics, jazz, 1, 10–11, 145–46
  in critiques on the number of musicians, 34

in exclusion and inclusion, 118–19, 130, 135, 159–60
as key listeners, 50, 53, 132–33, 136, 138, 155
Cuba/Cuban musicians, 2, 25, 26–27, 43, 80, 88–89, 159–61
cutting contests, 57, 62–63

Davis, Miles, 21, 56, 92, 98, 104–5, 108–9, 108f, 110–11, 112, 113, 166–67n.7
discrimination. *See* exclusion
distributed knowledge, 16, 17–19
downbeat magazine, 55, 162
"downtown" scene, 21–22, 52, 86–87
D'Rivera, Paquito, 5, 21, 25, 160, 164n.13

Ellington, Duke, 104–5
Ellison, Ralph, 16–17, 57–58
embodied knowledge, 16–17, 18–19, 133–34
ethnic community. *See* community
ethnic frames of listening, 6, 9–10, 30, 133–34, 135, 137–38, 145, 154, 156–57, 159–60
ethnic identity, 5–6, 8–9, 11, 15, 30, 66–67, 73, 75–76, 90, 93–94, 113, 114, 115–16, 117–18, 119, 120–21, 129, 132–33, 135, 136, 137, 154, 156–57
Evans Bill, 27, 58–59, 92, 108–9, 132, 143, 145
exclusion, 6, 10–11, 13–14, 73. *See also* borders
of Black migrant musicians, 55
of instruments, 62
of migrants, 10–11, 156, 160–61
of women, 12

Falcón, Leonor, 84–85, 87, 89–90
familiarity, 75–76
with the city, 1
as constitutive of scenes, 77, 159
with jazz, 94, 100–1, 106–8, 115
with multiple genres, 87, 89, 90–91 (*see also* competence)
with other musicians, 56, 71, 79, 141, 148, 155
with songs, 70–71, 85, 150
fans, 83, 159. *See also* audiences

of avant-garde, 144–45
migrant musicians as, 58
folklore, 58
as border, 114, 123–24
in representation of ethnicity, 122
free jazz. *See* avant garde
Freedman, Daniel, 25, 49–50, 147–48
fusion, 37
of African and European elements as essential to jazz, 14
as feature of 1980s jazz, 20–22, 26, 103
as "not jazz", 14, 21
in representation of ethnicity, 95

Gavrieli, Nitzan, 45–46, 56, 64–65, 66, 103–13, 130
gender
as border, 6, 10–15, 86–90, 103, 123–24, 157–58
as boundary, 11, 12–13, 27, 40, 58–59, 84–85, 95, 156–57, 159–61
in jazz performance, 9, 63–64, 72–73, 97, 134, 154, 163–64n.5
Genovese, Leo, 26, 27, 121, 124–25, 126–29, 132, 140–43, 162
genre
critiques of, 8–9, 132–33, 162, 167n.1
as discourse, 10–11, 94, 114, 117, 134, 137–38, 154
Gil, Mariano, 114, 121–24, 126–29
Gillespie, Dizzy, 21, 121, 164n.9, 164n.13
global jazz scenes, 14–15, 41, 117–18
González, Benito, 85
Goodman, Benny, 30, 146, 147–48, 149–50, 153, 154–55
Gordon, Lorraine, 137–38, 139–40, 146–47
Greenwich Village, 2, 3f, 21–22, 30, 49–53, 59, 92, 124, 137–39, 154
Gurvich, Uri, 26, 30, 45, 124, 126–28, 132, 139–46, 154, 167n.1

Haden, Charlie, 19–20
hangs, 16–17, 49–50, 55, 56–57, 64–68, 75–76, 79, 104, 158–59
Hargrove, Roy, 50–51
Harlem, 51, 57–58, 86–87, 120
Hekselman Gilad, 25, 102–3

history and historicization, 16, 57–58, 119, 137–38, 161
　as frame of listening, 6, 132–34, 145, 154, 156–57
　of migration, 57, 114–15
　in storytelling, 19–27, 30, 93–94, 96–98, 99, 100–1, 102, 103, 106–8, 109–11, 112–13, 114, 122, 123–24
home, 34, 65–67, 78, 86–87, 90, 120–21
　critiques of, 30, 80
　as felt by migrants, 86–87, 114–17, 120–21, 123, 126
　as performed by migrants, 122–23
　scenes as, 76–77, 79–80, 81–82, 90
　as sound, 6, 87, 89
house sessions, 28, 29, 86–87, 89–90, 106, 124, 157–59

identity politics, 117–18, 119–20, 135
immigration laws, 2–5, 29, 39–43, 44–45, 54, 55, 102, 158–59, 165n.9
improvisation, 14, 15–18, 57–58, 84, 90–91, 94, 96–97, 99, 109–10, 112–13, 115, 120–21, 137
incorporation, 11–12
　of migrants, 29, 57, 60, 61–62, 72–73
　of non-core elements into jazz, 14, 20–21
inequalities, 13, 73
　in access to music education, 43–47
　between clubs and schools, 49–53
　in influence of listeners on musicians, 10–11, 134–37
instruments
　association with ethnicity or nationality, 8, 88, 94–95, 96, 114, 119–20, 126–29, 134–35
　inclusion and exclusion of, 10–11, 14, 20–21, 67–68
　in teaching, 44–45
interaction, 15–16, 27
　on the band stand, 89, 96–97, 101, 112–13, 133–34, 137, 139, 141–43, 147, 150–52
　between musicians and audiences, 12–13, 30, 79–80
　between migrants of different ethnic backgrounds, 8–10, 11–12, 61, 79–80, 104, 163n.3
　in jam sessions, 68–71
　between teachers and students, 35, 41, 99
　on the scene, 15–16, 27, 28, 59, 65–66, 67, 77, 90, 161
Iridium (venue), 22
Ishito, Ayumi, 5, 40, 63, 89–90, 98–101

Jackson Heights, 29, 74, 77–78, 84–85, 86, 90
Jackson, Travis, 55, 138
Jam Sessions, 5, 29
　as educational spaces, 50, 57–58, 71–72
　as formative of interactions between migrants of different backgrounds, 58–59, 62
　as formative of networks, 28, 56–57, 64–68
　as proving grounds, 59–60, 68–71
Japantown, 103–4
Jarrett, Keith, 92, 105–6, 105f, 107f, 112–13
jazz
　as cosmopolitan, 18
　in exclusionary discourse, 13–14, 26–27, 97–98
　in film, 1–2, 13, 23
　as genre, 10, 11–12
　as narrative, 13, 14, 96–97
　as vernacular vs. Lingua Franca, 17–18, 80, 89–90
Jazz at Kitano (venue), 104, 130
Jazz at Lincoln Center, 1, 5, 28, 44, 120, 153, 164n.9
Jazz Gallery, 2
jazz schools. *See* academic jazz programs
Jazz Standard (venue), 2, 32–33, 81–82
Jewish music, 30, 117–18, 136–37, 140, 142f, 143f, 144–45, 146, 149–50, 153, 155
Jones, Elvin, 123
Juárez, Yuri, 80, 81–82

key listeners. *See* listeners
Klein, Guillermo, 49, 52
Knitting Factory, 21–22

knowledge, 23–24, 27, 59–60, 66–67, 70, 89, 99, 107–8, 110, 114, 126. *See also* competence
  of conditions on the scene, 42, 54
  as embodied, 16, 17–18, 133–34, 158
  as motivation for migration, 23
  as situated, 17–19

Latin jazz, 21, 22, 24, 26, 27, 89, 95, 116–18, 128, 160–61
Lawrence, Arnie, 50–51, 164n.9
Lefebvre, Henri, 77
Legal Aliens, 28, 126–29, 162
Lindner, Jason, 25, 49–50
listeners, 32–33, 51, 98, 114–15, 124–25, 126–28, 132, 137–38, 144, 159. *See also* audiences
  and aesthetic judgement, 10, 156–57, 159–60
  and categorization, 10–11, 117
  and construction of ethnic and racial identity, 11–12, 14–15, 134–35, 149
  and construction of gender identity, 134
  and frames of listening, 6, 145–46, 154
  key, 132–33, 134, 135, 136, 139, 153, 159–60
listening, 7–10
  of club owners, 52, 137–38, 139–40
  as constructed, 2–5, 6, 145–46, 154
  between musicians, 64–65, 69, 114, 123–24, 126, 131, 133–34
  power differentials in, 134–37
  to records, 102
  of respected musicians, 138–39, 143–44
Live at the Village Vanguard (as sign of prestige)
loop, 28, 33
Lovano, Joe, 19–20, 141

Mahavishnu Orchestra, 20–21
Marsalis, Wynton, 20–21, 113, 164n.9
Mel, George, 38, 47–48, 128–29
Mela Francisco, 26–27, 81–82, 132, 140–43
Menares, Pablo, 56, 64–65, 66, 130, 131
Méndolas, Juan, 19–21, 26
Metheny, Pat, 21, 102–3

methodological nationalism/ethnicity, 8–9, 75
Meza, Camila, 5, 124–25, 126
Micic, Alma, 45–46
Micic, Rale, 45–46, 68
Minton's Playhouse (venue), 57–58
Momoi, Hironori, 101–3
Monk, Thelonious, 61, 121, 123, 132
Motian, Paul, 19–20, 103, 106
multiculturalism (critiques of), 116–17, 119–20, 129, 136
music industry, 17, 34, 42, 117, 164n.11

narrative, 13, 14, 96–97. *See also* storytelling
nationalism, 118–20
neoclassical, 14, 21, 164n.9
New York City
  as city of immigrants, 57, 76, 78, 104
  as educational space, 23–24
  imaginations of, 1–5, 6–7, 16–17, 19–21
  as jazz hub, 1–2, 9–10, 23, 65
networks, 49–53, 65, 67–68, 74, 76, 89, 114–15, 148, 157–59
New School, The, 28, 35–36, 37, 38–39, 47, 48, 50–51, 52–53, 54, 66, 67–68, 164n.9
nueva canción, 26, 30, 124–25

Optional Practical Training (OPT), 41
overproduction. *See* loop

Parker, Charlie, 98–99, 100–1, 107–8, 123
Parra, Violeta, 26, 30, 124–26, 131
Perdomo, Luis, 2
Pereira, Vanderlei, 1, 2–5, 6–7
Perez Edward, 74, 79, 83, 85–86
Peterson Oscar, 21, 88–89, 92
place, 15, 17, 29, 72–73
  as constituted by immigrants, 30, 74–75, 76–77, 81, 104, 157–58
  as constitutive of jazz knowledge, 23, 24–25, 26, 27, 56–57, 58
  as history, 16–17, 58–63, 113, 114, 161
  for listening (within the music), 114, 131
  as movement, 17–18, 28, 115–16, 131
  of origin, 10–11, 87, 114–15

producers/promoters, 10–11, 117, 130, 135

Queens College CUNY, 47–48, 102

race
  changing demographics of the scene, 32–33, 46, 54
  as frame of listening, 11–13, 119–20, 156–57
  as musical border, 11, 117–18, 131, 134–35
  in jazz schools, 37, 47–48
  in jam sessions, 57, 60–64, 97–98
  as social boundary, 55, 60–64
Radical Jewish Culture, 136–37, 139–40
Ramaswamy, Prasanna, 5, 36–37, 39, 81–84, 86, 87–88, 89
recordings, 15–16, 20, 25, 26, 27, 40, 58, 74, 99, 101–2, 106, 108–9, 110–11, 120–21, 136, 137–39, 146–47, 148–49, 154
Redman, Dewey, 19–20
Redman, Joshua, 138
Rei, Sofia (Koutsovitis), 74, 80, 126–28
repertoire, 10, 11, 59–60, 68–71, 85, 104–5, 116–17, 119–21, 147, 149, 156, 159, 166n.2
Rhythmanalysis (Lefebvre), 77
Rosenwinkel, Kurt, 49, 137–38
Rossy, Jorge, 49

scene(s), 13, 28, 92–93, 114, 117, 131, 132–33, 136, 137–38, 157
  as constitutive of knowledge, 18, 23, 87, 103, 124
  in contrast to community, 9, 76–77
  economic conditions in, 3f, 7, 9–10, 17, 24, 29, 33, 35–36, 46–47, 50, 51, 53, 54, 157–58
  as rhythmic, 80, 83–84, 86
  as sense of belonging, 5, 6, 15–17, 49–50, 55, 63–64, 73, 79, 85, 146–47, 157–59
  as sociomusical groups, 20–23, 25, 29, 56–57, 64–68, 74, 104
schools of jazz, 5, 17, 28, 33–39. *See also* the academization of jazz; loop

  as agents of inequality, 47–48
  as formative of scenes, 42, 49–53, 66
  as facilitators of migration, 29, 39–43, 102
  socio-economic impact of, 29, 34–36, 48, 49–53
Shaw, Artie, 25, 149
sheets of sound, 110
situated knowledge, 16–19
Slavov, Peter, 26, 124–25, 126, 132, 140–43
Smalls (venue), 25, 49–50, 51–52, 54, 165n.1
sociomusical groups, 55, 59–60, 64–68, 74. *See also* scenes
sonic color line, 11–12, 135
son jarocho, 78–79
sonoracialization, 11–12
Spalding, Esperanza, 26, 162
Stone (venue), 52–53, 140
storytelling, 13, 93, 96–97, 113
Swarnabhoomi Academy of Music, 36–37, 86
Sweet Basil (venue), 2, 7, 19, 21–22, 49
Sweet Georgia Brown, 150–52, 150f–53f
swing, 14, 21, 25, 27, 44, 85, 88–89, 96, 97–99, 100–1, 102, 103, 105–8, 109, 113, 118–19, 131, 141, 146–48, 150, 153, 154, 155

Taller Latino Americano (venue), 20, 30, 126–29
Terraza 7, 28, 29, 74, 77–86, 88, 90–91
Tomi Jazz (venue), 28, 30, 103–5
tradition(s), 11, 17, 23, 29–30, 59–60, 90–91, 94–95, 116–17, 128–29, 130–31, 137
  jazz, 2–5, 13, 21, 26, 49–50, 62–63, 80, 96, 97–99, 103, 118–19, 132–33, 139, 147–48, 156–57
  Jewish, 136, 149, 153
  son jarocho, 79
trad(itional) jazz (also New Orleans Jazz), 21–23, 25, 106–7
transcription
  as mode of embodiment, 87–88, 92, 106, 114
  vs. physical presence, 1–2, 16–17
Trujillo Duran, Ariacne, 159–61

Turner, Mark, 49, 137–38

Valera, Manuel, 2, 80–81
venues. *See* clubs
vibing, 71–72
village. *See* Greenwich Village
Village Vanguard, 5, 21–22, 28, 30, 138, 140
   in the careers of migrant musicians, 132, 143–44, 145–47, 148–49
   as conservative, 144–45
   as core, 137–38
   as a focal point of the scene, 77
   as site of listening, 137–39
   as site of jazz tradition, 2, 133–34, 139, 146, 154
   as sound, 145
virtuosity, 69, 128, 152

visa, 2–5, 29, 38, 39–43, 44–45, 54, 102, 158–59, 165n.9
Vodou bar (venue), 28, 29, 56, 59, 60–65, 66, 67–68, 69, 70, 72–73

WeBop (JALC program), 44
Webster, Ben, 99, 100
Wilner, Spike, 5, 51–52, 54
Wong Deborah, 94
Wyatt, Alex, 56, 66, 105–8, 109, 110, 111, 112–13

Yoshitake, Kenji, 30, 92, 103–13
Young, Lester, 98–100
Young Lions, 147–48

Zawinul, Joe, 20–21, 40, 118–19
Zorn, John, 5, 30, 52–53, 68, 119–20, 132, 136–37, 139–46, 149, 154